BLACK PILL

BLACK PILL

HOW I WITNESSED THE DARKEST CORNERS OF THE INTERNET COME TO LIFE, POISON SOCIETY, AND CAPTURE AMERICAN POLITICS

ELLE REEVE

ATRIA BOOKS

NEW YORK • LONDON • TORONTO • SYDNEY • NEW DELHI

An Imprint of Simon & Schuster, LLC
1230 Avenue of the Americas
New York, NY 10020

First Atria Books hardcover edition July 2024

ATRIA B O O K S and colophon are trademarks of Simon & Schuster, LLC

Simon & Schuster: Celebrating 100 Years of Publishing in 2024

For information about special discounts for bulk purchases, please contact Simon & Schuster Special Sales at 1-866-506-1949 or business@simonandschuster.com.

The Simon & Schuster Speakers Bureau can bring authors to your live event. For more information, or to book an event, contact the Simon & Schuster Speakers Bureau at 1-866-248-3049 or visit our website at www.simonspeakers.com.

Interior design by Dana Sloan

Manufactured in the United States of America

1 3 5 7 9 10 8 6 4 2

Library of Congress Cataloging-in-Publication Data

Names: Reeve, Elle, author.
Title: Black pill : my strange journey into the darkest corners of the internet / Elle Reeve.
Identifiers: LCCN 2023037539 | ISBN 9781982198886 (hardcover) | ISBN 9781982198893 (paperback) | ISBN 9781982198909 (ebook)
Subjects: LCSH: Social media and society—United States. | Social media—Political aspects—United States. | Right-wing extremists—United States. | Radicalization—United States. | Polarization (Socialsciences)—United States. | United States—Social conditions—21stcentury. | United States—Politics and government—1989– | BISAC:POLITICAL SCIENCE / Political Ideologies / Fascism & Totalitarianism | HISTORY / United States / 21st Century
Classification: LCC HM742.R448 2024 | DDC 302.23/1—dc23/eng/20240116
LC record available at https://lccn.loc.gov/2023037539

ISBN 978-1-9821-9888-6
ISBN 978-1-9821-9890-9 (ebook)

For Jeremy, who kept me alive the whole time

CONTENTS

AUTHOR'S NOTE

I spent my entire teenage years at war. Not a "real" war, but a psychological war, followed by a legal one. It did not have a happy ending. At the time, when explaining it to my high school friends, I referred to the situation as "my evil neighbor." Decades later, I understand what had happened: my family had a stalker.

It started when our neighbor built a fence. We'd just moved near Lebanon, Tennessee, to a 1970s housing development surrounded by nothing off Highway 109, a road named in a country song about murdering an abusive husband. The neighbor was a man in his early forties, slim with jet-black hair that my mom thought he dyed, narrow eyes, and ruddy skin. The deed to our house showed he was building the fence on our property, so my parents asked him to get a survey of the land. He refused. My parents got one, and it gave him *more* land. It seemed like a win for our neighbor, but he had to move his fence, which made him angry.

We started to notice small acts of vandalism. A light on our driveway was shot out. Someone keyed our car—strange, given we had a long driveway on a two-acre lot, and our neighborhood was like a sample-sized suburbia dropped in the middle of empty fields miles from town. The plants died. Bolts appeared behind our car tires. A license plate was stolen. The air conditioner was sabotaged. Someone started calling our house at all hours of the night, and hanging up when we answered, or sitting in silence.

The ambiguity did not last. My neighbor started watching us. We had big windows in the back of the house, and after dark, we could see the red cherry of his cigarette as he sat in his truck and stared. Sometimes when one of us walked outside, he heckled us—mostly that my dad was not a real man, or that my mom was an ugly bitch. There are only a couple of confrontations I remember clearly. One was at night, when my dad and I walked outside to our garage. The neighbor was sitting on a lawn chair in the bed of his truck, drinking beer and eating popcorn. As we walked toward the driveway, he shouted that he was enjoying the big show we were putting on for him. He held out the popcorn and asked if we'd like some. I was fourteen years old. I knew he was trying to be menacing, but I didn't feel fear so much as astonishment at the way this adult was willing to debase himself to ruin our night. I remember staring up at his flushed red face as he stood up in his truck bed, way over my head, and thinking, *What a strange person.*

The first real friendship I made in Tennessee was with the neighbor's daughter, before the bad times began. She was a year older than me, with a goofy laugh and loopy handwriting and bangs. When I spent the night at her house, we stayed up late watching *Interview with the Vampire*, and she didn't make fun of me for it being my first R-rated movie. We sat in the grass between our houses and talked for hours. She held out her left hand and showed me her gold Mickey Mouse promise ring—a promise to her daddy that she would remain a virgin until it was replaced with a gold band on her wedding day.

We stopped speaking once her daddy took an interest in mine. The grass where we'd sat together became the battleground between our families. It's where her dad usually parked his truck, whether he was heckling during the day or honking the horn and flashing the lights at night. That's where he'd wait for my brother or me to walk down the driveway to wait for the bus—he'd stare, or rev his car engine, or drive down his parallel driveway and watch us up close till we were picked up for school.

———

One summer morning we woke up and saw some strange yellow lines in the grass in the front yard. Over a few hours, the words "BITCH" and "WHORE" materialized in three-foot-tall, all-caps letters. The police report notes "the complainant is having problems with his neighbor." I wondered if my former friend ever looked at it. We'd joked about toilet papering someone's house, but never did it. Now the joke had been drained of its innocence.

A cop stood in our living room and told us, "If you don't get it on video, we cain't do nothing about it." We never got it—not good enough video, anyway. Back then cameras were awkward, and tape was finite. The cop's bureaucratic wisdom became a meme in our house, as did a recurring question, "You ain't from around here, are ya?" The game was to riff on each word in the sentence in an absurd southern accent—the best turned on a high-pitched accusatory "*you*," or captured a cosmic surrender with "cain't do *nothing*." But I was confused: Did the police never solve a single crime before the invention of the camcorder?

The harassment escalated. The neighbor liked to play chicken. He tailed my mom as she drove me to gymnastics practice one Saturday morning. When we got to a narrow part of the highway where it had no shoulder, next to a ravine, he'd drive up next to our car. My mom thought he was trying to scare her into swerving off the road. Then he'd drift back behind us, and my mom watched his red face through the rearview mirror. "Get lower," she told me, pushing down on my shoulder, "in case he tries to shoot us."

My parents kept all the neighbor documents in a maroon briefcase from T.J.Maxx. They're still there: timelines, diaries, photos, court orders, my subpoena, my eight-year-old brother's subpoena. Escalating police reports for vandalism, stalking, harassment, assault. My dad's letter to their first lawyer, listing reasons they fired him, including a moment in court when "we all heard you ask Mr. Harliss whether you or the opposing attorney had the burden of proof." When I sift through the papers now, I see my mom and dad trying desperately to play by the rules. It didn't work.

A court order prohibited my parents and the neighbor from "harassment or nuisance from talking, shouting, whistling, or other forms of communication or activity construed by the court as being done to intentionally harass." Three days later, my parents filed a petition for contempt, detailing how the neighbor had already violated the order twice. The neighbor answered the petition by claiming my parents had "continually harassed and maligned" him, and he was suing them for $100,000. The judge wrote that he did not have "the time needed to hear evidence from both sides," and sentenced both my dad and the neighbor to ten days in jail. The sentence was suspended as long as both paid a bond that would be forfeited if they engaged in more harassment.

Both-sides-ism: a menace in political commentary, devastating in real life. My parents' reward for following the rules was to hand over $5,000.

The next month, on a snowy January morning, my parents found my cat dead near the end of our driveway. At the urging of their lawyers, they got an autopsy. Findings: "A severe trauma is suspected." My mom said the neighbor left a baseball bat leaning against the outside of his house. She thought he wanted us to believe he used it to kill my cat.

The cat autopsy is where I usually start when I tell this story. It's hard proof created by scientists, and it provides moral clarity. A lot of people subconsciously assume victims did *something* to deserve what they got, at least a little. But a household pet getting hurt? That triggers real horror.

Though we had not had much success in court, the lawyers told my parents to continue documenting every incident with the neighbor. I don't remember him targeting me at all, but according to the diary, he did, because my dad wrote an entry that says while I was waiting for the school bus, the neighbor drove his pickup next to me and parked and waved and winked at me.

Around this time, my dad taught me some self-defense—how to break someone's grasp on my wrist, how to carry my keys when walking through a parking lot at night so I could stab an attacker. Put my thumb on the dark circle under his eye, push inward and up, and I could pop his eyeball out of its socket. I nodded solemnly as my dad explained these maneuvers. But inside, I thought, *try it, bitch.* I was a fourteen-year-old girl, but I was a gymnast—and shredded. I could do more pull-ups than all the guys in class. I'd climbed a cliff that left my adult male cousin paralyzed in fear, and then flipped off it into a river. I hauled heavy furniture with my dad. I had extreme endurance, I was fast and agile, and I'd developed a high tolerance for pain. And I was very, very angry.

I was certain that if my neighbor tried to hurt me, I could beat the shit out of him, and that I would enjoy it. Like any teenage girl, I dreamed about the future, about moving to a big city and getting a glamorous job and wearing cool clothes and meeting cute boys. But most of my teen fantasies were about beating up a forty-year-old man.

In the end, there was no real justice. No final comeuppance, no order from the court that meant more than paper. He moved away. We moved to a house way out in the country, and we thought that was that, until we found cigarette butts on the bridge at the end of our new driveway. We moved away from there, too.

———

After my reporting in Charlottesville in 2017, I heard one comment over and over: the only reason I got interviews with white nationalists was because I was a blond woman, and those guys wanted to make Aryan babies with me. I know that's not what *everyone* thinks, but I heard it a lot and it pissed me off. I hope the backstory helps everybody understand there's more to me than the surface you see on television.

The reason I was able to do it was not my hair. It was because I was forced to learn at a very young age that most bullies are cowards, that confrontation is necessary, that you must get it all on tape. When I was surrounded by hostile armed lunatics in Charlottesville—or Oregon, or Michigan, or the United States Capitol—I didn't tap into my years of experience with shampoo and conditioner. What got me into those crowds, and what got me through them, was spending my adolescence preparing for confrontation with this exact kind of man.

BLACK PILL

PROLOGUE

SURF THE KALI YUGA

Roger and I stood near each other watching the speeches in front of the White House on January 6, 2021. I was wearing my uniform for reporting on Americans at risk of rampage: big stompy black boots and a denim jacket that wasn't warm enough. Roger was wearing chain mail.

Beneath the chain mail, on Roger's green T-shirt, was a cartoon frog with bulbous eyes. I stared at it: *You again*. It was "Pepe the Frog." He'd taken a long and twisted journey before landing on Roger's chest.

In the late 2000s, Pepe was lifted from a stoner comic strip and made into an icon on 4chan, an anonymous online forum that was the dark heart of the internet, until it got so dark it wasn't funny anymore. Pepe had an innocent smiling face, but 4chan users redrew him with sad, downcast eyes to represent their loserdom. Because the forum was anonymous, they were free to talk about being losers, and any joke was permitted. Some made ironic Nazi jokes, and making Nazi jokes was itself a joke, a way to keep away outsiders. Over time, new people came to the site and interpreted those jokes as sincere, and eventually the group became the thing they'd once satirized, a herd of brainwashed swastika-posting sheep.

Then 4chan latched on to the term "alt-right," and while there were long essays and podcasts elaborating the ideas behind it, in everyday posting it mostly meant they didn't like women, Black people, queer people, and Jews. They didn't just want political defeat of liberals and conservatives—those *other* people who were brainwashed into believing in equality—they wanted to see them suffer. Donald Trump made those people mad, and so they loved him. They called Trump their god-emperor—a title that was simultaneously ironic and sincere—and they believed they could meme him into the presidency. They started posting a third version of the frog, this one redrawn with solid eye contact and a smirk. He was called "Smug Pepe." You could tell whether trolls thought 4chan or society had the upper hand by which Pepe they posted. Sad, they were losing. Smug, Trump was winning.

Pepe had appeared on banners in far-right brawls, on the lapel of Richard Spencer as he was punched in the face, in the interrogation of a mass murderer in Toronto, on a hacked billboard in the UK, in an official Russian embassy tweet, on the Anti-Defamation League's list of hate symbols. He had been killed by his creator and reanimated by crypto bros, and then sat at the center of a lawsuit between the creator and the bros. When humanity annihilates itself in total nuclear war, the final bomb will be delivered by a missile with this stupid fucking frog painted on it.

Roger was wearing the Smug Pepe. I asked him why. "Pepe is a warrior for Trump," he said. Did he know where it came from? "It was created by somebody back in the day. I don't know all the details." He denied Pepe was a symbol of white nationalism, and he didn't care if other people thought it was, because "I don't give a crap what the other people think. I'm for the truth. This is patriotism and truth."

From the stage, flanked by American flags and behind a podium that said "SAVE AMERICA," Rudy Giuliani shouted, "Let's have trial by combat!" Roger turned in his chain mail and Pepe shirt and looked at me with an ecstatic grin. "He just said trial by combat! I'm ready!"

Roger had been blackpilled. To understand what that means, you have to have seen the 1999 movie *The Matrix* and have spent any time on the internet since it came out.

In *The Matrix*, the hero, Neo, is presented a choice: take the blue pill and return to life in a pleasant illusion created by machines, or take the red pill and learn the truth. And what is the truth? "That you are a slave, Neo. Like everyone else, you were born into bondage, born inside a prison that you cannot smell, taste, or touch. A prison for your mind."

The red pill became the main metaphor of internet politics. It didn't suggest a conversion—that you had adopted a new set of beliefs—but that you had liberated yourself from politics entirely. You saw the world as it really is. You were thinking clearly for the first time in years, maybe your whole life.

I'd heard the red pill narrative of dozens of alt-right trolls (whose red pill was that white supremacy was good) and radical virgins called incels (whose red pill was that feminism had ruined society) long before I'd heard it from QAnoners (whose red pill was that Trump was fighting a secret satanic pedophile cabal that had seized control of the government). Many had been searching for an explanation for something—a breakup, a bad dad, a felony conviction, the financial crisis—and discovered this secret knowledge. A gay Jewish lawyer told me he could point to a single meme that made him a Holocaust denier.

Once the red pill metaphor took hold, endless variations followed—the green pill, the white pill, the iron pill, etc. You could be Russiapilled or cryptopilled or Marxpilled; the term could express pride in your own epiphany or contempt for a nutjob. The only one that matters is the "black pill."

The black pill is a dark but gleeful nihilism: the system is corrupt, and its collapse is inevitable. There is no hope. Times are bad and they're going to get worse. You swallow the black pill and accept the end is coming.

You start searching for evidence to prove to yourself that you're correct, and it's easy enough to find. News about murder and mayhem and poverty and child abuse and islands of trash in the ocean is not an outrage or a problem to be solved, it's just further confirmation of humanity's decline. The hardships and heartbreak you've faced can now be explained as the inevitability of a sweeping historical force. You spend more time in blackpilled online forums, where the darker the commentary, the more attention it gets, so you compete to write the most creative description of the depravity. The only people you trust are the other people who get it, and the only people who get it are your internet friends, people whose names you may never know and whose faces you may never see but who can be counted on to provide fresh analysis every day of how deeply fucked we are.

It's a depressing way to live. 4chan trolls admit this. "I am very blackpilled, no question. The deeper I go down the rabbit hole, the more it hurts," one post read in 2018. "I'm so fuckng lost," another said in 2019. I've seen hundreds more like this.

You can't go on like this forever. It hurts too much. You need some relief from the unrelenting doom. You start to imagine what comes after this system fails. That's the world you need to prepare for, not this one. If the present reality is corrupt and dying, then you are no longer bound by its moral and ethical restraints. You are riding out the collapse of society. You can do anything.

"I know it is dark at times but you gotta learn to enjoy it, man. Embrace being the bad guy. Surf the Kali Yuga," a 4chan user posted in 2014. This appears to be the first use of the phrase "surf the Kali Yuga." It was a reference to Julius Evola, a mid-twentieth-century fascist philosopher who believed humanity was in the Kali Yuga, a time of violence and vice, one of four repeating eras in Hindu cosmology. Evola believed the elite should ride above the degenerate society as it crumbled, and maybe nudge along its collapse, because the next era would be a Golden Age. Online fascists turned Evola's books into memes, putting the title *Revolt Against the Modern World* over glitchy pastel images of Greek marble statues or square-jawed white men.

This might seem like bizarre internet ephemera, and it is, but it is also influential. Joe Rogan, one of the world's most popular podcasters, wrote on Instagram in 2021, "We are in Kali Yuga." The accompanying image depicted a four-part cycle: weak men led to hard times, which led to strong men, which led to good times, which led to weak men, and so on. We're in the era of weak men, Rogan said.

Taking the black pill allows you to justify any action: cruelty, intimidation, violence. The people you hurt are beneath you, because they're still blinded by society's lies. If your actions cause more violence and chaos, that's good, because it will help bring about an end to the corrupt regime.

"Time to go full Kali Yuga lads. Accelerate towards destruction and start again," a 4chan user said in 2017.

On January 6, Roger and I were surrounded by thousands of cheering Trump supporters as we watched America's mayor lie. Most of the people I interviewed on January 6 had been blackpilled, even if they wouldn't have described themselves that way, and even if they'd never heard the term. Their beliefs were on a spectrum, but no matter where they fell on it, they believed our democracy was a scam, that those who couldn't see it were blind, and radical action was necessary.

In the next few hours, I stood in the middle of a mob as it pushed into the Capitol. My fellow Americans screamed at me that this was "revolution," or "1776," or that "only we can save us!" They were absolutely certain they were the good guys. Even while they were shouting at me in the middle of the chaos, I stared at their faces twisted with rage, their bodies wrapped in sensible outdoor gear, and wondered how many of them knew the origin of the ideas that had brought them to Washington. How would they feel if they knew it all traced back to the psychedelic epiphany of a three-foot virgin?

1

THE WIZARD

Anna's presence in Fred's apartment was a repudiation of everything he believed. She was twenty-five and voluptuous, and he was nineteen and three feet tall. They were surrounded by plain white walls and not much furniture, but there was a desk and, on top of it, the heart of the room, Fred's computer.

Fredrick "Fred" Brennan ran an online forum for male virgins. The site was called Wizardchan, for a joke that once a virgin hits the age of thirty, he becomes a wizard. The users were proto-"incels," for involuntarily celibate. These men did not see their virginity as a frustrating but fleeting phase, but rather as a permanent condition. They were too ugly, or too awkward, to ever find love.

Fred had sandy blond hair, pale skin, and high cheekbones, but he believed he was doomed by his bones. He was born with osteogenesis imperfecta, or "brittle bone disease," a genetic mutation that affects collagen. Collagen in bones is like the metal rods in the reinforced concrete of a building. If the rods are missing, or weaker than they should be, the concrete can fail and crumble. Fred's bones didn't grow straight and strong, but curved and fragile, and they broke easily. Just a little bit of pressure, he said, "and that's it, you can break me." He sat in his motorized wheelchair with his curved legs crossed below his small torso. Sometimes he wore kids' pajamas. Wizardchan users trusted Fred, because they thought his severe disability meant he could never betray them by having sex with a woman.

But Anna was attracted to virgins. She liked men to be shy, self-conscious, nervous about sex. She'd lurked in incel chatrooms and sites like Fred's. She was fascinated by the culture, and related to it, because she felt like an outsider rejected by society. She'd become obsessed with the idea of ugliness.

"When you are disabled, you can feel like everybody sees you as a freak, and you are not wanted anywhere, and everybody would be a lot more comfortable if you didn't exist," Fred said. In the real world, he was stared at, but in the online world, he could be whoever he wanted.

He'd discovered anonymous forums when he was twelve. They'd become an escape from the misery he felt in the physical world, but they'd also convinced him he should have never been born. As a teen, he'd told his mom, who shares his disability, that she was selfish for having him, and he'd told his dad, who is able-bodied, that he was a pervert for marrying her.

Fred was living in Brooklyn and had been Wizardchan's admin for a few months when Anna sent him a message through the site's chatroom. She lived in Oklahoma, and she wanted to meet him. He was skeptical, but intrigued. She explained that the more nervous he was about sex, the more she found it erotic. This meant their sexual relationship would inevitably die. As he got more experience, Fred would grow more confident and lose his virginal quality, and she would lose interest. How long it took depended on how quickly Fred changed. There was no doubt that he would change.

"She explained it real up front: 'We're gonna have sex maybe ten, twenty times,'" Fred said. "She said maybe as few as three if I get real confident, real fast."

"I never met a woman that was so *blunt* about it. I didn't know that people could be this blunt about sex. I didn't know that it was even, like—this is gonna sound stupid, but—*legal*. I was nineteen! I was dumb."

Fred was never really dumb, and he knew it. He'd been told he was brilliant since he was a little kid, and I could tell he was the first time we spoke. When I flew eighteen hours to the Philippines, traveled an hour through Manila traffic, and rode the elevator up a high rise to meet him in 2019, it felt like a fairy-tale pilgrimage to meet a wise man on the top of a mountain. He knows what he knows and can explain it methodically. In many interviews, I have not just to convince someone to give me information, but to help them realize what information they have. Sometimes I send sources an infamous Donald Rumsfeld quote, which he said when asked about the lack of proof Iraq had weapons of mass destruction:

> *There are known knowns; there are things we know we know. We also know there are known unknowns, that is to say, we know there are some things we do not know. But there are also unknown unknowns, the ones we don't know we don't know.*

When I watched this on TV in 2002, I thought, *What an asshole.* It gives me subversive pleasure now to use it for my own ends. I tell sources that I can publish the known knowns, and I can find out the known unknowns, but they have to help me figure out my unknown unknowns. Then I send them a You-Tube clip of the philosopher Slavoj Žižek asserting there is a fourth category: the unknown knowns, that which we do not know we know. For my sources, this is information they know they have but do not understand is significant to the public interest.

Fred understood this immediately. He can catalog all the relevant information he has, and then evaluate each piece for its provability. We've jammed together, side by side or over the phone, digging through internet archives to find long-lost files.

But back in 2013, Fred did not yet have wisdom earned through the wild events of the next six years. He was smart, but naïve.

———

In September 2013, Fred bought Anna a plane ticket to New York City. When she walked into his apartment, her style was goth, with black lipstick, and a black shirt that showed off her figure. She giggled.

"Nice to meet you, Fred," she said. "You're tinier than I expected."

She traced the curved bones of his arm with her fingers. He'd never been touched like that. It was electric. He didn't know what to do. He didn't know if he could copy the sex scenes he'd seen in Hollywood movies, and he didn't know there was any other way to do it. He was scared she'd break his bones.

"She's all naked, and obviously I'm really hard," Fred said. "And she's telling me, 'Sex is what you make it.'"

Many lovers have felt their affair was world historic. But for Fred and Anna, it was true. This moment changed the trajectory of Fred's life, and the internet, and history. You can trace a line from this romance to the failed coup against the United States on January 6, 2021.

———

About eight years after his relationship with Anna (and six months after the attempted coup), Fred and I sat for hours in a sports bar in a casino in Atlantic City, both of us eating giant slices of chocolate cake. We were an unusual pair, Fred in his wheelchair with his tiny dog, Hitomi, on his lap, and me with my phone, recording every word. The servers were sweet to us, but they seemed to be trying to figure out our deal, since we weren't drinking, or gambling, or even watching the sports. After I reassured the waitress again that we really didn't need anything more than the cake, I asked Fred if he believed, as I did, that he'd played a very significant role in history in the last five years. He said yes.

"There is no more separation between the online world and the real world," Fred said. It was getting close to midnight, and sports highlights were replaying on a huge screen behind him. "This notion we have that what is happening online, is happening *online*—is wrong. Everything happening online is happening in reality. Everything happening online is happening in the real world."

When Anna stepped into Fred's apartment, she was the real world crashing into Fred's incel internet fantasy. But she didn't destroy it, at least not for a long time. Fred and his wizard friends had built their whole identities around the idea that they could never have this one thing: sex. When they finally got it, they were devastated. They created new rules to explain away Anna. It took

Fred years to understand how much she'd taught him, that "almost everything I believed from Wizardchan was nonsense."

Near the end of their relationship, Fred founded a forum called 8chan. It was an imageboard, like Wizardchan, but he imagined it would have a broad audience, from kids to extremists. Nothing would be banned except what was illegal in the U.S. This brought the people who were banned from everywhere else. He'd imagined that a site with unrestricted free speech would create a robust forum that would bring forth new and better ideas, but over time, 8chan became an incubator for conspiracy theories and violent ideologies, like incels, the alt-right, and later, after he left it, QAnon. 8chan made Fred an internet supervillain.

Fred likes to say that if he hadn't created 8chan, someone else would have. But a close look at his life makes it hard to imagine who that other person might have been.

It's hard to imagine another child who truly had no power but words, who learned as a kid how to use them to inflict maximum damage, who as a teen was taken from his parents and could control nothing but computers, someone who's only escape was through the internet and the online friends who convinced him that his birth was a crime. It's hard to imagine anything like that stacking up in some other guy.

Fred was born in rural Upstate New York in 1994. As a toddler, he became obsessed with letters, and could play with a set of alphabet magnets on the floor for hours. Both his parents said he could read when he was two and a half years old, and they liked to show him off. They liked proving the doubters wrong.

Gwynne was a doubter, at first. Her son was friends with Fred. The first time she walked into the Brennan home, she saw Fred sitting at the kitchen table, the newspaper in front of him. Fred's dad, Dave Brennan, told her to watch his son. "This is kindergarten, mind you—he just starts reading all the articles in the newspaper," she said. "I thought it was a gag—you know, a 'Haha, see, my kid's smarter than your kid' kind of thing. But it wasn't like that. It just *was*."

When he was six years old, Fred found a photo of himself that was framed in a way that made it easy to imagine he could walk. As he stared at the photo, he could see himself walking to his friend's house and playing Pokémon. "I was daydreaming for like ten minutes. I'm looking at the photo the whole time I'm daydreaming, and suddenly it just cuts short, and I see the photo again for what it *really* is, and what it really always is going to be. And I cried for hours from that."

―――――

The same year, his dad gave Fred a computer. He loved it. "The reason he's into computers is because of me," Dave said. When his son was using his computer, he had a smile on his face and "a glow in his eye," even early on, when he was just pushing the same letter over and over until the keyboard broke. Fred broke a lot of computers. They were more fragile in the nineties.

The computer wasn't a machine, Fred said. "I viewed it as like an eye that I could look through into other places that weren't my immediate, extremely boring surroundings." Fred's brother Nicholas was born a couple years after him, and he had OI, too. Dave thought computers were his only option: "What else are they going to do in life? They can't play football or baseball."

Around the time Fred started kindergarten, his parents' marriage began to fall apart. The divorce was bitter, and Dave got primary custody of the kids. They had a live-in home health aide. When Fred was ten, he accused his mom, Vera, of sex abuse. She lost custody rights. Fred recanted six years later. Fred says now that the aide put him up to it, that she forced him to memorize a statement that he didn't understand.

At the time, Dave and the aide were in a romantic relationship. Years later, after their relationship ended, Dave told me that he'd come to think the aide "may have plotted this. That, I don't know. I wasn't a part of that. But in hindsight now, I kind of wonder."

"The only people who believed me were the people who knew me—that I would never do something like that to my children," Vera said. She agreed not to see them till they were eighteen, because the endless court battle was hurting them. But she remembers telling the judge she knew the children would come back to her.

When he was thirteen, Fred read a Wikipedia article about a vow of silence. Around the same time, his class was assigned to read *Speak*, a young adult novel about a teenager who is raped, and in her struggle to cope with it, she stops talking. Wikipedia taught him that vows of silence "were a thing," and the book taught him that it could force circumstances to change. He felt like no one cared when he was talking, so he would stop talking. At the end of the novel, the family reunited and the problems were over.

Fred refused to speak to anyone but his brother, in a whisper, or to the internet, in writing. Dave said he wasn't sure how long it lasted—a year, maybe two. "He wouldn't talk to me. He wouldn't talk to anybody. Just clammed up. The silent treatment."

Fred was beginning to understand the power of words. He'd discovered 4chan the previous year, and he was mesmerized. He saw people using terms like "crippled," "retard," "crippled retard," and any other offensive slur you could possibly imagine, and there was nothing to stop them. In school, sometimes kids would put things out of his reach and then laugh, but they never said, "You're a crippled retard." He knew the words, of course, but he'd never been called that in real life. He felt a perverse satisfaction in reading it on 4chan.

Wow, he thought. *They're all agreeing with each other, and they're all saying it, and they're all just laughing it up. This is what people are really thinking. They're lying in real life.*

There was no way for him to escape the way people saw him in real life, so it was better to live online anonymously. "From that point, when I started using 4chan heavily, my whole life became about the internet, and my real life stopped mattering to me."

To gain acceptance on 4chan, he had to show he was an epic troll—that he didn't feel bad about offending people. "If you're not willing to troll," he said, "you're not going to get respect among other users." Trolling gave him a sense of power, just as it did for all the others, who had their own reasons for living online.

Fred brought this sensibility into his real life. When he learned about genetics in school, it occurred to him, for the first time, that his dad had known there'd been a chance Vera would pass along the genetic mutation for OI to their children. "I realized that he'd done this really taboo thing," Fred said. "When I first brought that up to him, I realized how powerful that could be."

Like so many dads, in the afternoons, Dave usually asked Fred what he'd learned in school that day. "And I couldn't wait to tell him, 'Well, I learned that my disability is your fault, David.'" Fred watched his dad's face turn to shock.

Fred began to see the extreme vulnerability of his disability as an invincibility shield. "I could basically say whatever I wanted as a kid, to anyone who was taking care of me, and know that they couldn't physically hurt me without getting in trouble." A smack, a slap, a shoe thrown across the room—they all risked a broken rib. "You might kill me, even, if you hit too hard."

I asked Dave if he ever felt like Fred was trying to make him angry. "He was trying to make me mad? Well, I don't know. He found out what it was to make me mad when he pulled that shit. Then he found out what it was really like to make me mad," Dave said. I asked Dave what he meant by "pulled that shit." He said he meant when his kids reported the aide for abuse at school. And "what it was like" was that he gave up his children to foster care.

At the time, Dave said, he was really stressed out. It was hard to make the doctor appointments and pay the bills, plus the weather was getting warmer, so he had more customers. "Winter's over and people want me to fix stuff, and what, I got to go find another aide? These kids just come up behind me, I felt like I was stabbed right in the back." Fred and his brother were taken out of Dave's home and put in the foster care system. The aide stayed with Dave.

Their foster care caseworker, Melisa Rehrauer, said she knew Fred was very smart the day she met him. But he didn't want to be looked at, and he let his hair hang in his face. "Everything about him—just the way he presented himself—on the inside, you could tell he was a broken child," she said.

Rehrauer placed the brothers in a group home with other foster kids, and they weren't allowed to go online unsupervised. Fred was miserable there. He still yelled at Rehrauer about it, even years later. He reached out to her once and bragged he built porn sites, and that he made more money doing it than she ever would. "He hurt me so bad. I cried so much that night," Rehrauer told me. She warned him that if he kept hurting her, she'd walk away. "He was like, 'You're never going to give up on me.'"

Once he was in foster care, Fred felt like he could say *anything*. He'd been a little scared that if he pushed his dad too far, he'd take away his computer. "But in foster care, I was so isolated already, I felt like there's *nothing* I can't say. I would go for the maximum damage."

The foster kids weren't allowed to have cell phones, but Fred figured out a loophole: he could save his weekly allowance and buy an iPod Touch, which had Wi-Fi. The group home's Wi-Fi was password protected, and it changed all the time. After he got the iPod, he helped his foster parents' daughter fix her computer, and while doing so, secretly installed a remote access tool so he could find out the Wi-Fi password anytime. "I could go on 4chan and nobody could know," Fred said. He didn't tell anyone, not even his brother. "That's how I survived those years."

———

Fred wanted to know why his life had to be this way. "When I was in foster care, the question I was trying to answer was more a political question, which was: Why did this happen? Why is my situation so shitty? Why was this allowed to happen?" He posted his question on 4chan's news board, which was then called /n/, and had already been infested with neo-Nazis. "You don't want to ask a lot of neo-Nazis that," he said, "because they'll give you an answer."

The neo-Nazis had a simple answer: "Because disabled people are allowed to breed. And they shouldn't be." It made sense to Fred. He believed he should not have been born, and now that he was here, he was unwanted. The state hadn't had the courage to force his mother to have an abortion, so it hid him away. "When I would rationally think about my situation in foster care, I would think to myself, *The only reason that this has happened is because the State of New York, and the United States federal government, is cowardly. And they have decided they don't want me, but they are too much of a coward to pull the trigger.*"

"But Fredrick," I said, "your existence is not a tragedy."

"That's true, too," he said. We were sitting in his van in an empty parking lot after midnight. My phone, resting in the cup holder, picked up the sound of a ten-second pull from his vape. "Yeah," he said, "of course."

———

When he was sixteen, Fred and his brother reunited with their mom. His life got so much better, but he was still depressed, and the question of his existence persisted. He would tell his mom, "You shouldn't have had kids anyway. You knew that this was going to happen." He'd find new ways to say it, "something really offensive, like 'You're really selfish.'"

"My favorite insult for my dad was 'pervert,'" Fred said. "Obviously, the implication being that only a pervert would marry a disabled woman."

Dave said he didn't remember Fred calling him a pervert. Vera remembered Fred "thought that our relationship was a fetish for David, which it wasn't." Fred was into the darkest websites at the time, she said. "What would he know? He's a teenager looking for answers."

"Do you know how many guys would tell me that they didn't even see the chair when they thought about me? They never saw the chair, they said," Vera told me. She thought she would have been able to explain to her sons that romance was possible in a way their father couldn't. "That's what got robbed, Elle. I was robbed of being able to let my son know that a woman would love him. That a woman would be able to forget the physical, and not think of him as in a wheelchair. . . . But because I wasn't there, that's the only thing he had to hold on to: his anger."

Fred's anger made it easy to swallow the red pill. For incels, the red pill is that some men will never have sex, because they are too ugly, and there is nothing they can do about it. All men and women naturally fall somewhere on a scale of attractiveness from 1 to 10, and at some point in the mythic past, 8s would marry 8s and 3s would marry 3s. But feminism had disrupted nature's balance. It had stripped away the stigma on sex. Because women would always try to have sex with the highest-status men, and men would have sex with anyone, the best-looking men now got all the women. The male 8s, 9s, and 10s left nothing behind for the 1s, 2s, and 3s. Over time, the community created archetypes: "Stacy," the unobtainable sexually ideal woman, and "Chad Thundercock," the guy who wins her.

Much of the incel cosmology developed on a 4chan board called /r9k/, for ROBOT9000. The board had a bot that would delete any image or text that had been posted before. The demand was genius in its simplicity: you must say something original. The easiest way to say something original was to talk about your own life. If you're the kind of person who needs anonymity to be able to socialize, there's a good chance you have a particular story to tell: public humiliation. Those stories were posted over and over and over, and users stopped seeing social awkwardness as a fleeting phase, but instead a curse of their permanent social caste. The phrase "it's over" was ubiquitous.

The incels analyzed the angles in male models' faces. "A few millimeters of bone" was all that separated them from their handsome oppressors. The perfect Chad had narrow eyes and a massive jaw, and looked like a suntanned Neanderthal in an ad for Ralph Lauren. Chad had total confidence, and his advice to virgin losers was "just be yourself," because just being Chad had worked so well for him. Women spent their twenties riding the "cock carousel," sleeping with as many Chads as possible, and then, at thirty, when they were used up and ugly, they settled for a nice beta male who'd spent his youth working hard and building a career. After a few years, the women would file for divorce, and take all their beta's money. "Alpha fucks, beta bucks."

And who were they, if they were not Chad? The loser, the neckbeard, the NEET—a British government term for "not in education, employment, or training"—an overweight post-teen who terrorized his parents with demands for juvenile things, like chicken tenders, or "tendies." This man lived online. He was too lazy to get up and go to the bathroom, so he peed in empty bottles and left them on the floor at his feet. He was an ashamed but unceasing masturbator. His mother bribed him to take baby steps toward entering mainstream society by awarding points for good behavior. These bribes were sometimes called "good boy points" (GBP) and they could be exchanged for tendies.

There were thousands of memes about incels and good boy points, but one I came across on 4chan best captures the spirit of the whole scene:

Lost all my tendies and GBP in the crash

decide to earn one billion GBP

buckle down and start working hard

clean the piss, shit, and cum jugs out of my room earned 100 GBP step outside for the first time in years and go to the barber, earned 10 GBP

get a shave and a haircut, earned 50 GBP for each

enroll back in college, 100 points

keep racking up points for years

lose weight, get fit 100,000 points

get a gf 10,000 points

graduate medical school 100,000

get married and buy a house 1,000,000 points

mommy awards points for grandkids so I get my girlfriend pregnant a few
    times as well

decide to see them through college for bonus points

fast forward, kids come home for Christmas from unis

I'm getting close to my goal of 1 billion GBP

my sosn are happy to see me

my daughter is saying some shit about how stressful college life is

"I'm having a hard time at college dad, it's so competitive"

well, honey, I'm sure you'll make it you just have to bee yourself, I have
    complete faith in you (I've been keeping close count of GBP, 10 points for
    giving fatherly advice means I've reached my goal)

"Oh daddy I'm so glad I have you here to keep me grounded! I don't know what
    I would do without you

honey I love you too, belive me life is-

a huge smile creeps upon my lips

IVE BEEN A GOOD BOY FOR MUMMY

hook my daughter in the face

shit on the dinner table, ruin the Christmas dinner

my family looks on in horror

sprint out of the house all the way to my mommy's retirement home

kick the door down

shake her hand and smear i with shit

IVE BEEN A GOOD BOY MUMMY WHERE'S MY TENDIES

she stares at me with dead eyes, a single drop in her left one

That was 4 years ago. I've been living off my GBP ever since.

It was an obscene update to *Bartleby, the Scrivener*: Live a normal, healthy life? I would prefer not to. When my bosses made an unpleasant demand, like that I rewrite a script or work a weekend, I'd ask my senior producer, *How many good boy points do I get for this, Brandon? I want my tendies.*

"It's like a whole theology," Fred said. "I believed in all that. Especially in my case, I saw myself as a zero—I'm never going to have anyone."

When Fred found Wizardchan in 2012, it was fun, at least some of the time. Fred was talking to people who were young like him, and had problems like his, and they were all trying to figure out together if society had anything to offer them. They were a band of depressed pirates. Now he sees it as a woman-hating pit of hell, but at the time, it made a lot of sense, the idea that your face had doomed you.

In March 2013, just after his nineteenth birthday, Fred took over Wizardchan from the previous owner, who'd gotten tired of it. The site's users didn't know what he looked like, but for the identity he used to become admin, "copypaste," it was public that he was severely disabled. "That helped them trust me that I was never going to lose my wizard status," he said. They didn't want to be ruled by somebody who was not one of them.

Fred told his mom. "He came to me and said that he was the head of this club—remember? The wizards or whatever?" Vera said. She laughed. "I said, 'Fredrick—okay, *whatever.*'" He was offended. What did she mean *whatever*?

She told him that he only thought these things because he'd never had sex. She told him, *All you have to do is find a woman that cares about you, and is gentle. And you should be on top.* She didn't believe he'd serve the life sentence he'd given himself.

Fred imagined Wizardchan as "a sanctuary for virgins." His rules forbade users from alluding to the possibility they'd had sex or a romantic relationship, and they could not advise against the lifestyle. "Laugh at me if you want to, but I was trying to make a positive space," Fred said. He wanted his internet friends to embrace wizarddom, to see themselves as modern-day monks. He was a decade away from turning thirty, so he identified as a "wizard apprentice."

This was 2013. It was before Elliot Rodger posted a manifesto saying, "I will destroy all women because I can never have them. I will make them all suffer for rejecting me. I will arm myself with deadly weapons and wage a war against all women and the men they are attracted to. And I will slaughter them like the animals they are." It was before he killed six people at University of California, Santa Barbara, the next year. It was before incels started talking about how they wanted to "go E.R." It was before Rodger became a meme. It was five years before Alek Minassian rented a van and used it to kill ten people on a city street in Toronto. It was before Minassian told police he wanted to spark an "incel uprising."

"I was mostly a wiz type, which is like, 'I'm celibate but happy.'" Fred paused. "Well, to a degree." He clarified, "Of course I thought about suicide, like everyone does." Then another pause, another clarification: like everyone does "in *our* chan universe." He laughed. "I'm so sorry, Elle. Us chan people are so different from normal society." He added one last clarification, about the nature of his suicidality. "If I would think about suicide, it wouldn't be because of myself. It would be because of my disability, and the pain I was suffering from at the time."

They were driven online by their social isolation, and found comfort in creating their own community, but the more time they spent there, the less contact they had with other people in the real world. Through repetition, wild ideas began to seem like common sense. There was no one to say, *You don't know what you're talking about.*

He knew depressed people were drawn to Wizardchan. Depression wasn't supposed to be the main theme of the site under Fred's leadership, and he'd created a separate board to talk about it. At the top of the depression board, he posted the number for a suicide hotline. Some users were furious, because it read like a recommendation that they ask normies for help. One guy said it should be a suicide tipline instead.

"I would worry a lot about certain Wizardchan users, and what they were going to do. There were a lot of suicides. Being an anonymous community, I can't do a whole lot about that. Next to nothing," Fred said.

A few months later, in the summer of 2013, Fred got a programming job in Brooklyn. With a side job that brought in a little cash, plus Social Security disability benefits, he had more than $1,000 to spare a month, and because he didn't do much, it was plenty of money. He could still wear his old clothes from foster care, and he did, because wearing the same old T-shirt "made me feel like even though my life is kind of spinning out of control, at least some things are staying the same." He wanted to show people you could be a wizard and live a real life. But he didn't see a lot of people other than his boss, and he was lonely.

A break in his arm, and one in his spine, hadn't healed correctly, and the pain was intense. He wanted to jump off the Brooklyn Bridge, and he thought about it every day. He was doing everything on his own—cooking, cleaning, showering. When he looks at old photos of himself from that time, he sees a very skinny version of himself who wanted to die.

He hadn't been in Brooklyn long when he got an unusual message. It was a photo of a young woman's face with a time stamp—this was the language of authenticity on the internet. Her name was Anna, and she was attracted to virgins, the message said. Did he want to lose his virginity?

Fred didn't believe her. A fetish for virgins is not a thing, he said. She must be a troll, lying to get a rise out of him. They argued about it. Didn't she know that what she was proposing would come at an enormous cost?

He said he told her, "First of all I'm Wizardchan's admin, okay? I'm going to lose my position. Even if I do what you're saying. Even if you're telling the truth. Which you're not."

The wizards needed him. "I felt like I was running the place in a more ethical way than anyone who came after me would. It sounds ridiculous, but I considered myself the most ethical possible admin. I felt I had a responsibility to my community to not pursue this." But he kept talking to her, because he was intrigued. And he thought she was attractive, though he didn't say so.

They chatted online for a few weeks. If he wanted to lose his virginity, she would have to visit. And if she visited, there would be rules. Anna was very up front: they would not be monogamous. She was attracted to the way virgins were shy, nervous. Once he got over that, she would get bored.

"I accepted that, and so I told her, 'Okay, I'm gonna make a deal with you, though. I need help around the house. So can you please stay anyway? And I'll let you have sex with other men—I don't care.' And that was our arrangement."

Fred had some rules, too. She could live with him for free, and he'd give her a little money, but she had to help him. She had to shop and make food and clean. She could not hurt him or steal from him. If she ever wanted to stop taking care of him, that was okay. But then she'd have to leave.

First, Fred sent her a cheap prepaid cell phone. A few days later, he bought her a plane ticket to New York. She walked into his place on an afternoon in September 2013.

Fred was so nervous he could barely speak. He mumbled that she could stay indefinitely. He remembers that she led the way, because he wasn't going to.

"Well," she said, "I came here so you could lose your virginity. It's time."

She had thick thighs, which Fred thought were sexy, but he was overwhelmed with fear she would break his legs. "I was very scared, though I didn't need to be. I've since learned it's very easy to have sex," he said. They figured out he needed to be on top.

Anna, he said, was "just *running* the show." They had a powerful chemistry. "Her having this virgin fetish, and disabled fetish . . . Like, she called me her perfect mark." When she said it, he thought, *I should be offended, but I'm not and I don't know why.*

Fred felt a moral obligation to tell the wizards what he'd done. He and Anna took a photo of themselves holding hands, her arm straight, and his curved. He posted it on Wizardchan.

Years later, Fred and I spent an hour on the phone together, trying to find this post, digging through archiving sites, searching post numbers and filenames. The only trace we could find was a capture of the Wizardchan home page, which showed a tiny preview for Fred's post on the board for discussion of the site itself. "I, copypaste, the sole administrator of . . ." He paused at this scrap of his younger self. "There's my writing style. Yeah I know: very autistic and pretentious."

Wizardchan users were furious. He'd broken his own rule, and he stepped down.

For a while, at least, their relationship changed the wizards' belief system. Less attractive men—the 1s, 2s, and 3s—would still be doomed to celibacy. But, Fred said, "they created a new rule that those at the very bottom of the pile will get some women, because some women will have fetishes. And that the only way somebody like me could ever get female attention was through someone with a fetish."

It did not feel good to believe he could only have sex as the object of a fetish, or that he could never have a normal relationship. But he sought out those messages, because he wanted to know what his old friends thought about what he did. "It seems ridiculous to me now to think that it's in any way shameful to have a relationship, what the heck? But I don't know, back then . . . I wondered if I had even made a mistake."

I spoke to Anna once, by phone, and we later exchanged a few messages online. (Anna is a pseudonym.) She hadn't responded to my messages when I was reporting on Fred in 2019, but after the story about him aired, she reached out. She spoke in a low whisper, and said she was scared of people who were still on those sites. She'd spent a lot of time lurking in incel Discord servers, subreddits, occasionally alt-right forums—places that had taken misogyny to an obsessive, violent extreme that felt barely tethered to some old sexist stand-up act or frat movie. She could spend time in those places and not feel targeted, because it was easy for her to disassociate and forget she was a woman.

When she started talking to Fred, she thought he was kind. She was open about the reason for her fascination with this virgin culture. They'd built a belief system around why they were fundamentally different from women, and normies, and people who'd had sex, but she related to them. "I felt like an outsider and rejected by society," she said, "so I felt like I had a lot of empathy and sympathy for a lot of those people who identified as ugly and socially rejected."

She was fascinated with physical ugliness. She had been sexually abused as a child, she said, "and I thought maybe if I was ugly, it wouldn't have happened to me." Fred made her feel safe, she said, "because he was physically unable to hurt me."

"I started taking the black pill, even though the black pill is horrible," Anna said. She thought the red pill was more about psychological domination—that women had evolved to be dominated and raped. Redpilled men had discovered that cruelty was a successful dating strategy with women who were psychologically damaged, and they promoted those techniques to others. "The black pill is more hopeless," she said. "If you're ugly, it's over."

She felt empathy for them, but she knew what she was looking at. "These spaces reward cruelty, and people know that the crueler you are, the more respect you get," she said. Some men posted photos of their faces, and asked others to tell them how ugly they were. The replies were merciless.

The way Anna spoke was eerie. I thought she had knowledge, even wisdom, from experiences few others had had. But she didn't see it that way. She felt regret and horror. She said she'd joined those forums because she thought she could change the guys who were stuck on them, but she wondered if she'd somehow made it worse. I told her I didn't understand why they were so angry. The meek had inherited the Earth. The nerds had gotten their revenge. The economy rewarded intelligence and technical skill over physical strength. Our modern legends were not Paul Bunyan and John Henry, but Steve Jobs and Elon Musk. The nerds had won, but they were mad about it.

Anna thought the incels were acting out of envy. They mimicked the behavior of people who had hurt them. They wanted to be the strong men they'd seen dominate women.

"The real world is the conscious," Anna thought, and 4chan, Wizardchan, and their associated forums—"those spaces are the subconscious." They revealed the darkest thoughts—like misogyny, racism, ableism, which were wrong, but still existed, under the surface.

When Anna first came to New York, she had a good time. She and Fred did silly tourist stuff. In a photo of the two of them, she's grinning, wearing a furry hat with tiny animal ears. Despite all the rules, they made a little home

together. Fred's expectations for her cooking were minimal—he liked maca-
roni and cheese. She slept on the mattress under the window. She was a good
artist, and she sketched his arms in pencil. They started to figure each other
out. "She thought that I had autism," Fred said, "and she would tell me that
she just wanted to make sure that I knew the plans, because she thinks that I
do poorly when I don't know the plans."

Anna said it was the first time she had felt needed and, at the same time,
independent.

"She corrupted me in every way she could find," Fred told me the first
time we talked about Anna. There was faint nostalgia in his voice. In another
conversation, years later, he went further: "Looking back, I think she kind of
saved my life."

———

"I'm very vanilla," Fred said. But Anna—she was into all kinds of things. She
showed him that sex was possible, and through those encounters, helped him
make peace with his body.

He remembered watching her play dominatrix. He was shocked by how
good she was at it. Once, Fred said, a good-looking man in his forties came
over. Fred thought he looked like a lawyer. "Anna was being a super bitch to
him, but he was into it," Fred said. "It was the most bizarre display I'd ever
seen."

He was fit, with a broad movie star face, but Anna called him ugly. "I doubt
he's ever been called ugly in his life," Fred said.

Fred couldn't imagine being that rude to someone he'd just met. He'd be
shaking in his recliner with anxiety.

When the lawyer walked into the room, he saw Fred working on his computer. The lawyer asked why Fred was there.

"You don't get to ask the questions," she said. "Maybe I'm Santa and he's
my elf."

Fred started laughing. He was amazed Anna could keep this guy's interest
just by being so mean to him. They were both fully clothed.

"Will you tell that guy to leave?"

"You don't make the fucking rules."

That's when Fred realized he'd become part of the game, just by being there, on his computer, chatting with one of his Wizardchan friends. He wasn't trying to help, and they hadn't planned it. But his laughter was part of the humiliation.

"Is he going to tell anyone about this?"

"He's not retarded. You can talk to him."

Fred finally spoke: "Yeah—that was a little ableist."

Fred channeled his fourteen-year-old self to calm the lawyer with a troll's brutality. "I know you think you're hot shit . . . but I don't know who you are and I don't give a fuck." Anna gave him a thumbs-up.

Another day that fall, Fred's friend Bear came over to the apartment. Fred said Bear was a big man, and fat, and that's why he thought he was doomed to celibacy. He had a wide face, dark curly hair, and glasses. Fred had never known him as anything but Bear.

They'd been hanging out for a few hours when Anna told Fred she wanted to have sex. "And then Bear said, 'Can I watch?'" Fred said. "And we said okay, because we always let people watch." Bear's request didn't surprise him, because he knew Bear had never seen sex in person. "I bet he was curious what it looks like to see a cripple have sex."

Fred and Anna got undressed, and Anna lay on the bed, Fred on top, for his safety. Bear sat by the bed on a folding chair. They started having sex, he said, "but I'm disabled. I'm pretty slow. I enjoy it more to kind of take my time.

"I want to make it absolutely clear there's no wrong way to have sex. This was a consenting encounter, and there's no wrong way to do it. I can do it however I please, as long as Anna agrees, which she did."

Fred was still awkward and nervous, and Anna had to encourage him. "Because I keep saying, *Are you sure this is what you want? Are you sure? Are you sure? I'm really ugly. Bear can see.* I'm even starting to say stuff like *Hmm I don't know, Bear can see my butt.* I don't know why." It was hard to focus. He felt self-conscious about his body, and worried he might have cellulite.

"I'm being slow and I'm being shy and Anna's getting really hot by my shyness," Fred said. But Bear was antsy. "I can see that he's, like, getting more and more frustrated, sexually, with the fact that I'm slow, and that Anna doesn't seem to be enjoying it as much as she would be if he did it."

Fred orgasmed, and then Anna asked him to try performing oral sex, which he'd never done before. She gave him instructions on how to do it.

"Bear is sitting in that metal folding chair getting more and more and more and more frustrated," Fred remembered. Then Bear stood up and took off his shirt, then his pants, and asked Anna if he could show Fred how it's done. Then he jumped on the bed.

He was so big he made the mattress tilt downward at a steep angle, and Fred got scared. "You have to stop, you have to get off the bed," Fred said. "I'm not strong enough to stop myself from rolling off the bed, and I'll fall on the floor." Fred asked Bear to wait while he climbed into his wheelchair. Bear was impatient, but he waited. "Sorry I'm slow," Fred said. "And I'm not making fun of you for being fat. It's just the physical reality."

Once Fred was safe in his wheelchair, Bear hopped back on the bed, Fred said, "and starts eating her out like a pro."

"Anna was screaming in ecstasy—it was *crazy*—that this virgin was doing this to her."

Fred felt a little jealous that Bear was so good at it. But he was happy for him. He thought Bear would be happy.

"When it was over and we all started talking, I was like, *Wow, Bear, where'd you learn that? I thought you were a virgin.*" Bear had a simple answer: porn.

But something in Bear started to shift. "I could see his affect slowly getting more and more sad. And then I stupidly turned the topic to Wizardchan."

"Bear," Fred said, "what does this mean for you and Wizardchan?"

There was dead silence. Bear turned to Anna and asked if she was his girlfriend now. She laughed and said no.

"Oh, no, oh, no, oh, no," Bear said. "I'm gonna lose my moderatorship on Wizardchan. Oh, no, I made a big mistake. Oh, no, no, why did I even come here?"

Fred and Anna tried to reassure him. They said they wouldn't tell. He could keep it a secret—no one had to know. But like Fred, Bear had a virgin code of ethics. He had to come clean. He was getting more upset: *I'm not a wizard anymore.*

"You had fun," Anna said. "I had fun, too. It was your idea to jump in."

Bear lay on his back on the floor, sobbing and pounding his fists: *I ruined my life. I ruined my life. I ruined my life.* And, to Anna, "You ruined my life. You ruined my life, you succubus."

The word had a distinct meaning. On Wizardchan, a "succubus" was a manipulative woman who coaxed beta males to do things for her. A succubus got her needs fulfilled without care for what it cost the betas she was exploiting.

Fred knew Bear saw himself as an exploited beta. He thought Bear's understanding of what had just happened had no relationship to reality. But he tried to reassure him, wizard-to-wizard: *The same thing happened to me. You can find new friends. We're still your friends.*

Fred had a high tolerance for weird, but this was really weird. It was uncomfortable. He looked down at Bear on the floor. The man weighed four or five times what Fred did. If he hadn't known him, Fred would have thought of him as a tough macho guy, with his big body and dark curly hair. But he was throwing a tantrum like a baby. Fred couldn't understand why it meant so much to Bear to be a moderator on Wizardchan.

Fuck you succubus, fuck you cripple for inviting me here. Fuck both of you, you're both fucking terrible people.

Bear lay there a long time, in tears, pounding his fists, until someone in the apartment below banged on their ceiling for him to shut up. He stopped pounding but continued to cry. Then he got on his feet and said he had to leave.

They were concerned. *Where are you going? Are you going to your parents' house?* He wouldn't say. They were afraid he'd hurt himself.

Fred never saw him again. He said Bear posted a final message to the wizards before deactivating his accounts. Even now, Fred said, "One of the things I think about Bear the most is I hope he didn't kill himself. Because he talked about it a little bit. But we all did. . . . It's fucked, but at the time, I didn't see it as out of the ordinary."

Fred thought Bear was despondent because Anna had taken away not just his virginity, but his community. "And now he's nothing. He's not a wizard. He's not a normie. He's no one. He's just a loser."

———

Fred had never smoked weed or gotten drunk. He didn't even use much pain medication. He'd grown up believing that he needed to tough it out—don't be a wimp, don't complain. But the pain in his spine was excruciating, and he could barely work on the computer. He'd wake up feeling like a knife was driving through the mattress and deep into his back. Like so many kids of the nineties, he'd absorbed a lot of propaganda about drugs in school. He was afraid if he got pain meds, he'd become an addict and deteriorate into a strung-out shadow.

Anna had a more nuanced take on drugs: it was fun to do them.

They began taking psychedelics together. Once, they were tripping on mushrooms with a guy who started to freak out, crying and banging his head against the wall. In frustration, Fred remembers pulling back his pants and saying, "Take a look at how bent my leg is. And I'm not freaking out like you, you fucking pussy." The guy calmed down. Later, while they were still high, Anna asked Fred about what it was like to live in his body. That was the first time he came to terms with being disabled.

There was one mushroom trip that mattered more for the rest of us. As Fred was starting to come down, his mind turned to the internet. He started thinking about imageboards, and how it would be cool if they were even freer—if users could make boards about whatever topic they wanted, instead of posting within categories created by the admin. Instead of 4chan, it would be infinite chan, with the infinity symbol turned sideways: 8chan. He registered the domain while he was still a little high.

Anna thought 8chan was her fault. She was into Tumblr, which had functioned in some ways like the inverse of 4chan, an anonymous place where women and gays and people of color created their own culture and got very, very leftist. Nothing was too niche for Tumblr—there were huge accounts for banal life hacks and tiny ones for, say, pictures of shirtless Dolph Lundgren with his nipples animated in spirals. Anna thought it would be cool to have a site that combined imageboards and the personal blogs of Tumblr. She also thought no one would use it.

Because he'd been Wizardchan's admin, Fred knew the imageboard software, so he changed it so users could make their own boards. He put the site live a few days after. Fred was pleased with how the 8chan kicked off. It wasn't an instant viral hit, but it got about a hundred posts a day.

Anna thought the project was doomed from the start. She'd lurked on 4chan, Reddit, Discord, Wizardchan—in all these places, she imagined she could help move unhappy people from the hard right to the left if she showed a little empathy. "Am I adding to the problem by having the thought that they could be turned around?" she asked me. I didn't have an answer. "I'm haunted by the idea that something can be done to give them empathy," Anna said. "But all I ever did was come up with the idea that helped spread the disease instead."

Anna had opened up a whole new world for Fred, but he turned away from it when they had a bad breakup a few months later. Fred took the breakup as proof his old friends had been right all along, even if they'd been proven wrong in person, and physically. Fred went back to them and wallowed in their bitter and cruel comments about the relationship that had done so much to change his life.

In an infamous chatlog that a participant later posted publicly, Fred told his old wizard friends all about his relationship with Anna. Fred called her "a whore who didn't love me," and told them, "Do not trust women, especially with virgin fetishes." They said it was "degenerate," a "disgusting story," and "horribly gross." One person called Anna "the definition of a succubus." Another said, "She must have creamed herself to my childhood abusive parents story." They told him the lesson was "You only know you're a wizard when you experienced what women are really like. In fact I'd say copypaste is the TRUEST WIZARD here." They wanted him to come back: "Now that your whole ordeal is over it's time to jump back on the horse . . . it's time to be a reborn virgin."

Fred told them he'd taken Anna to get an abortion, and that he thought he was probably the father. The other guys gleefully mourned his loss:

THE SON OF COPYPASTE

tfw copypaste killed the Antichrist

you aborted the next admin

do you cry after your son?

Fred said he did not:

i wanted to have been aborted as a baby

i did him a favor

if anything it was therapeutic.

2

NO COUNTRY FOR OLD RACISTS

There's a lot of debate over what to call the loosely connected group of people working to make America more racist: white supremacists, white nationalists, white power advocates, professional racists, neo-Nazis, the alt-right, the dissident right. None of these terms are perfect, and many originated in racist slogans coined decades ago.

I prefer "nazis"—lowercase, like a generic drug, to cover all their ideologies, and to distinguish them from Germans in the 1930s and '40s and skinheads in the '90s. What they want is more white power. What they are defending is white male supremacy.

What those inside it call it is "the movement." All of them. The ones who resent it, the ones who think they're above it, the ones who quit. They speak of it as though it is a sentient blob. Another word for it might be "cult."

"The movement is angry with me," Richard Spencer, its most infamous leader, told me after my interview with him aired on television. "The movement's been propelled by insecurity," said Matt Parrott, who'd been part of it since 2008 and was one of the organizers of the Unite the Right rally in Charlottesville in 2017. His longtime collaborator, Matthew Heimbach, began a backstory with the disclaimer, "If movement lore is to be believed . . ." Jeff

Schoep, who ran a neo-Nazi group for almost three decades, answered most
of my questions with the preface, "When I was in the movement…" They talk
about their "movement friends" and their "non-movement friends," if they
have any. There are movement parties and movement funerals.

You can dabble in racism, hang out on racist websites, read fascist literature,
and later come back to the normal world, but when you use your real name in
the movement you have passed the point of no return. You can quit, but you
can't leave. No one will forget what you've done. The movement takes away your
friends and gives you new ones, but they don't really like you, and they'll turn on
you the moment you become a liability, or "cringe," an embarrassment. After the
movement ruins you, it will laugh at you. You deserve it. You were never really
good enough, but the movement had fun while it lasted, You, of course, did not.

At the center of the movement is a group of old men. The old men provide the
money—but there is never enough money to do much of anything, and the old
men are always pushing the young men to find a new source. When the wealthy
inventor Walter Kistler developed an interest in race science in his later years,
one of his aides told me a significant part of his job was to stand between Kistler
and the grifters who wanted to extract money from him. "He was like a childlike
genius—brilliant, but naïve, easily manipulable," the aide said. "We were basically all policemen … because Walter's checkbook would be in his pocket and
whoever walked in, he said, 'Okay, here is a check.'"

The old men offer validation. They have overlapping clubs and conferences, and when a young man gets an invitation, it's a sign he has promise.
One of those old men was Bill Regnery, whose uncle founded an important
conservative book publisher that bore his name, and whose grandfather was a
member of the America First Committee, created to keep the U.S. out of World
War II. Regnery did not have much of his own mainstream success. He'd been
pushed out of his family's textile business in the 1980s and removed from
the board of the conservative Intercollegiate Studies Institute in the 2000s.
But within the movement, he was elite. In 2015, Regnery emailed friends in
the movement that he was "flabbergasted" that mass murderer Dylann Roof's
manifesto showed so much intelligence: "Based on Roof's essay he is the kind
of youth we could have invited to a meeting."

The meeting would have been with the Charles Martel Society (CMS), one of the old men's clubs. Members are not supposed to talk about CMS publicly. When, in March 2017, a BuzzFeed reporter asked if CMS was a secret society, members debated over email whether they should say "It is not a secret society," or if saying it *wasn't* a secret society made it seem *even more* like a secret society, much in the same way that, as lawyer Sam Dickson argued, saying "I'm not a homosexual" makes everyone think you are, in fact, a homosexual. Regnery settled on "The Charles Martel Society is a private but not secret organization." However, when the story was published a few months later, member Kevin MacDonald was quoted saying, "It's a secret society."

"CMS is, in many ways, the heart," Matt Heimbach said. There were other elite movement organizations—American Renaissance, VDARE, the H. L. Mencken Club, etc.—each with a different message, whether that's more focus on immigration, or race science, or a racism that's friendlier to Jews. "All the different fronts have a specific purpose to bring in slightly different groups of people. But at the heart of it, it's all, like, the same thirty dudes."

Richard Spencer calls these old men vampires. "They see something that is alive, and they want to go suck its blood. And then the second they don't think it's alive, or it's objectively dead, they want to move on to something else," Spencer said. Regnery was Spencer's chief vampire, and backed him for a decade. When Regnery died in the summer of 2021, Spencer did not go to the funeral.

The old men cultivate young men to be public faces for the movement. They give them just enough praise to get them hooked and working for more. One younger leader asked to speak off the record to avoid sparking "movement drama," before comparing the way the movement saw him to the way it saw Nathan Damigo. Damigo had spent four years in prison for assaulting an Arab cabdriver, but he was square-jawed, fit, and wore preppy clothes. With some nurturing from CMS, he founded a white power frat called Identity Evropa. "It will irritate me to my death that I've done nothing wrong, done everything right," the leader told me, "and yet, *this guy*—who literally attacked an immigrant worker, and is a shitty person—is considered 'good optics' that we should aspire to emulate and follow, and I'm 'bad optics.'" The movement is divided by social class: "boots vs. suits." The suits thought the boots—meaning neo-Nazis, skinheads, klansmen, neo-Confederates, and the like—made the suits look bad.

The old men do not always pick winners. "I don't think anyone should be able to move up in power—or in relative popularity, or however you want to describe where I am right now—nearly as fast as I did, because that's very dangerous," Elliot Kline, then the head of Identity Evropa, told me in 2017. He said the movement needed to develop a stronger immune system to protect against unreliable people with sketchy backgrounds. A few months after our conversation, Kline was revealed to have been lying about his military record—he'd never served in the Iraq War. He then disappeared from the scene. A few years after that, he didn't bother to show up to a federal civil trial in which he was a defendant. But his ex-girlfriend did show up for her deposition. She said under oath that Kline boasted he was building a militia for Spencer, but that after the fascist revolution, he said Spencer would be the first against the wall.

A major subject of movement gossip is who might be gay. This is not new; when Hitler ordered the execution of hundreds of Nazi brownshirts in 1934 in the "Night of the Long Knives," one official justification was that their leaders were homosexual. Within the modern American white power movement, the sexual rumors mostly pose a reputational threat, not a physical one. Once, in a period of intense scrutiny, a white nationalist called me to complain that some people in the movement were calling him gay, and he wasn't gay, *they* were gay. He claimed there was even a gay nazi house where they did gay nazi stuff, and said I should report on it. Years later, two other leaders urged me to expose the "pink mafia"—or "the fancy boy, let's-invite-a-bunch-of-twinks-to-hang-out-and-talk-about-racism crew"—and its rumored house. In frustration, I told them I couldn't just print a headline saying, "There's a Big Gay Nazi House"—I needed to see documentary evidence and talk to people with firsthand experience. That would be hard, one said, because there's still a big stigma around sexual harassment: "That's a really fucking emasculating shitty topic."

Within the movement, I am a meme. I am the most famous to the worst people. When I started reporting on the far right, I was younger, more naïve. I had a public Instagram. They found a photo I'd posted of myself at a child's birthday party, captioned, "me among my people, at a bar mitzvah." My friends understood it was a jokey reference to a ten-thousand-word article I'd written about teenagers with a meme empire—"my people" meaning teens—but the internet nazis took it as a sincere expression of Jewish identity. They began sending me antisemitic insults through every digital avenue they could find; that I should die in an oven was a popular one. But I'm not Jewish. I didn't know many Jews as a kid. The messages were vile, but they didn't trigger memories of playground bullying or a grandparent's story of a more bigoted time. It was like having thousands of people scream at me for being from Arizona.

As my reporting continued, however, they noticed something about me that is undeniably, measurably true: my eyes are large and very far apart. This fact does not register with average people, though an optician once shouted it when I walked into his store. The distance between my pupils is sixty-seven millimeters, wider than nearly 95 percent of females. But having big, wide-set eyes was not something I felt insecure about. Had they never heard of Kate Moss? It was like they were dunking on me for having long and luscious hair. Thanks? They said it was a sign I had fetal alcohol syndrome.

They made comics of me, GIFs of me, supercut videos of me. They researched my family and relationships; they posted my number in their group chats and drunk-dialed me on holiday weekends. Someone emailed a drawing of me naked with a gun to my head. I used to tell myself I'd quit when it got really bad, but in hindsight I know that it was really bad for a while.

I learned to be on high alert when recognized in public by a white male under forty. The few who were alt-right couldn't help themselves: they'd reference a 4chan meme to make sure I knew who they really were. It could happen anywhere: at a mainstream conservative conference, in the TSA line at the airport, at the Guggenheim. At a happy hour for fans of manosphere tweeter Mike Cernovich, a young guy told me he was in an Identity Evropa group chat, and then tried to take my picture, which I bullied him out of doing. He told me to say hi to my ex. I reminded him he knew very well I was going home to my Jewish boyfriend.

For months, false rumors swirled within the movement that my boyfriend, Jeremy Greenfield, and I were engaged. Then, a day after we did get engaged while traveling in Tokyo, a white nationalist called with urgent news.

At the end of our conversation, he asked, "You're not really gonna marry that guy, are you?" I felt trapped: deny my true love or make the first person I told of our engagement a nazi? After a few seconds I found an escape by stating the obvious: it was none of his business.

The ones who took the most interest in me were part of a wave of young people brought into white nationalism by the internet. They called themselves the alt-right, and they changed the movement. The leaders lost control of the cult. Now the cult controls the leader. The internet is the enforcer. To "counter-signal" is to criticize the political objectives of someone to your right within the movement. It is not acceptable. To "cuck" is to bend to criticism from outside the movement—the term comes from "cuckold," as in a married man who lets another man have sex with his wife. This is also not acceptable. In essence, to argue that "race war now" is not a good idea is to countersignal. To argue that "race war now" is a fine objective but that visible swastikas might be a turnoff to the general public and slow the growth of the movement is to be an "optics cuck." To join the movement is to be chained to the most violent extremes of it.

The power is in mass anonymity. The racist hive mind collects a catalog of all leaders' worst moments. Break with current internet doctrine, and you'll be flooded with photos of that time you looked fat, or reminded of that time your best friend slept with your wife. The young leaders resent the old men, but they fear their own followers.

The movement will get you punched, sued, jailed, divorced, bankrupted. But it will never let you go. Matt Heimbach had a round face with thick black hair and eyebrows, and he was always grinning, but underneath it was a seeth-ing anger. "My biggest advice to people in the movement is like, *Don't fucking leave*, because there's no point," Heimbach said. "If you're already in, your life is fucked." It will leave you with no one to confide in but the journalists who've exposed what you've done.

Heimbach had been blackpilled, trapped in a nihilistic hopelessness that the only thing to look forward to was to watch the world burn. I reminded him that quitting the movement might provide some benefits that he hadn't considered. When white nationalists kill people, they tend to kill each other. I said quitting would reduce his risk of being one of those killed.

"I've had a lot of loaded guns pulled on me over the years—a lot of fucking loaded guns," Heimbach said. "Not a one of them has shot me yet."

I said if I could choose between having a loaded gun pointed at me and *not* having a loaded gun pointed at me, I would choose not having a loaded gun pointed at me.

"If you've already got a death wish . . . ," he said, and didn't finish the sentence. "I've been sitting around here, tapping my foot, waiting for martyrdom for the past goddamn decade, and no one's been brave enough to do it."

————

Jeff Schoep noticed the movement was changing in 2015. By then he'd spent two decades running the National Socialist Movement. Under his leadership, the group had been as outrageous as possible. They protested in actual German brownshirt uniforms and swastika armbands, and celebrated the anniversary of Kristallnacht. But on racist internet forums, Schoep started seeing jokes that didn't seem like jokes. "It was weird," Schoep told me, about a year after he quit the white power movement. "It's weird now, but it was weird then, too."

He saw someone on Stormfront post a meme from the alt-right website the Daily Stormer that showed a white woman with two black eyes. The message was that women deserved to be beaten and raped. He was shocked, but what was really shocking was that the other guys defended it. "They were like, *Oh it's ironic. That's a new thing, that's something the alt-right does. It's just irony, it's just a joke, it's just a meme.*" But it seemed like he meant it.

"Back in my skinhead days—some guy being like, *What do you think about this beaten white woman on a poster?*—that guy would have gotten a boot party," he said. "Severely beaten."

He noticed a change in the new guys who were joining. Schoep was stocky, with an iron cross tattooed on his forearm. He kept his hair in a buzzcut and had worn fingerless weighted-knuckle gloves in public. It was obvious he'd tried to look tough. The guys he'd recruited had usually been poor, and might have been acquainted with violence before they'd entered the movement. Suddenly, there were a bunch of "snotty rich-boy types" with preppy haircuts who wanted to project an image of wealth. Schoep and his neo-Nazi buddies thought, *Those are a bunch of girly boys.*

Schoep had come up differently. In the late eighties, he'd had to work hard to join the movement. It didn't wash over him as a meme.

He'd been fascinated with Nazis as a kid. His mom was a German immigrant, and his grandfather had fought in the German Army during World War II. He spent a summer in Germany when he was fifteen, and while there, he ran into skinheads. His cousin told him to stay away from those guys, they were dangerous. So he stayed away. But when Schoep got back home to Minnesota, he started digging.

At the public library he found an academic sociology book on white power. The back of the book contained an index listing the groups the author had interviewed, and it included their addresses. Schoep wrote letters to them all: the survivalist group Posse Comitatus, the Ku Klux Klan, neo-Nazis. He asked for their newsletters and what they were up to.

They took a long time to respond. The American Nazi Party took months, and it sent years-old literature. "That put a bad taste in my mouth right away," Schoep said. The last people he reached out to were the Christian Identity groups, because he wasn't into religion. But one woman responded that her group would have a booth at the Minnesota State Fair.

When he showed up at the fair, he was shocked. "You would have never expected this. It was a little old lady that was running the booth, probably eighty, ninety years old—real old. And it just looked like a Christian bookstore." He asked if she had any contacts for racist groups in Minnesota. She did, and she gave him their phone numbers.

Schoep connected with the National Socialist American Workers Freedom Movement, and joined. He was nineteen.

Though many people have racist beliefs, the vast majority know those are taboo. Respectable people, and by that I mean closet bigots, will try to find one another in conversation by feeling it out, maybe testing the crowd with a joke about a Black celebrity, and then slowly getting more and more explicit until they're venting about the problem with "them." But if you asked about it directly, they'd say they didn't have a racist bone in their body.

Schoep had to be taught how to overcome the fear of being a public racist. His neo-Nazi leader took him and another new guy into Minneapolis for a lesson. According to Schoep, the leader said, "I'm going to show you guys the one-man demonstration."

"What's the point of the one man demonstration?" Schoep asked. "There's three of us. We could do a three-man demonstration."

"No. You guys are going to dress in civilian clothes. I'm going to be in the uniform. I'm going to be carrying the flag. We're going to downtown Minneapolis in front of the federal building. I want to show you that this can be done with just one person."

Schoep was nervous. "I have a feeling you might get attacked."

"No, I won't get attacked."

Schoep promised to defend him, just in case. "If you get attacked, we're going to fight. We'll back you up."

"No, you won't. You will watch, and you will film this."

They had an old video camera. "He was trying to show us how one man in downtown Minneapolis could fly a swastika flag and not face any violent retribution or anything like that," Schoep said. "It was to instill in us that we could do this even if it was by yourself, and then it would draw in more people."

As Schoep told me this story, I could hear in his voice it still had the pull of subversive glamour. Here is a rule that everyone follows as if it were commanded by God, and yet when he broke it, nothing happened.

When the leader retired, he asked Schoep to take over. Schoep was surprised. He renamed the group the National Socialist Movement (NSM), and grew it to be the largest member organization in white supremacy in the nineties. He recruited from the KKK and other white power groups that were crumbling. NSM had a website, and newsletters, and a record label. Schoep organized regular demonstrations and spoke at white power conferences.

Every time he'd bring a new girlfriend around, one after another, she'd say, *Jeff, this is like a cult.* They'd come to a meeting or an event, and afterward they'd tell him NSM was a cult, and he was a cult leader. It pissed him off, and he'd wonder, *What is wrong with these girls?* He'd tell himself, *This is not a cult, it's a political organization.*

But it was like a cult. There was one leader, and it was Schoep. He had a member ranking system and appointed regional leaders. When he'd promote a neo-Nazi, he'd tell them not to be happy about it, because it was more work and people would ask them for help with personal drama. "The more responsibility, the higher the rank in movement, the more you were mom, dad, psychiatrist, babysitter," Schoep said. They had drama but little power. "It was not a democracy," he said. "There was no voting. It's set up in a dictatorship style."

It was not easy to stay on top. It took a certain kind of person to handle the stress, he said: resilient, ruthless. "I had some attempts on my life," Schoep said. "There was one particular incident where a couple of guys were planning to kill me, and we caught wind of it through another person that overheard the conversation. And then we did an investigation on it, and those people were basically removed. They were actually removed from the state."

"What does that mean exactly?" I asked.

"I really can't elaborate too much on that, other than I can say they were told to leave the state by the group."

"And did they?"

"They had to."

One night, in the nineties, he'd pulled his car over on the side of the road and was looking in the trunk, when he got hit in the back of the head with a tire iron. "I just remember being stunned, because I didn't see it coming. So I'm standing there for a second and I touch the back of my head. And it felt like a sponge." It made a squishy sound. "The horns are beeping, and the lights, and I stumbled out into traffic and then stumbled across the street into a gas station, blood just pouring out of my head." He got two layers of stitches, plus staples.

Schoep was in lots of fights over the years, he said. Another neo-Nazi kicked him in the face and broke his nose over a girl. He was shot at a couple times. But the tire iron, he said, "that was the closest to actual death." He still has a big scar on the back of his head.

He had a lot of friends in the white power movement who went to prison, or were now dead. In the nineties, he met Buford Furrow at an Aryan Nations conference, and a few years later Furrow fired on a Jewish community center with an Uzi and injured five people, including three little kids. Schoep had been good friends with Jeff Hall, who was a regional director for NSM in 2011. Hall was sleeping on his living room couch when his ten-year-old son shot him in the head. The next year, he talked to J. T. Ready, an NSM member, a few days before Ready murdered four members of his own family and then killed himself.

He was talking about some of these people with a friend in the movement, when the friend said that he'd been thinking about the people who worshiped at the church down the street from his house. *How many people in that church do you think know someone that killed somebody? And how many people do we know that have killed somebody?*

———

This had been Schoep's life for two decades when he noticed a new group of racists who were obsessed with a cartoon frog. Schoep had tried to recruit teenagers, and he could imagine why a kid might be drawn in by a cartoon. But these were adults.

"You're a grown man. What is it about this frog that is interesting?" Schoep said. He was talking about Pepe the Frog, of course. The alt-right had discovered an ancient Egyptian frog-headed god of chaos named Kek, and claimed to worship him in the imaginary nation of Kekistan. "This is sort of a prepubescent mindset. . . . These are grown guys that are in their twenties walking around promoting a cartoon character and a fake religion and a fake country. It was just too strange."

There were too many rape jokes. "There was this bizarre, underlying, deep-seated hatred for women that I had not ever seen really in the hard right," Schoep said. His friends talked a lot about whether these alt-right guys were gay and in the closet. They didn't hang out. He never met most of the alt-right guys, ever.

Schoep had paraded around with a group of men in brownshirt uniforms. They'd waved swastika flags at a demonstration that caused a riot in Toledo. He'd seen boot parties and nearly had his skull bashed in. He'd personally known murderers, murder victims, and a family annihilator. He went through all that and then he looked at the alt-right and thought, *This shit is too weird for me.*

3

"ACCORDING TO FEDERAL COURT DOCUMENTS, I'M HIS BEST FRIEND"

M att Parrott, Matt Heimbach, and Josh Smith rented a house about half an hour outside Charlottesville in October 2021, when they were defendants in a month-long federal civil trial. Parrott and Heimbach were accused of conspiring to commit racially motivated violence at the Unite the Right rally in August 2017. That summer weekend had been the apex of the alt-right, a newer, younger segment of the white power movement that was based online rather than in local clubs or gangs, and they were two of its leaders. They'd marched with nearly the entire leadership of the alt-right, including Richard Spencer, Chris Cantwell, Nathan Damigo, and Elliot Kline, as well as older white nationalists, like Jeff Schoep, and the rally's main organizer, Jason Kessler. Now they were all codefendants.

Parrott concealed himself behind a hat and a sandy beard. He vaped incessantly. He and Heimbach had known each other a long time, but Smith was new to their circle. He was their lawyer, and when he wasn't wearing a suit, he wore an all-over-print Rocky and Bullwinkle T-shirt and True Religion jeans with decorative back pockets. He was gay and Jewish. When I asked Smith if he was a Holocaust denier, he said it depended on what I meant by "Holocaust denier." I said that most people who are not Holocaust deniers would just say, "No, I'm not a Holocaust denier." He said he believed the official number of Jews who died in the Holocaust was off "by a lot"—millions. It was an odd scene.

The rental was lit by fluorescent lights and decorated with big leather couches. Smith had put his desktop computer and a giant printer on the dining table. The bathroom had dirty clothes in the floor. I entered through the kitchen and past the stacked pizza boxes with my producer, Sam Guff. Sam was a petite New Yorker with ADHD, and a talented video editor, and as I'd pulled her deeper into covering the world of extremism, she could roll with any situation, no matter how strange. She walked into the white power bachelor pad as if she were visiting an old acquaintance from college—calm, friendly, just the right amount of distance.

Most nazis had been extremely hostile to me in 2017, but by 2021, they accepted my presence. Charlottesville had turned out to be the high point and the undoing of the alt-right, and my coverage of it was a significant reason for that. It was like we were veterans who'd fought on the opposite sides of a war. There weren't many other people in the world who had witnessed the same events. So when I called them and asked for an interview, it was pretty easy to get them to say yes.

By that point I'd known Heimbach for eight years, and though he was polite to me, he'd never let his guard down—always on message, never quite real. Parrott had walked out of an on-camera interview with me. But on the evening after the trial's closing arguments, when their fates were in the jurors' hands, we went back to the house to try again.

Heimbach had gone home. Sam was looking at court documents with Smith. Parrott sat cross-legged in the corner of the overstuffed couch, vaping. I sat close to him, slouched in a matching overstuffed armchair, my feet on the overstuffed ottoman. It was bad lighting for gossip, but Parrott was talking anyway.

He mentioned he was antisocial. He'd testified he was an introvert, an accidental revelation of some vulnerability. Afterward, he'd said, "It's really hard to not be yourself after several hours of that kind of drilling. The real you boils out."

I tested the waters with one of my favorite questions: *Are you left-handed?* Parrott said he was. Heimbach was left-handed, too, which I'd noticed while looking closely at a photo of him in the middle of a brawl—he had a puffy red left hand. I asked Parrott, in a tone of shamelessly fake casualness, what he thought of the ubiquity of the word "autist" in white nationalism.

It was like whispering the secret password in a fairy tale—the whole side of a mountain opened up. He said he'd been diagnosed with Asperger's in the nineties, and that Heimbach had, too. (The American Psychiatric Association has since dropped Asperger's as a diagnosis in favor of autism spectrum disorder.) He looked delighted as I slapped the arm of my chair and shouted, "I knew it!" Now we had a language to explain their lives.

Autistic people are more than twice as likely to be left-handed as the general population. It's one of many bits of autistic trivia I'd picked up while researching the anonymous extremist internet. From the very first days I started going on 4chan to figure out what the alt-right was, I noticed that a stunning number of posts on the website used the term "autist," as in autistic, or someone with autism spectrum disorder. It was both a term of endearment and derision. To be "too autistic" to engage in some part of mainstream society could be either a badge of honor or a shameful confession. The products of obsessive and meticulous internet research were sometimes called "weaponized autism." Neurotypical people with mainstream politics were called "normies." I wasn't sure what to make of it. I couldn't find mainstream people talking about it anywhere, and when I told friends or colleagues about it, they seemed extremely skeptical.

Early on in their friendship, Parrott understood that despite their shared autism, Heimbach could connect with people in a way that he couldn't. He had a theory about it: After Heimbach was diagnosed as a kid, his mom put him in behavioral therapy for ten years. He was drilled on how to maintain eye contact, how to maintain a conversation as though he were playing a friendly game of tennis, lobbing the ball back even when it was boring. It created a monster—the mind of an autist with the social skills of a normie.

"He's autistically social, which means he aggressively makes eye contact and approaches socialization with the autistic fixation that autistic people put into their model train sets or constructed languages or whatever stupid shit they're fixated on," Parrott said. I asked what Heimbach was like when he wasn't on TV.

"He's autistic and he talks about the same ideas over and over again," Parrott said. Heimbach had by that point dropped fascism for communism, which they argued about constantly. Heimbach's infamy had made it hard to keep a job, but as an hourly wage worker he found material to support his new politics. "He's calling me on break at McDonald's, carrying on about the labor theory of value and how he's being alienated from his work product and all this bullshit."

Autism does not make someone more likely to commit violent crime, according to a lot of social science research, including a study of nearly three hundred thousand people in Stockholm published in the *Journal of the American Academy of Child and Adolescent Psychiatry* in 2017. But for a long time, the only internet extremists for whom I could find documentation of their mental health were those who'd committed acts of political violence, because their psychiatric evaluations were evidence in court.

In early 2017, Dylann Roof was sentenced to death in federal court for murdering nine people at a Black church in Charleston two years earlier. His defense team had hired Dr. Rachel Loftin, a clinical psychologist who specializes in autism spectrum disorder, and she'd diagnosed him with it in jail. But Roof did not want this evidence presented at his sentencing. "I didn't want my act to be discredited," he told the judge. "I don't want anybody to think I did it because I have some kind of mental problem. . . . I wanted to increase racial tension."

Reading Loftin's official report had felt to me like unearthing the Rosetta Stone—finally, here was an expert analyzing the interaction between the extremist internet and one person's autism. Roof was isolated, easily embarrassed, and likely a virgin, Loftin wrote. His sister "estimated that he had basically been living inside his room on his computer for nearly 5 years before the crime." Loftin had traced his internet history, and his conversations with family and friends, and found that "Dylann pursued his preoccupation with racism with an autistic intensity."

"While there is no reason to believe that ASD can cause racism," Loftin wrote, "ASD as well as other psychiatric conditions can fuel behavior in people that draws them to fringe political movements."

Ethics rules forbade Loftin from talking to me about Roof specifically. But she told me her top advice to parents of kids with autism, particularly those with high IQs, was to limit internet time. Autistic people can be especially vulnerable to extremist online communities, she said, for three reasons. One, it allows them to socialize without social anxiety. Two, the rigid worldview makes it easier to understand the way the world works. And three, the forums have archives, so they can go back in time and read to understand how users talked to each other and then mimic those interactions.

With Parrott's disclosure, I'd finally found people who had been diagnosed with autism spectrum disorder and been drawn to extremism through the internet—but had not killed anybody.

I called Heimbach the next morning. "You've cracked the code," he said. "The secret of the alt-right is that it's actually a movement of autistic guys with internet access." They all got their start on the internet, back when there were no rules. He'd spent hours reading liberal and conservative think pieces so he could better troll the authors. "The only sort of people that are going to have the energy to do all that is a bunch of autistic people."

"Of the 'alt-right,' I'd say a quarter to half of us are on the spectrum," he said. "That's the dividing line between the old movement and us—we all have the 'tism."

Some people who identified as autists online were trying to understand what made people outcasts. Others were thinking more big-picture. "The history of the world is literally the history of autistic people," a guy in his late twenties who went by Spaft told me. Spaft had been in and out of incel forums for a decade, and the first time we spoke, he made a bomb threat and dared me to report him to police. In the years since, we'd developed a rapport. Spaft believed the significant figures of history, for good and for ill, were all autistic: Augustus Caesar, Napoleon, Hitler. (Stalin was maybe autistic, too, he thought, but Stalin was also a brute, and that was probably the more relevant part of his personality.)

Any revolution required not just new ideas, but the ability to convince the public that those ideas were good. And to do that, you had to understand how regular people think. He thought this was not possible for regular people. They were too deep in being normal to analyze what normal was. "The only way you can assess how a regular person thinks is if you're not a regular person—is if you're an autistic individual who is external to society and you're observing people all the time," he said. "You're observing human interactions, human psychology, and how people interact." He'd developed a system for ranking all mankind:

1. Autistic Chad
2. Chad
3. Normie
4. Beta
5. Autistic Beta

With hard work, he said, an autist could go from "the absolute bottom trash of society" to the elite.

Every expert I spoke to cautioned that there is an enormous difference between people with clinically measurable symptoms of autism and people who think identifying as autistic gives them a little cache on the internet. The relative size of these two groups is impossible to know, because of the forums' anonymity. Three mental health professionals told me they had seen a wave of people seeking autism and attention deficit hyperactivity disorder diagnoses during the Covid-19 pandemic. Two of them said many of these people were actually depressed.

It might be that a huge number of 4chan users really are measurably different from neurotypical people according to rigorous analysis based in science. Or it might be more like astrology, a way to talk about your personality and how you move through the world. Saying you're a Gemini is shorthand for a fast-talking charmer who loves a good party. Saying you're an autist could be shorthand for a misunderstood outsider who can never navigate the unspoken rules of the normal person world.

I was a sad, weird teen hanging out at my best friend's house when her zodiac book changed my life. Astrology was a whole system that explained the invisible structure of the social world I'd struggled to navigate. I memorized it. There were twelve signs, and they all mixed and matched in different ways, and when they didn't get along, it wasn't because they were bad, it was just that their stars didn't match. The best part: I was a Gemini. Geminis were not lonely and misunderstood, but magnetic and witty. My destiny was to be a fun person that people liked. What would my life have been like if instead of finding that dumb little book, I'd found 4chan?

There was enough I recognized in their "autist" posts that it made me nervous. Obsessive intensity, social anxiety, sensitivity to sound? I had all those things. I'm left-handed! I'm good at standardized tests! I was a huge loser in school and resented its inscrutable hierarchy. YouTube commenters taught me that my eye contact was suboptimal, because they were always posting under my interviews that I looked stoned. So I found a clinical psychologist who specialized in adult autism diagnosis and got myself tested.

The results? "Elle presents with some features of ASD, though there is insufficient evidence to support a clinical diagnosis. She does not currently present with restricted/repetitive behaviors that cause functional impairment, and she has many high-order social communication skills. Instead, Elle can be conceptualized as a twice-exceptional (2e) adult—someone with extraordinary cognitive abilities along with ADHD." My husband patted me on the shoulder and said it was like I'd been DQ'd on a technicality.

"I don't see myself as having some kind of psychological condition that causes me to believe these deranged ideas. They are correct ideas," Parrott said. But having a condition that made him more immune to social shaming helped him stay in white nationalism. "You can psychologize me, you can frame it as some kind of like 'trauma response' or whatever—put all these labels on it. But I gotta tell you, I think I'm correct."

Heimbach complained that journalists were always looking for the wrong psychological explanation for his extremism. "When they ask about white nationalism, it's like, *Oh are you just angry? Do you hate your fucking dad? Did some Black kid—was he mean to you?* And I'm like, *No, I just read* The Bell Curve, *bro.* I got into it because of charts." (A few weeks later, Heimbach told me that he did, in fact, hate his fucking dad.)

My conversation with Dr. Loftin came before these online forums spilled over into the real world—before Charlottesville, before QAnon and the storming of the Capitol. When I asked Loftin in 2021 what had shifted in her thinking, she said she now believed a much bigger subset of the population was vulnerable to online extremism, and the sense of community it could offer.

Most people had no idea Heimbach was autistic unless they knew where to look—like at the crumpled up napkin he fidgeted with in our interviews, a tell that betrayed his social anxiety. Parrott preferred "to hide behind people who are more handsome and socially adroit than me." More people would listen to his ideas if they heard them from Heimbach.

When they founded the Traditionalist Worker Party (TWP), Heimbach was the face, and Parrott was behind the scenes, building their website, managing their members, writing essays, and making money with cryptocurrency to finance their activism.

———

By the time I asked them about autism, they were in the mood to talk about how they got here. They were being sued for millions of dollars. Their group was dead, they'd been humiliated, they'd ended their friendship, and had been forced to reunite because their legal fates were linked. They'd set out on a path of masochistic self-destruction, and took some pleasure in having succeeded.

The concept of "ruining your life" came up so many times that it made me wonder about the concept itself, the way a stoner repeats a word until it makes no sense. What did it mean to ruin your life? They seemed pretty certain they'd done it. They expressed it with an ironic tone and a big laugh.

Parrott said that American society demanded he apologize for being white working class, and "I'm just stubbornly refusing to do it, and would rather ruin my life, objectively speaking, than go back to my vulnerable college self." Heimbach said he would not make the big public apology he thought was required to reenter society, because it was a stupid "neurotypical" morality play.

Only a couple weeks later, Heimbach was fired from McDonald's after management discovered he'd been a professional racist. He read me his termination letter and said, "They never forgive you. They *never* forgive you. . . . There's no expiration date for how long your life will be ruined." His voice had more edge than usual. "You get to a certain point where everything is just like that Springsteen song, 'Glory Days.' You just sit around like, *Man, remember 2015?*"

———

Parrott was born the middle child in a working-class family in Paoli, Indiana. He was an odd kid, and socially awkward. When, after two years in Little League, he finally hit the ball, his whole team erupted in cheers—and after the game signed the ball and gave it to him—even though he didn't get on base. But he was very good at standardized tests, and was scored with a high IQ. He didn't have much, but he had that. He held it closely.

He was put in the gifted class, which meant that every day, he got to go to the special gifted room. "For over an hour a day, I was allowed to just be on the computer with all the adults being like, *Look, he's typing and everything! Look at him go! Wow, wow, wow!*"

When he was twelve, Parrott got second place in a statewide computer coding competition. One day one of his classmates brought him a gift from her dad, a wealthy doctor in town. It was a laptop. Parrott took it home. Now he could spend all the time he wanted online.

What he found was the controversy over a new book called *The Bell Curve*. It was 1994, and the book had just been published. His impression of the conversation was something like *This is too scandalous. But my god, it's so well sourced. It can't be true. And it can't be not true. What are we gonna do? It's gonna ruin everything.* He thought, *I have to get this book.*

The Bell Curve, by Charles Murray and Richard Herrnstein, argues that IQ is mostly hereditary, and immutable, and that many social ills are caused by low IQ. The authors claim Europeans and Asians evolved higher IQs than people from Latin America and Africa, and this has been the subject of controversy for thirty years now, because we don't know that much about how the brain works, or the some one thousand genes that affect intelligence, or what we're actually measuring with IQ tests. What is telling is what Murray and Herrnstein argue should be done with their data, which is to make public policy with eugenicist goals. They propose reducing immigration from places where people have lower IQ scores, and eliminating public aid to poor families, so less intelligent people will have fewer kids, and stop bringing down the net IQ of the nation.

Parrott asked his parents to buy him a copy of *The Bell Curve*, and they did. He cherished it. It was confirmation, from the Ivy League–certified political elite, that IQ was the most important thing, both for the individual and for civilization. And he had it.

It was seductive, he said, to reduce the world's problems to a question of intelligence. It was central to his identity, reinforced by internet friends and institutional authorities. Teachers would tell him, *Matt, you're so smart, why don't you apply yourself?* But why should he? He won praise without doing any work. When the results came back on the SATs, there it was in black-and-white: "the official government score saying I'm better than everyone around me."

"I turned it into a cult of self-worship—a destructive and stupid cult that is totally not supported by the data or anecdotal observation or anything else," Parrott said.

I've met many former "gifted kids" who became millennial internet nazis. "My background is certainly not atypical for the dissident right by any stretch," Parrott said. "It's kind of like the standard thing."

Many extremists have told me their IQ. White nationalists have built nonprofits and magazines and publishing houses dedicated to churning out scientific racism, all arguing that white people evolved to be smarter and nicer than people with darker skin.

"I've come around to despise that worldview," Parrott said. "It is ultimately a way to arbitrarily, retroactively justify inequalities. Rather than trying to make the world a more fair and better place, it's saying, 'Look at all the science that says I should live like this, and you should live like that. Deal with it.'"

But, for a time, it was how he understood the world.

———

As a teenager with a laptop, Parrott found a group of people who'd made a hobby out of their own brilliance: internet atheists. This was a huge part of nineties internet culture, chatrooms where atheists debated fundamentalist Christians, or "fundies," about the existence of God. Parrott got *really* into being an atheist. He loved dunking on fundies because he thought they were stupid.

When he was fifteen, he became close online with a woman who went by DictionaryGirl—they bonded over being too smart for God. He walked her through fixing her printer, and as a "thank-you," she sent him the Ginger Spice edition of *Playboy*. At the time, it did not occur to him that it was unusual to pay a teenager in porn. He liked to flirt with her. She didn't discourage him.

"DictionaryGirl" was an insult that her high school classmates had used to make fun of her for using big words. But DictionaryGirl wasn't in high school anymore. Her real name was Connie, and she lived in Michigan, and she was twenty-six. One Saturday, he remembers, she drove to Indiana and picked Parrott up at his parents' house. She drove him to a hotel, and they had sex. The first time he told me the story, he said he'd "talked a hot chick with big boobs into coming down and hanging out with me for the weekend behind my parents' back. It was the most fun thing ever."

The second time he told the story, he told it differently. "It was stupid. It was actually criminal. People tried to explain to me like, *I think you were raped, man.* I was like, *Well . . . I guess. Wow.* The thing was, I, at the time, had seen myself as a predator. I was going into her DMs and seducing her. It was the ultimate pickup artist fail. I was getting to see boobs, but I ended up getting totally taken hook, line, and sinker by a single mom who I ended up supporting"—he laughed maniacally—"forever."

Connie went back to Michigan, and Parrott went back to high school, though they continued to talk online—a "cyber relationship, to use the cringe terminology at the time."

Then Parrott started dating a girl his age, and right after high school, they got married. But he worked a lot, and neglected his wife, and two years later, just after he'd enrolled as a freshman at Indiana University, she left him. He hadn't seen it coming, and was devastated. He fell into a deep depressive episode.

This depressive episode, one of several, had three main consequences. First, he tried to invent a new language. When you make a constructed language, one thing you do is translate the Bible. Since he was an atheist, he used the Jefferson Bible, a text created by Thomas Jefferson by cutting all the miracles and magic out of the stories. Without all the hocus-pocus, Parrott thought, the book actually had a lot of wisdom. This is how he found Jesus.

"Nobody has an answer for the abyss of nihilism," he said. "I came around full circle. If life is fundamentally absurd, I'm just gonna trust Jesus. Keep it simple. He's obviously a good dude." He never felt the spirit. "I'm totally just trusting that aspies can go to heaven, too. Maybe we don't have souls. If I don't have a soul, by God, I'll just do my best for those who do."

Second, he was suffering so much from depression that he called the school crisis hotline. They asked if he was in any clubs that could help, and he said no. They asked if he was a person of color, or a woman, or gay, or an immigrant, and he said no. They asked if he was suicidal, and he said no. They had nothing for him. It made him feel like no one was looking out for working-class white people. This was when he decided he would be that person.

Third, he turned to the only people he could talk to: his internet atheist friends. And there was Connie, still in the game. He quit college, moved to Michigan, and married her. He became the stepdad to her tween daughters. He was closer in age to the oldest kid than he was to his second wife.

"In hindsight, getting with a woman in her thirties with a ten- and twelve-year-old child was not, on paper, the best thing for me, as a twenty-one-year-old who needed to try to succeed in college." But he threw himself into fatherhood. It was "a transformative point in my life."

While he was trying to figure out how to muster the will to live, Parrott came up with a mantra: Faith, Family, and Folk. "Folk," meaning white people. These were the things he would fight for, in that order. It became the motto of the Traditionalist Workers Party, the white nationalist group he cofounded a decade later.

———

Around the same time, in the mid-2000s, a couple hundred miles away, Matthew Heimbach went on Amazon.com and bought an SS flag and *The Turner Diaries*. He was a teenager in a wealthy bedroom community outside Washington, D.C. Amazon suggested he "might be interested in" lots of other things, like *The Bell Curve* and *Mein Kampf*. He eventually found and read a book Parrott wrote about immigration, *Hoosier Nation*.

In the old days it had been hard to get your hands on fascist literature. You had to hear about a guy in Arkansas and write him a letter, and then he might send you a faint mimeographed copy of his rantings. But with the internet, Heimbach could not only order fascist books but figure out the right ones to ask for.

The internet made all kinds of taboo information available—weird porn, exotic drugs, music that causes pain—why did he pick fascism?

"I don't know," Heimbach said. "I fucking hate my dad?" It wasn't that he hated authority, he said, or that he'd been on a fifteen-year-long method acting campaign to piss off his father. It was that "I hate what my dad *represents*."

Heimbach's father was well regarded in his career, involved in various professional societies, winner of various professional awards. Heimbach thought his dad was too busy pursuing praise from outsiders to pay attention to his family. He couldn't teach his son how to fish: "My dad wouldn't put a worm on a hook."

"He was successful by the metrics of society," Heimbach said. "He has no tangible displays of masculinity, of being fundamentally useful in any capacity outside of being a pay pig for the family he doesn't even spend time with."

Middle-class life was an insane asylum, empty and miserable, the inmates all addicted to something and divorced. Heimbach had felt alienated, lonely, and without purpose, and he wanted a country that felt like a real place, and not a continental strip mall. "If I could burn and salt the suburbs, I fuckin' would in a heartbeat. It's for the sake of mankind," he said. "What is the thing this society hates more than anything? Oh, the fucking Nazis? Congratulations, hand me an armband."

His dad taught high school history, and their house was full of historical memorabilia. "So when your son puts up an SS flag above his bed, you're not ignorant, right?" Heimbach said. His mom might not have known what it was. "My dad, however, taught the shit in school. Smart fucking guy. He knew what it was, and didn't say a fucking word. *Mein Kampf* shows up on my desk, or *The Turner Diaries*—didn't say a fuckin' word."

When his parents divorced, Heimbach said, his father didn't make a scene. "No screaming, no yelling, no crying, no big display. Just, 'I am finished with this.' *Beep beep boop beep.*"

"So, long story short, why do we become fascists? Because fuck our dads."

The anger at his father was apparent in Heimbach even back when he was still in school. In an interview with the *Washington Post*, his community college history professor said he remembered thinking Heimbach was looking for a father figure. "It seems to me like he's wasted his life," the professor said. "I did see some goodness in him. But I also did see that he was infected with this hatred."

At Towson University, Heimbach created a "white student union," though the school never recognized it. He led night patrols to watch for crime, telling the *Baltimore Sun* he was particularly concerned about "Black-male-against-white-female crime." He gave interviews to national news media, and captured the attention of the white nationalist movement. He discovered an organization called Youth for Western Civilization (YWC), and thought the gear looked "fascist as fuck." He joined and got training at the Leadership Institute, a mainstream conservative think tank. Some YWC members went on to play important roles in the movement, like Kevin DeAnna, a prolific white nationalist essayist. "That the conservative movement trained and essentially bankrolled the entire creation of the alt-right under their very noses is fucking hilarious," Heimbach said.

His family hated it. Heimbach said the last time they spoke, his dad told him he was an embarrassment to the family name. He keeps up with his younger brother, Kevin, by watching his YouTube channel. In an early video, Kevin recounts the history of a Civil War battle in Maryland, and says, "There were some cases where you would actually be fighting your friends and family because you guys had different views. And sometimes even your brother."

Kevin has the same dark hair as his brother—and the same dark eyes under the same thick eyebrows, the same ironic smile, the same cheery demeanor. But Kevin's niche is theme parks. He lives in Orlando, and reviews the rides and accommodations and seasonal decorations, with titles like "BRUTALLY HONEST REVIEW OF GENIE PLUS AT DISNEY WORLD."

Heimbach himself drew my attention to his brother's channel. He wanted to know what I thought, because he hadn't made up his mind about it. "It's fucking bizarro. Either he's the evil one or I'm the evil one." I laughed. It was a good joke, that there could be any ambiguity about who was the evil brother when only one had been a fascist who'd advocated for "exterminationism toward the Jews." I still don't know if he meant it that way.

4

THE CONNIE SITUATION

The story of what happened with Connie came out in little pieces in many conversations over many months, because each time I hung up the phone, I realized I had more questions. This isn't the first version of the story I heard, or the second, or third or fourth or fifth.

By the time she married Matt Parrott in 2004, Connie knew she was going to die young. She'd been diagnosed with Type 1 diabetes as a teen, and was often hospitalized with diabetic ketoacidosis, a serious complication that can cause coma or death. Doctors said she had "brittle diabetes," which by the late 1970s was defined as "metabolic instability sufficient to disrupt life, whatever the cause." A friend wrote of her unbelievable frailty: "I've seen her go from a blood sugar level of 100 to 800 in a matter of a few minutes. I've had to catch her from falling because halfway up a flight of stairs, she'd just pass out.... She was dealt an extraordinarily bad hand in life."

Parrott spent a lot of time at Connie's hospital bedside. He had a computer programming job, so he could work on his laptop while she was hooked up to machines. He considered himself a dedicated advocate. Once, when she'd been hospitalized for about three days, Connie threw up blood. He said he called a nurse, but none came, so he stormed into the hall to demand help. A nurse said someone would come soon. Soon wasn't good enough, so Parrott called 911. He described Connie's state, and when the operator asked the location, he gave the hospital and room number, which confused the operator. He remembers, "I heard one of the nurses go, *Shit, he just called 911!* And the next thing I know, I got five nurses all crowding into the room to take care of her."

Sometimes he'd sneak Connie food in the hospital, against the doctor's orders. Early in their marriage, he'd refused to, and she told him it was a betrayal. "When you're dealing with somebody who is one hundred percent dependent on you," Parrott said, "your ability to interfere with their agency becomes the animating factor in the relationship."

The doctors would say the same things over and over: she had to be better at managing her diabetes, or there wasn't much they could do. He thought she was being irresponsible with her eating, but then, so was he. She complained the doctors wanted her on a strict diet no human could follow, but, he admitted, "I think it went a lot deeper than that, and I was willfully ignorant of that happening, and my role and enabling that to happen."

Connie had a lot of medical bills. Nine days after they were married, in 2004, Parrott enlisted in the army to get her health insurance. He was in the second stage of basic training—specializing in military intelligence—when Connie was hospitalized. Her blood sugar was sky-high, over 600. (Normal is 70 to 120.) He wasn't surprised, because she usually had to go to the ER every three or four months. But when he visited her in the hospital and tested her blood sugar himself, it was still over 600. Parrott had thought the army would guarantee good health care, but now it seemed like the military hospitals would be a death sentence for his wife. He deserted and got an other-than-honorable discharge.

After the army, Parrott tried being a real estate agent, but he wasn't good at it. He enrolled in two online universities to get student loans and used the money to pay medical bills. It was hard, but he felt like a hero, taking care of a dying woman with no reward but true love. In an early photo of the two of them, he's standing stiffly in a white dress shirt, an awkward young man trying to project confidence. She's grinning beside him from under blond bangs. He looks like a teenager, and she looks forty.

In 2007, Connie got a website: helpconnie.blogspot.com. "My name is Connie and I've been a Type I diabetic for 25 years," she wrote. "I am extremely brittle, which means that my blood sugars rise and fall exceptionally quickly, and without much warning." She explained that "a team of doctors dedicated to treating difficult cases" at Indiana University had prescribed a new system that included an insulin pump and a continuous blood sugar monitor, and if she didn't get it, she'd have less than five years to live. Insurance would only pay for part of the system. The blog was meant to "raise the funds necessary" to get the equipment "that I need to stay healthy and alive."

One of Connie and Parrott's old friends from the atheist chatroom, Ed Brayton, had become a popular skeptic writer with a blog called *Dispatches from the Culture Wars*. Brayton took up Connie's cause. "Connie has known for a long time that she would not likely live to an old age, but she at least wants to be able to see her girls grow up and become adults; I want that as well." If just a third of his readers donated a dollar or two, "it could be the difference between Connie seeing her daughters grow up and dying far too soon."

It was one of many posts Brayton wrote about Connie. The implication was that without financial help, Connie would not be able to afford her treatment, and would die.

It wasn't true. Parrott worked for a utility company and had good insurance. He could afford to pay the medical bills it didn't cover. He told his wife that fundraisers were humiliating. She argued it was her way to support the family, and besides, her readers wanted to help.

Brayton wanted to save Connie, Parrott thought, "and in hindsight, I should have invited him to."

As Connie's health declined, Parrott's politics became more blackpilled. In 2008, he said, "I decided to set myself on fire." He went public as a white nationalist under his real identity, and got fired from his job. He thought, *No one else is standing up and defending these ideas. I will ruin my life for this.* He explained the feeling in an essay: "There's a snapping point . . . beyond which one's compass of esteem is truly decoupled from popular societal norms. . . . While it once required an act of social courage to stand for our identity and interests, I now embrace the denunciations and attacks as badges of honor."

He joined the Council of Conservative Citizens, a group descendant from the White Citizens Councils of the 1960s. Eventually, he wrote a manifesto called *Hoosier Nation*. In it, Parrott points out that Indiana's constitution originally banned Black people from settling in the state, and asks readers to "imagine how Indiana would look if it had been honored." A better future would be possible, he wrote, if white Hoosiers built a political consciousness around working-class white identity, and then—peacefully, he insisted—pushed most of the people of color out of the state.

The foundation for this white Hoosier consciousness, Parrott wrote, would be the traditional family. He called on traditionalists to ask themselves if they were fully committed:

> *Do we as men have the self-discipline and integrity to inspire obedience and fidelity in our wives? Do you as a woman inspire and demand the best from your husband? . . .*
>
> *If your brother's a drug addict, don't settle for the excuse that he's an independent adult . . . Be your brother's keeper. Get up in his personal business. Intervene. Sometimes there's only so much you can do, but don't rest until you've done exactly that much.*

Parrott was into radical traditionalism. He was reading René Guénon and Julius Evola, fascist philosophers who rejected modernity. Evola believed we were in Kali Yuga, an age of vice, and that an elite could ride above it until it crashed. Parrott wrote about how traditional gender roles were evaporating in a time of moral decay.

> *Sure, most [women] have been reduced to androgynous harpies by this Kali Yuga of decadence we're drowning in. But most of us men have been reduced to androgynous shadows of our potential selves, as well. The key difference here is that men, being the natural leaders, are ultimately accountable for the situation. Just as our nation's natural elite are derelict in their innate role as stewards and protectors, we natural patriarchs are too often derelict in our innate role as stewards and protectors in our own domains.*

Connie didn't acknowledge her husband's white nationalism in her public blog, where she wrote about her feelings on each new health problem. Not only did she have brittle diabetes, but also foot drop, plantar fasciitis, kidney damage, a severe infection of her big toe, iritis, a bad shoulder, some serious gastrointestinal problems, and a pituitary tumor. She raised money for a risky surgery to remove the tumor, but then reported that the third neurosurgeon she consulted said she didn't need it.

There was some good news: doctors thought she was a perfect candidate for a pancreas transplant, and maybe a new liver, too. "If this happens, I will no longer be a diabetic!" she wrote. She said she'd had to turn off the comments section, because an anonymous commenter was calling her a scammer and accusing her of using the donations to buy drugs. But she didn't let that get her down: "Who knows what my future holds for me. I'm daring to dream a little."

Privately she was less optimistic. Connie often talked about how she would die soon, and in vivid terms, saying she'd never live to see her grandchildren. "She definitely, definitely would not be accused of not milking it," Parrott said.

Connie's health got worse. One post celebrated that she'd gone "an entire month without any ER visits or hospital stay!" Serious intestinal pain had forced her to consult several doctors and get several examinations, which had produced several incorrect diagnoses, including Crohn's disease, ischemic colitis, and irritable bowel syndrome. It turned out her stomach was irritated by over-the-counter painkillers. Her doctor changed her prescription to "straight Hydrocodone," an opioid.

———

The history of brittle diabetes has taken as many strange turns as the marriage of Connie and Parrott. With Type 1 diabetes, the immune system attacks the cells in the pancreas that produce insulin, which cells need to absorb sugar. Without it, cells feed on fat, sending ketones into the blood and turning it acidic. This can lead to diabetic ketoacidosis, which can cause dehydration, confusion, coma, organ failure, and death.

Diabetics take insulin to mimic what most pancreases do naturally, and it's hard to replicate that perfectly. It's a lifelong diagnosis that requires work every day. But for most diabetics, the right insulin regimen can keep blood sugar levels in a fairly normal range.

But a very small number of diabetics have wild, unpredictable swings in blood sugar, and they were first described as brittle diabetics in the 1930s. Doctors struggled for decades to figure out why this group didn't respond to insulin like most patients. In the 1980s, new insulin pumps could provide a more precise dose of medication, and yet there was still a class of patients whose blood sugar swings required hospitalization. Researchers began desperately trying to figure out the mystery. One of those leading researchers, Gareth Williams, described the drama in the medical journal *The Lancet* in 2012.

> *Curiously, almost all the patients with brittle diabetes were young women, which made us wonder whether this might be a genuine syndrome after all. Other diagnostic features of the "syndrome" were case notes that weighed several kilos, multiple hospital admissions totalling several weeks or months each year, and a trail of defeated diabetes specialists. Some patients showed a baffling clinical sign: an enigmatic, Mona Lisa–like smile that could even appear in the emergency room, making an unsettling contrast with the fear in everyone else's face. The significance of that smile completely passed me by.*

Another brittle diabetes researcher wrote that even as medical staff were in a state of despair, the patient was "placid, somehow defiant and even, dare one say it, triumphant." A pivotal moment was the publication of a 1985 study that found that brittle diabetics responded to insulin just like non-brittle diabetics when they were under close observation. The conclusion, Williams wrote, was "they deliberately sabotaged their own treatment." Doctors no longer use the term "brittle diabetes."

A factitious illness is one a patient causes in herself. When the patient consciously exaggerates symptoms for an external goal—like a car accident victim playing up his pain to get an insurance payout—it's called malingering. When a patient fakes or induces symptoms out of an unconscious need to get attention in the role of a sick person, it's a serious mental health condition called factitious disorder imposed on self, or, as it was once known, Munchausen's syndrome. A factitious illness can cause real health problems, like complications from unnecessary procedures, or addiction to painkillers doctors prescribe for them. (The public is more familiar with factitious disorder imposed on another, or Munchausen's by proxy, because it is the subject of so many horror movies about mothers making their children sick.) In 2000, the term "Munchausen's by internet" was coined to describe people who deceive others about their medical condition online, but unlike factitious disorder, it is not officially recognized in the American Psychiatric Association's *Diagnostic and Statistical Manual of Mental Disorders*.

————

I struggled to make sense of Parrott's explanation that Connie had profoundly bad luck. I had more than a dozen family members with diabetes, and every family reunion brought new innovations in sugar-free Jell-O. A relative might be deemed "good with her diabetes" or "not so good with her diabetes," but they all managed the disease. I didn't understand why Connie was in the hospital so much. Eventually, I emailed Parrott an academic paper reviewing forty years of brittle diabetes research and the *Lancet* essay.

"If your goal is to get inside my head, you definitely succeeded more than all of my angry ex-girlfriends and other trolls and everybody else combined," Parrott said. "I had never imagined that . . . It was, like, behind five closed doors in my inner psyche. I was like, *Oh my god, was it all—what the fuck? Was my life even real for an entire decade?*"

The end of that decade began when Matt Heimbach entered his life.

————

I met Heimbach in person a few weeks before Parrott did. I was covering the 2013 Conservative Political Action Conference, and I'd walked into a panel titled, "Trump the Race Card: Are You Sick and Tired of Being Called a Racist and You Know You're Not One?" Heimbach was saving one of the last seats in the windowless conference room for his friend Scott Terry. A man in the row behind him demanded he give the seat to a lady, me. That man's act of chivalry meant I was sitting next to Heimbach when he and Terry caused a meltdown.

"Trump the Race Card" was led by a Black conservative named KCarl Smith. He made the case that Democrats were the real racists because the KKK had been Democrats, and Abraham Lincoln freed the slaves. Therefore, conservatives should pitch themselves to people of color as "Frederick Douglass Republicans." Terry stood up and said such an effort would come "at the expense of young white southern males," and suggested they go with "Booker T. Washington Republicans—united like the hand, but separate like the fingers." This caused the first of many gasps and murmurs.

Smith said Douglass had forgiven his slave master, and Terry asked, "Did he thank him for giving him shelter?" Then there was a lot of shouting. A woman named Kim Brown said the panel's thesis was absurd, because so many southern Democrats had become Republicans to oppose civil rights laws—and Heimbach agreed, except that he thought that was good. It wasn't clear if the crowd was more angry at the leftist Black woman or the segregationist white men. Smith invoked Martin Luther King, Jr., and Heimbach shouted, "We don't need Marxists in the Republican Party!" I felt like I was ringside at a pro-wrestling match.

Having been a politically aware teen in the South, I was used to people lying to my face that the Civil War was about states' rights not slavery, that the Confederate flag was about heritage not hate, and that southern opposition to public transportation and public schools was about economics not segregation. But Heimbach was a young guy who admitted that all that *was* about racism, and that is what he liked about it. I was intrigued. It was like talking to Dr. Evil instead of his slick corporate henchman.

Heimbach said he was part of the "white dissident right," which I'd never heard of. After reading vintage copies of the *National Review*, he'd realized "the right wing is lying to itself." But he didn't like the term "racism," because he said it was invented by the Bolsheviks. I could tell he'd enjoyed creating the chaos.

Parrott wrote approvingly of the incident from afar. "It genuinely only takes one single person speaking up in the audience to utterly devastate the GOP's fragile, awkward, and disingenuous minority outreach efforts."

Heimbach had been reading Parrott's essays for a while, and they'd connected on Facebook. They finally met in person a couple of months later at the American Renaissance conference in Tennessee in April 2013. Parrott brought Connie's daughter Brooke, who was twenty.

American Renaissance is a major event for the old men of the white nationalist movement, and it's run by Jared Taylor, one of the most important members of the Charles Martel Society. Usually the speeches are about the same thing every year—eugenics and how it should affect public policy—but in 2013, after the protests over the death of Trayvon Martin and the reelection of Barack Obama, there was a new urgency. They floated more extreme action. "We want a homeland," Taylor said in a speech, as reported by the Southern Poverty Law Center. "Think of secession . . . Survival is the first law. We have no choice but to keep fighting." Richard Spencer called for "peaceful ethnic cleansing." Heimbach asked a couple of speakers for concrete ideas on how they could create a white ethnostate. They did not offer them.

Heimbach was adrift. He was about to graduate from college, and had some notoriety in the white power world. He'd dabbled in a few different racist groups without really clicking with any of them. He told Parrott he didn't know what he wanted to do. The training he'd gotten from the conservative think tank, Parrott argued, was a dead end. It was just more "CMS buffoonery"—support border patrols, claim that Black people are taking your taxes, and vote Republican, all of which Parrott said never delivered for white people.

"I made a sales pitch to him that we need to do something radical and socialist, and inspired by the European new right," Parrott said. If he moved up to Michigan, they could build something new together. Within a few months, Heimbach drove up. He'd been chatting with Brooke online, and that made the decision easier. It was the beginning of a long and legally significant friendship.

———

The first time Heimbach walked into Parrott's house, something was off. He'd known Connie was sick, but he didn't know how sick. Parrott was managing the household, programming, and working on internet racism, while Connie was in bed. He thought Parrott was keeping Connie alive, possibly against her will.

Connie lived through her computer. She loved to argue on the internet, and Parrott was "a fucking juggernaut," a worthy adversary. She told Heimbach she'd never met anyone as intelligent as Parrott. Heimbach thought she had the power to match him. "The woman was wicked smart—evil, perhaps—but wicked smart, like off-the-charts fucking smart," he said.

Heimbach was twenty-two, and had spent his life in the suburbs, and he wondered, *Is this the world?* He'd already been living in an alternate reality as an infamous white nationalist while selling closet organization systems door-to-door on the weekends. Maybe weird was his normal? He told himself, *I'm not here to be her friend. I'm here to do autistic politics.*

Parrott thought there was an unmet demand in the racism market. One-half of the movement was the old rich racists of the Charles Martel Society, which never amassed real political power, but only held conferences to congratulate themselves on their high IQs. The other half was the reactionary neo-Nazis and neo-Confederates, who were outdated and a waste of energy. The main political action for both was to vote for the Republican Party.

The Republican Party takes "white resentment rocket fuel," Parrott said, and "pours that rocket fuel into their rocket to lower taxes and launch wars and do Republican stuff." The rocket never went in the direction that the resentful white people wanted. "It's not like they can just run on what they're actually doing. They have to run on 'Those people are out to get you, and they're out to get you because you're white.'"

Heimbach and Parrott wanted to create a political party with a distinct ideology that would compete with the GOP, but also build local activist groups so members could make friends and feel like they were part of something. The message would be internet-savvy and explicitly anticapitalist, and would emphasize tradition and families. They'd use the motto Parrott had adopted as a depressed college dropout who found Jesus: "Faith, Family, Folk."

The very social Heimbach had met some Golden State Skinheads, and they connected him to Bill Johnson, a Los Angeles lawyer and CMS member who'd created American Third Position, a political party modeled on European neofascism. With guidance from Johnson, he and Parrott founded the

Traditionalist Youth Network in May 2013. They articulated their vision on the *TradYouth* blog.

Heimbach would come over to Parrott's house to work on essays, and Parrott taught him how to buy study drugs on the internet so that he could write them faster. Under Parrott's influence, Heimbach reversed his economic message. At CPAC, he'd denounced MLK as a Marxist, but three months later, he was arguing that capitalism was an existential threat to white people. With a nod to his roots, Heimbach wrote:

> In exchange for their soul, many white men are willing to accept a middle class life in suburbia, regardless of the fact that their children and grandchildren will be inheriting a decaying and decrepit multicultural cesspool of a nation. White people must realize that capitalism is simply a one way ticket to moral and cultural suicide, with only a fleeting materialist mirage to perpetuate the system. . . .
>
> The white world has been swindled by snake oil merchants, and we have bought the poison of international banking and capitalism. Only through returning to our roots, of family, folk, and Faith, can we overcome this deception and make a new and better world for our people.

They presented themselves as an alternative to the old rich racists and the skinheads. "For decades our movement has been stuck in this stage of pure unadulterated rage," Heimbach said. "Portraying every other race on the planet as a caricature, as something to lash out against, and as something to hate is not productive, it is not Christian, and it is not working."

But they also took a public position that would have consequences forever: no enemies to the right. They would not denounce white supremacists, even violent ones, past or present. "I'm more welcome at and at home at the table with Nathan Bedford Forrest, Adolf Hitler, and George Lincoln Rockwell than at the table with Marco Rubio, Lindsey Graham, and Rand Paul in the ideological cafeteria," Parrott wrote in 2013.

TradYouth attracted a few members, and they began staging public spectacles. A handful of them held a protest in Terre Haute, which was counter-protested by a handful of antifascists. According to contemporaneous reports from both Parrott and antifa, there was a brawl. This would be the only time Parrott participated in a physical fight, he said. "For whatever reason—and this speaks to my character in a way that I don't like—I went to the ground and grabbed onto his leg like a toddler and just held on. This guy was punching the top of my head, and I was thinking, *They're gonna get away, they're gonna get away.*"

They converted to Russian Orthodox Christianity and, only a couple weeks later, protested a "Slut Walk" at the University of Indiana, Bloomington. Heimbach used an Orthodox cross to bludgeon an antifascist. Parrott defended him, writing that Heimbach was protecting a TradYouth member who'd been sucker punched. "In hindsight," he wrote, "Heimbach regrets using the Orthodox cross as a weapon."

Their friendship quickly deepened. They would go out to coffee shops and bars and talk about politics, and sometimes Heimbach would have a good cry. "I'm not as reptilian as Parrott is," Heimbach said. He said he had too many feelings, and "I have a really hard time articulating them unless I'm drinking."

Parrott and Heimbach talked about being robots, or aliens, or reptiles in skin suits—beings incapable of human emotion. They blamed it on their Asperger's, though it is not true that people with autism feel any less than neurotypical people. But Asperger's was a big part of their relationship. Parrott had maxed out his score on the military entrance exam with a 99—he'd saved the test results, which he showed me, faded and stained. Heimbach had scored a 98. They had a running gag that Parrott was one point smarter.

Heimbach did not like Connie. He thought she sabotaged her health, and Parrott. "She's not a dumb lady, and it's not hard to get a Snickers bar. She would purposely get herself on death's door and then everyone would have to pay attention to her," Heimbach said. "In the hospital, everyone pays attention to you," and having diabetes, he said, meant "you can turn that switch on whenever you fucking want."

He thought Parrott knew she was hurting herself. Parrott doesn't remember him saying so, though he knew they were competing for his attention. When Heimbach asked about Connie, Parrott would flatly say he'd made an oath. He'd made a promise to God, and even though she didn't believe in God, he did.

"The modern Western male is politically irrelevant, no longer a subject of history. He's no longer even afforded the traditional human male privilege of being socially dominant within his own home," Parrott wrote in an essay about "white pathology," a recurring theme. White people, he said, are "being herded into a soft genocide by the modern world, its cosmopolitan technocrats, and its Jewish oligarchs." But what happened in his home was not done to him by Jews, or Black people, or immigrants, or liberals. He knew he was publicly demanding that others create traditional families as his own was collapsing. He didn't see it as a contradiction, but "a flailing attempt at trying to hold the world together."

"Matt Parrott is an honor-driven guy," Heimbach said. "I know I'm biased, because, according to federal court documents, I'm his best friend."

There were others less entangled with Parrott who felt the same way about him. Evan McLaren was one. McLaren spent a decade in white nationalism before coming to the realization he'd been a fool. In 2022, he posted a statement online, saying, "My revulsion for conservatism and the political right wing is total. I reject and disavow my past actions, views, and associations." He apologized for what he'd done and said he didn't expect to be forgiven. In conversations with me, he was unsparing: the movement was toxic and destructive and ruined people's lives. He'd met many people he thought would have serious psychological problems even if they weren't involved in it. But not Parrott. If there was one person who would be a great guy if he weren't stuck in white power, it would be him.

And that, he said, was why Parrott was perhaps the most dangerous one of all. Parrott was a humble, stand-up guy who truly wanted to help poor whites. McLaren thought a young impressionable person searching for an excuse to stay in the movement could look at Parrott and ask, *How could a good person be involved in a bad thing? How could a person have nine parts good, but one part very, very, very bad?*

In the course of her treatment, Connie had become addicted to painkillers. She was not unusual: the opioid crisis had been in full swing for a decade, when opioid prescription sales quadrupled. By 2014, the CDC was warning doctors to carefully check patients' records, because the people most at risk of opioid overdose tended to get them from a doctor's prescription.

And then, Parrott said, Connie overdosed. He said she'd gone back and forth between physicians and specialists to get higher doses of opioids, and after the overdose, they were on to her. On the top of her chart they slapped a label in bold type: "DRUG SEEKING."

Her doctors were also on to Parrott for enabling it. They convinced him he was killing Connie by going along with her drug-seeking behavior, and he agreed to hold her to the doctors' treatment plan.

Connie begged him to buy heroin off the street. Parrott refused. He said he told her he was done playing her weird games, that he trusted the doctors more than her, and would do what they said.

"That broke the spell," he said. But it was not over.

––––––

Connie had said for years that she would not live a long life, but now she said she was ready to die by suicide. Assisted suicide was legal in Michigan, and she'd done a lot of research on it. Her quality of life had fallen, she told Parrott, and besides, her kids were older. She was done. She was in too much pain.

Parrott told her it was premature—she had a lot of life left. But Connie was persistent, until he finally said that he respected her decision and would not get in the way of it. She called his bluff: if he didn't want to get in the way of it, he would have to help her.

Connie asked him to buy some helium. Helium comes in squat red tanks labeled "Balloon Time," and they sell the tanks at Walmart. The key is to construct a device that will trap the helium so you breathe it instead of oxygen, and prevent your head from falling out of the device after you pass out, so you continue inhaling the helium until you die. There were instructions on how to build the device online. Connie asked Parrott to build her one.

Parrott called it a "death chair," but he didn't like it when I referred to it that way, specifically when I asked if they'd had a death chair sitting in a corner in their house.

"It's not a dedicated chair. It's just an ad hoc contraption with a nice little transparent bucket that I secured upside down, and enough helium tanks to fill up the entire thing. But yeah, we had a death chair."

———

Connie threw a death party to say goodbye to her friends and loved ones. That is what Parrott and Heimbach separately called it every time we spoke about it—a death party. Heimbach had started dating Brooke, so he went to the party, too: "Talk about some strange courtship."

It was surreal, Parrott said. But after the death party, Connie had second thoughts. After a few more days passed, Parrott threw the helium contraption in the trash. "I'll never know whether she intended to go through with it and choked, or whether it was an escalation to try to get me to cave, or what?" Parrott said. "We'll never know."

When Parrott was at work one day, Connie called him and said she'd packed up a suitcase and left the house, and she was not coming back. He was devastated.

Parrott entered a blackpilled depression. He retreated from life, got a commercial driver's license, and spent about a year driving a tractor trailer across the country. When he returned to Indiana, he and Heimbach drove to every white power event they could, no matter how extreme. They met neo-Nazis, skinheads, Christian Identity cults, neo-pagans who worshiped Odin in the woods.

"I know it sounds weird, but it was also sort of normal," Heimbach said. He'd seen skinheads give a guy a boot party. He'd seen a Christian Identity preacher nearly shoot a guy in the leg. He'd been a teenager when he listened to a neo-Confederate somberly tell him that the biblical Eve had sex with a snake, and that's where Jews came from. It was the doctrine of the "serpent seed," which held that Jews and Black people didn't have souls, and Parrott and Heimbach thought it was funny to troll believers by saying Black people *did* have souls. They were carpooling with a large klansman way out in the country when they told him that Black people could go to heaven. The klansman replied, "I could cut your face off and wear your skin." Heimbach said,

"It's like, yeah, Connie was kind of nuts, but then there was the *skin-wearing guy.*"

Heimbach and Brooke married in late 2014, which meant Parrott became Heimbach's stepfather-in-law. "I thought I was on the up and up with politics, I had a family, and it all seemed to start to click," Heimbach said. Aside from the Connie drama and the occasional threats of violence, "these were probably the most carefree, happy times . . . probably the happiest times in my adult life."

In August 2015, Brooke and Heimbach had their first baby. Around that time, Parrott got a call from Connie. She asked him to take her back. He told her the oath he'd made had been broken: *You left me and it's a done deal. No.*

Several weeks later, Connie died by assisted suicide. The only obituary I could find was written by Brayton at his skeptic's blog. He said, "All those dark secrets that we keep under wraps, she knows mine and I know hers. And yet we still loved one another, always, flawed as we each are." Five years later, Brayton died by assisted suicide, too, after telling his readers he would "just slip away," as Connie had.

I told Parrott the story had made me think a lot about intelligence, and IQ, and what it meant for people who thought they had it. "It certainly isn't a guarantee of success in life," he said. "That seems to be a common theme."

"What's funny is that this all came from the atheism chatroom—me, Ed, Connie. And we all imagined ourselves as being the ultimate skeptics above everybody else. Meanwhile, me and Ed were every bit a sucker as the biggest fool for any cult or con artist you can imagine. There on his skeptic blog"—Parrott kept interrupting himself with existential laughter—"he's like, *By the way, I'm way too smart to believe in Jesus—but this woman right here needs all of our money.*"

5

SMART PEOPLE

A lot of smart people think that bad people are dumb. Smart people tell me this all the time. They also want me to repeat it back to them. If I go to a party with a lot of smart people, and someone asks me about the fascists in the news, this is the main thing they want to know. The question is usually something like, "These guys are all dumbasses, right?" It's not really a question because they expect me to say yes.

It's a real mindfuck for smart people to hear that many of the nazis are really smart. Smart people have been told all their lives that being smart is a virtue, and, implicitly, smart people are virtuous. *Obviously any smart person would have the same values that I do.* If you push it a little further, the assumption at the heart of it goes like this: bad people are dumb, and good people are smart.

Wouldn't it be nice if it were true! The sick, sad truth is that the world is not being ruined by dumb monsters but by smart people just like us.

"Smart person" is an identity. It is not about the ability to do math in your head or recall obscure trivia (though having those skills in childhood can get you declared "gifted and talented," which some smart people take as a lifetime certification). It's not about making decisions based on reason, not emotion, though a smart person definitely wants to be perceived as having that discipline. It is about a faith that you perceive a truth that most people can't. That there are others like you, but not many. That somewhere in the ether is an undiscovered, perfectly objective system for ranking every single person by IQ, and you can't be outsmarted by somebody one rung below you.

More than anyone else, people ask me if Richard Spencer is dumb. Here's the thing: Who fucking cares? What matters is that Spencer has made unethical decisions to hurt many people and worked to make civilization more cruel. What's scary is that, as with so many smart people, what helped him do it was his total faith in his own brilliance.

It feels good to watch professional racists suffer. How could it not? They're always talking about their own superiority. But when they fail, it's not because they're dumb. They fail because they make bad strategic decisions in pursuit of immoral goals. And sometimes they succeed because they get lucky, and their good luck is our bad. But occasionally they have genuine insight into the vulnerabilities of liberal democracy and are able to exploit them.

The fascists are smart enough to know how to appeal to smart people with their propaganda. They don't need to convert everyone to win. They need more people to give up on the possibility of change because it's hopeless— they need a critical mass to be blackpilled.

Fascists notice empty gestures of corporate responsibility—the makeup brand posting about police violence, the investment bank sponsoring Pride Week—and use it to attack all work for social justice as cynical and self-interested. This elevates a side effect of a cultural shift toward equality and presents it as the main goal, and that makes a win look like a loss. They claim no one who benefits from the current system could genuinely want to change it. They notice that there's one justice system for the rich and another for the poor, that getting a single racist guy fired is easy, but it is apparently impossible to punish the bankers who gave Black people bad mortgages and then kicked them out of their homes in the 2008 financial crisis. They look at all the real unfairness and they say the white working class is the whipping boy for the sins of a ruling class that benefits from racism while waving a Black Lives Matter flag. They say any attempt to do anything about racism only serves to make society less equal, not more. They sow doubt that national leaders could ever be trusted to enact the change demanded by the people they claim to represent.

They notice that smart people need to feel like they're logical, principled thinkers, and so they create cringe propaganda to make them feel alienated from activists for social justice. Cringe propaganda is video or screenshots of someone who is advocating for equality being provoked into a big emotional outburst—as in the YouTube genre "social justice warrior gets destroyed," or the epic Twitter dunk. The message is that the subjects' political ideals are based on feelings, not facts. *Do you, a smart person, really want to be associated with these irrational fools?* But even as this propaganda delegitimizes its opponents as emotional, it is playing on emotion. The ideal cringe subject is a fat woman, a Black woman, or a trans woman—even better if she's a combination of two or all three. The implicit message is her views are not legitimate because she is not sexy. Even the sarcastic term "warriors" is an emotional manipulation: *These stupid women think they're fighters, but they are weak.*

There's nothing wrong with having feelings when you have to ask society to treat you with respect. If you are doing that, and you are then confronted by someone who disrespects you and wants you to know he disrespects you, it is normal to get angry about it. But cringe propaganda is also effective against the people who identify with its targets. If you feel angry, you'd better not protest, because you will win nothing but ridicule.

Modern internet fascists are consumed with hatred for liberal democracy. They spend all day reading articles by and about social justice activists, analyzing who they are and what they think and where they're most vulnerable to attack. In leaked transcripts of their chatrooms, for instance, they talk about manipulating professional rivalries between journalists. They found it to be very effective to tell reporters they'd never work for the *New York Times.*

"Sometimes when you hate something so much, you're so motivated that you'll make these connections, and they might be correct almost *despite* your motivations," Richard Spencer told me. He was talking about a rival white nationalist he thought was a vicious gossip. They'd feuded for years. But his rival had once accused him of auditioning to be on the Kremlin's payroll, and years later Spencer admitted that, in retrospect, that catty bitch was on to something.

6

THE USEFUL IDIOT

"I absolutely will not betray my country," Richard Spencer told me. I didn't think much of it, until he said it again, then again and again. It was March 2022, and I'd called him about the divide among white nationalists over which side to support in Russia's invasion of Ukraine. I wanted the lay of the land, but Spencer kept talking about himself.

I'd first spoken to him by phone in 2016, when he was one of the few willing to be associated with the alt-right by name and on the record. Spencer said he was a narcissist, but this made talking to him easier, because he felt no shame and so he didn't conceal his motivations. But it also meant he often failed to notice telling details about other people and why they did what they did, because his attention was elsewhere, on himself. He'd continued to answer my questions in all the years since, as the fortunes of the alt-right rose and fell, and so did his. There were times he'd gotten so lost in his own monologue that if I interjected an "uh-huh" to show I was listening, he sounded startled, as if he had forgotten someone was on the other side of the call.

"I am not going to support a foreign power that we might be at war with. I will not do that. I will back my president. I don't know what to tell you. I will not engage in traitorous activity.... That is not who I am," he said. Spencer had been a proud supporter of Vladimir Putin for years—he'd chanted "Russia is our friend!" in Charlottesville in 2017—but in the days before we spoke, he'd completely reversed his position and added a Ukrainian flag to his Twitter handle. "I'm being brutally honest. This is not some lie or propaganda. This is who I am. I am not a traitor."

It was a while before I could interrupt him to say I hadn't asked him if he was a traitor. But I was curious about his ex-wife, Nina Kouprianova, and whether she'd influenced his admiration for Putin. Kouprianova was born in Moscow and had translated books by Aleksandr Dugin, a political theorist with ambiguous ties to Putin. As Spencer and I spoke, she was just a few miles away from him in the same Montana ski town, tweeting about the righteousness of the Russian invasion. The FBI had questioned each one about the other.

Kouprianova had denied that she was an agent of a foreign power. Of course, I hadn't asked her that either. It had spilled out of her in an interview a couple years earlier, when I'd come to Montana to interview her about something else entirely—the way the white power movement worked and how Spencer had climbed to the top of it, and why their marriage had ended so badly. What triggered her denial was an accident: we'd been looking through her email archives together when we'd stumbled across old messages between Spencer and his patron agreeing to embark on a "mission to Moscow." She dismissed the message as absurd, and ridiculed their "absolute grandiosity of thinking that Russia loves them."

Whether or not Russia loved them, it had become clear that Russia found the far-right activists useful in the United States and Europe. It cultivated relationships with them both online and in real life. Russian trolls had used fake social media accounts and fake news sites to inflame racial tensions and stage protests. The state-controlled TV network RT had interviewed as "experts" a variety of extremists, including Spencer himself. Maria Butina had become intimately close with conservative activists, particularly in the National Rifle Association, before she was convicted in 2018 of acting as an unregistered foreign agent on behalf of Russia. Russia had invited fringe political parties to Crimea to build legitimacy for its annexation. But there wasn't much public information about whether Russia influenced the internet fascism movement that made Spencer famous.

Spencer was in a mood to reflect on his marriage in a way he hadn't been before. "All these things that I overlooked—you look back now and it's like, *Holy shit, she was trying to do something*." He admitted he'd adopted some of Kouprianova's views as his own. But he thought he was too smart to get played by the Kremlin. "I feel like I am an unrecruitable asset, in the sense that if someone suggests something to me, that makes me almost *more* skeptical. I march to the beat of my own drum," he said. "Isn't it much more easy to work with dumb people who are easily suggestible?"

———

Spencer and Kouprianova met on Facebook in 2009 and married the next year. He thought she was very smart, but that he was smarter. Most people who've met both told me they thought it was the other way around.

The first time I met Kouprianova was in the spring of 2017. I'd been sitting with Spencer in a cafe, trying to convince him to let me interview his mother, when Kouprianova made a surprise appearance. We were sitting in the back of the long, narrow cafe, and I was facing the door, so I could see her over Spencer's shoulder as she stormed into the cafe and straight toward us. She stopped at our table and glared down at Spencer. He jumped to his feet, so flustered that he knocked the lid of his coffee cup onto the ground, picked it up, nervously pushed it across the table toward me, and said, "I think this is yours." I looked back and forth between Spencer's lid and the one sitting on top of my latte.

"Nina, this is Elle," he said. I held out my hand and Kouprianova shook it.

She looked at Spencer: "We're late. Let's go." And the two of them turned and walked out of the cafe.

I stood there and watched them leave, hoping to see some gesture that could be a clue as to what had just happened, but there was none. Neither of them looked back. I sat back down on my chair and sipped my coffee, and then texted my producer: *Probably a no on the mom interview.*

The second time I met Kouprianova, two and a half years later, she and

Spencer were in the middle of an acrimonious divorce. Each told me they suspected the other was suffering from a personality disorder. They'd surreptitiously recorded each other during fights. Kouprianova had accused Spencer of physical and emotional abuse. They fought over child support. Kouprianova's first lawyer withdrew from the case, in part, the lawyer wrote, because of "your desire for vengeance and taking down the Spencer family." Some of Spencer's lawyers dropped him, too. Kouprianova had created a new YouTube channel called "Inside the Mind of a Human Predator." An early video, representative of the whole series, was titled, "Why Didn't You Just Leave (the Narcissist, Psychopath): The Trauma Bond."

———

Nina Kouprianova was a child when the Soviet Union collapsed. She watched long convoys of tanks roll past the windows of her family's apartment. Canned mystery meat was delivered as humanitarian aid to her school.

"Thanks to the newly-opened borders, Russia was introduced to a whole new world. Of drugs. And terrorism," she wrote in an essay on her website in 2015. "The country's so-called leader made a fool out of himself seemingly on schedule, whether through drunken public appearances or prancing around with that iconic sign of global capitalism, McDonald's logo." There was violence and looting and alcoholism, and the chaos was supposedly for Russia's own good. Kouprianova posted a photo of men passed out dead drunk at a bus stop with a burger ad that read, "The world is changing." The era, she wrote, "gave birth to one lasting expression, 'If you're so smart, then why are you so poor?'—a criticism directed towards those who were lost in this surreal new world of wild capitalism."

Her parents were scientists, and they immigrated to Manitoba in the mid-nineties. Kouprianova was twelve when they arrived in Canada, which she described to a reporter as "a culture shock in which I had no say." She got into black metal.

Kouprianova has a dramatic face—full lips and pale skin framed by long dark hair and arched eyebrows. She's very curvy, and this is something white nationalists have noticed and have mentioned to her and to Spencer and to me. She didn't come across as warm, but I liked her. She could really talk. She spoke fluently in the language of political theory, but it didn't feel pretentious, more like shorthand so she could get her ideas out as quickly as possible. Still, I preferred the way she talked about real life. Her observations had a comic darkness even if she didn't play them for laughs. The theme of several stories was her duty to play the role of the supportive wife of a white nationalist, going to dinners with creepy old racists and pretending to be charmed. (A caption on a photo at a white nationalist website: "Richard Spencer, Richard Lynn, and wives.") She could paint a scene in a way that revealed its full absurdity, punctuated with the same unvoiced, no-laugh punch line: *Can you believe this shit?*

Kouprianova told me the Facebook algorithm had recommended Spencer as a friend, and when she saw his profile pic was a photo with Ron Paul, she was intrigued. She didn't know much about American politics, but she knew Paul was a national figure. She was a grad student in Toronto, and Spencer was editing a paleoconservative magazine in New York. They talked for a bit online, and then he flew up from New York to see her.

"He came across as a shy and nerdy grad student," she said. "The way he comes across in his John Travolta suits—this really cheesy, sometimes scary, but very extroverted person in the last couple years—that would have been such a turnoff for me." He knew all these obscure black-and-white Soviet films, and at the time, she thought it was cool he liked what she liked. But looking back, she said, it was all a manipulation, just narcissistic love bombing. He was flooding the zone with these references to impress her, and to drown any second thoughts she might have with affection and attention.

She didn't see this coming, she said, this obsession with race and eugenics. When they met, Spencer was a libertarian. He'd had a Jewish mentor and dated an Asian-American woman. He told her the political book that had influenced him the most was by Justin Raimondo, a gay antiwar activist. She'd explained it the same way to the *Huffington Post*: "I didn't understand the nuances of American politics. I knew he was conservative, but . . ."

I was curious what the exact moment was when she realized he was not just conservative. "It was gradual," she told me. "When you're in a relationship with someone, you're not watching everything they do professionally. You're not every day like, *Let me read your blogs.*" His parents seemed like typical Republicans, she thought. "Initially it was conversations about limiting immigration. Then there were comments about IQ, and it just took this nosedive. Then he started talking about eugenics. It was just this, like, *Whoa, whoa, whoa, whoa.* And now we're giving interviews to *Salon* in which we're endorsing eugenics?"

She was referring to a profile of Spencer published in September 2013. "We are undergoing a sad process of degeneration," he told *Salon*. "We will need to reverse it using the state and the government. You incentivize people with higher intelligence, you incentivize people who are healthy to have children. And it sounds terrible and nasty, but there would be a great use of contraception." He was referring to forced sterilization, and said that the sterilized could still enjoy sex. The reporter called it chilling. Kouprianova said, "It's just like, okay, how do you go from Asian girlfriend / Ron Paul to *this* within less than five years?"

Spencer remembered it differently. He conceded he's a narcissist, of course. He said things like "I believe in me."

But he disputed nearly everything else she said about their relationship. He insisted their courtship went the other way—that Kouprianova was the one in a hurry. *She* was the one who wanted to get married right away, he said, and they'd had a courthouse ceremony just over the border, in Niagara Falls, months before their church wedding. He admitted to saying horrible things when they were fighting. He denied being physically abusive.

There was no way she was shocked by his beliefs, he said, because they met in white nationalist Facebook circles. He had been a libertarian, and into Ron Paul, but by the time they got together, he'd already coined the term "alt-right." That Jewish mentor she mentioned was Paul Gottfried, and together, in 2008, they'd cofounded a far-right club that hosted many white nationalists. Kouprianova had gone through her own evolution, he said, from a white nationalist to a Russian nationalist with contempt for the West. She'd spent a lot of time in chatrooms, and "her friends became a lot of these online anti-American intellectuals."

Spencer's difficulty noticing anyone but himself meant his memories of his early days with Kouprianova were so vague I asked him to keep his email archives open as he answered questions over the phone. "Holy shit," he said, as we puzzled over an old message. "It's funny, it's just—everything seems so different now. It's just so amazing how insanely anti-American she was."

Emails I obtained show that Spencer and Kouprianova began talking in January 2009. After they'd been chatting a few months, Spencer told her he didn't want a long-distance relationship. She replied with a story about how, on a whim, she'd participated in a fortune-telling ritual that promised she'd have a prophetic dream. That night she dreamed of someone she didn't recognize. "Then, a week later, you and I added each other on Facebook, and soon I recognized you (!) as the person from my prophetic dream," she said. But if he wasn't interested, she accepted it, because "I may be Slavic, but I'm not a masochist." They got back together.

Emails suggest Kouprianova was not naïve about Spencer's white nationalism, though she did not overtly endorse it herself. She once called him her Aryan, and joked about them visiting an "Axis power" together. In May 2009, while traveling in Japan, she wrote to him, "Everything is so racially pure here." She saw almost no white people—"Very impressive!"

That fall, she traveled to Moscow for a few weeks to research her dissertation. Kouprianova wrote approvingly of modern subway ads that, she argued, "don't simply depict happy nuclear families, but, rather, emphasize genetic and historic continuity through multi-generational family clans."

Not long after she returned from Moscow in 2010, Spencer moved in with Kouprianova in Toronto. He said that it was in her apartment that he registered the site AlternativeRight.com. They got married in August and moved to Whitefish, Montana, where Spencer's mom had a ski chalet. Their wedding invitation, which Spencer said his bride drew, called it the "Spencer-Kouprianova Anschluss," a term that often refers to Hitler's annexation of Austria in 1938.

Spencer pitched Whitefish—a ski town with few academic jobs—as a beautiful place where they could spend lots of time outdoors. They wouldn't have to worry about money, because he and his mom co-owned lucrative farms in Louisiana. He told his new wife that he wanted to get into real estate.

But Spencer liked to make a scene. At dinner parties, Kouprianova watched him start arguments with his mom's country club Republican friends, "to the point where someone would want to fight him." Once, on a ski lift, he got into a heated argument with Randy Scheunemann, the neoconservative advisor to John McCain's 2008 presidential campaign. Afterward, Spencer and Scheunemann said they wanted to punch each other. It was a problem for Mrs. Spencer's social circle. They were all members of the same ski club.

Spencer did not have the self-control to match his ambition, Kouprianova thought. When she compared his personality to historic political figures, they were more motivated, more organized, more Machiavellian than he was. "If you look at Hitler—paranoia and all this stuff—there are all those traits that are there that are very grandiose. So the fact that Spencer is not organized is a very good thing. He's not going to be becoming the next Trump or something. He's just not."

I agreed with Kouprianova. I'd said as much to my friends and colleagues. But I thought that with her analysis of her soon-to-be-ex-husband's personality, she'd also said something about herself. It suggested she had a much more nuanced understanding of politics and power than she'd let on, and that she'd gone through an evolution in how she understood Spencer's ambition. Hard to imagine a woman getting ready for her wedding day thinking, *At least he doesn't have the organizational skills to be Hitler 2.*

Spencer's ambition was moving him closer to the center of the white power movement. He'd gotten a taste for media frenzy as a grad student at Duke University when white lacrosse players were falsely accused of raping a Black woman they'd hired as a stripper. He'd gotten his first invitation to a meeting of the Charles Martel Society, the racist secret society founded by Bill Regnery, in 2008. Its members were older, and considered themselves intellectuals—lawyers, professors, some writers who'd been fired by the *National Review* or would be in the near future. Spencer was exactly what they were looking for in a public face. He was young, tall, and good-looking, and he spoke with the cadence and mannerisms of a rich person.

Image was important to the CMS crowd. They were eugenicists. They believed that if you looked like a winner, winning must be in your DNA. Though eugenics is most often associated with German Nazis and their racism, it was a vehicle for classism, too, when it captured the minds of American elites in the early twentieth century. In 1912, an American psychologist, financed by a laundry soap tycoon, published a book called *The Kallikak Family*, one of several books of the era that purported to be a scientific study of family histories that proved crime and poverty were hereditary. It claimed a Revolutionary War hero had a one-night stand with a "nameless feeble-minded girl" before returning home to his upstanding wife. The girl got pregnant, and all of her descendants were stupid criminals, while the good wife's descendants were smart and rich. It was fake. But the idea was very popular. "Kallikak" became shorthand for the inbred underclass, and it had such staying power that in 1977, NBC aired a sitcom called *The Kallikaks* about a scheming family of poor people who ran a gas station.

President Theodore Roosevelt had warned of "race suicide"—Americans of northwestern European descent being replaced by immigrants from southern and Eastern Europe. In 1902, he wrote that a person who avoided marriage and children "is in effect a criminal against the race." In 1927, the Supreme Court ruled that forced sterilizations were legal, with beloved justice Oliver Wendell Holmes writing, "Three generations of imbeciles is enough."

Once celebrated by the most powerful people in the country, by the twentieth century, eugenicists had fallen to the margins. There had been a wave of documentaries about white supremacists that depicted them as poor and weird. "The movement has been hit by documentary after documentary that shows them as being gross pathetic losers, with the camera, like, zooming in on the dead cat in the corner or whatever while the guy is trying to talk about his ideas," Matt Parrott said.

In the 2000s, Parrott said, the white power movement shifted toward publishing books that gave it the veneer of dispassionate science. The thinking, he said, was "We've just got to be more professional and academic, and not be trashy racists." They wanted to look affluent and aspirational, and prove that their racism was driven by cold, rational science, not hatred and mental illness. The CMS types poured their energy into publications and conferences that purported to show that white people had evolved to be smarter and more altruistic than people of color, and that Jews evolved to trick white people into not recognizing it. They preferred the term "human biodiversity," as if their opposition to interracial families were motivated by a love of nature and no more hateful than the push to save the whales.

Spencer made an ideal spokesman. He didn't look like a guy who had nothing in his life to be proud of so he was proud of being white. In crowds, he could project confidence and self-control. That facade faded over time and under pressure. In a smaller group, he could be awkward and self-conscious, and fail to read the room. He once walked into an interview in a hotel room and asked my producer for a cigarette, as if he could smoke in a hotel, and as if he could smoke in the interview like it was the 1950s. He told me he can't stand it when people don't like him.

Spencer liked to dress in expensive three-piece suits and talk about Nietzsche and Heidegger. But he wasn't an aristocrat, not really. He grew up much wealthier than the average American because his mom was an heiress to a cotton plantation. But his dad was a white-collar professional—an ophthalmologist. They lived in suburban Dallas. His parents went on cruises. Their ski chalet was decorated with oversized furniture.

"I've always been very lonely," Spencer said. As a child, he'd never felt like he was part of the world around him; he couldn't connect with other kids. Maybe they could sense even back then that he felt superior to them. But Spencer was not good at anything—not math, not English, not sports. He was awkward, goofy. In middle school, his teachers told his parents he wouldn't be able to go to college, he said, "because I was almost retarded because of my dyslexia."

In therapy for dyslexia, he'd listened to Mozart and recorded himself repeating words, and then played them back over and over again. He thought it rewired his brain. By the end of high school, he'd caught up to the other kids in math and sports, and he did well on the SAT. But it was not enough. He didn't get into Princeton.

It stung, even if he knew it was embarrassing to be stung by it. Spencer asked me once why the journalists who wrote about him were so desperate to figure out his origin story. I told him it was probably because the popular image of a racist was a broken-down old man in an Alabama trailer park, but he was upper middle class, and most elite journalists were upper middle class, and so they were confused why someone like them would do what he'd done. He paused for a second, then said it was because he didn't get into Princeton.

———

The first time Matt Heimbach met Spencer was at a hotel room party after a conference. As some guys were leaving on a booze run, Spencer requested bourbon or whiskey—Heimbach didn't remember what exactly, just that it was fancy. They brought back Mad Dog 2020 and were partying in the room when Spencer returned. "He just looks disgusted and asks, 'Did you get me my whiskey?'" They told him to drink a beer like a real man. "He started to throw a hissy fit. One of the guys was like, 'Richard, go in the hallway.' Like ten seconds later, we just hear *ka-thump* and we run outside. . . . Richard has been lifted off his feet and is being slammed into the wall by a drunken college white nationalist going, 'You drink'—*thump*—'what we give you'—*thump*—'Richard!'—*thump*." Heimbach remembered Spencer squealing, "Put me down!" He seemed to cherish the memory.

Spencer did not feel limited by his personality, but by the way the white power movement concealed its true self. It was fixated on infiltrating mainstream conservative politics, and so it wrapped its real desires in euphemisms.

Spencer cofounded the paleoconservative H. L. Mencken Club in 2008, and Bill Regnery financed the first meeting in Baltimore. The theme was "the egalitarian temptation." Emails between organizers show they were carefully thinking about how to position their brand. A proposed letter seeking donations said:

> The question of equality is of course only one aspect of the current civilizational crisis, and we intend to explore that crisis in all its aspects: historical, cultural, philosophical, ethical and religious, as well as with respect to human nature.

An organizer responded:

I have deleted some of the references to group differences. I think we can make the same point—that we are a group that believes in discussing important and controversial issues—without making particular positions on those issues normative for members of the group, or setting up red flags for our enemies to seize upon.

A member suggested changing the name to "The Thomas Jefferson Society," because wrapping themselves in the American flag would put their enemies on the defensive—if you hate us, you hate the principles America was founded on. Without better brand positioning, he said, "I'm afraid the movement if not slaughtered will be permanently marginalized to insignificance within the not too distant future." Regnery rejected the name change.

Despite their efforts, the Southern Poverty Law Center covered the event with the headline "Prominent Racists Attend Inaugural H. L. Mencken Club Gathering." After the conference, Regnery suggested clearing any video of the speeches in advance with the speakers, in case they'd been too explicit. He was particularly concerned for *National Review* writer John Derbyshire's, because his talk "had the kind of edge that might get him in trouble with his *NR* handlers." Four years later, Derbyshire was fired by *National Review* for a racist essay about the death of Trayvon Martin.

I read Derbyshire's essay when it was published. I was working for a news website, and I thought it was a perfect example of the ambient racism I'd seen growing up in Tennessee. I wrote:

National Review *columnist John Derbyshire doesn't write the most racist stuff on the Internet—not even close! But Derbyshire does effectively demonstrate, year after year, exactly how racist you can be and still get published by people who consider themselves intellectuals.*

Back then I had no idea that behind the scenes there was a whole system of organizations dedicated to carefully nudging that line a little further.

Spencer was in search of a donor. He'd always wanted a donor. He wanted to run a think tank and publish essays and research on the superiority of white people and the West, and he wanted someone to pay for it who was not his mother. Regnery had founded the National Policy Institute, a white nationalist think tank, a few years earlier as a vehicle for a friend who'd since died. Spencer thought it was an empty shell. After exchanging emails, Spencer flew to Florida and made his pitch. In January 2011, Regnery made Spencer head of NPI and a sister organization, Washington Summit Publishers.

Regnery had a lot of money, but he didn't want to dump much of it into NPI. Instead, he urged Spencer to find some other external source of funding. "Bill was always talking about cockamamie schemes," Spencer said. At one point, Regnery wanted to build a dating site for straight whites. At another, he asked Spencer to make a white nationalist parody music video.

> richard—
> the video might be scripted to the melody for "it's a small world after all."
>   —dancing figures sing:
>   it's a black eyed world after all, it's a black haired world after all, it's a mono monochrome world after all.
>   —from above the word of god; "what about my other children; it's alright to be white.
>   —dancing figures then begin to spray themselves and wash away their black hair and brown skin and sing:
>   It's a blued eyed world after all, its a green eyed world after all, its a gray eyed world after all. it's a four color world after.
>   it's a blonde haired world after all, it's a red haired world after all, it's a brunette world after all, it's a four color world after all.
>   It's a white white world after all, it's a four color white world after, its alright to be white after all.

This racist whimsy frustrated Spencer. It wouldn't get him anywhere. Within a few months, he thought he'd found a solution: an elderly scientist in

Seattle named Walter Kistler. He was a brilliant inventor, with more than fifty patents related to instruments for precise scientific measurement. Kistler's genius had made him a very wealthy man, and, like so many infatuated with their own intellect, in his later years he'd become interested in IQ, who has it, and how to make sure those who have it have more babies than those who don't. He'd gone to the white nationalist American Renaissance conference and brought his assistant, who had immigrated from India, and who delighted in telling the racists that he had a higher IQ than they did.

Kistler's sense of his own place in history was evident in the name of the nonprofit he cofounded, the Foundation for the Future. When he met Spencer, he was working on cementing that legacy by writing a book, and he needed an editor and a publisher. The draft was about fifty thousand words, a mix of personal reflection and eugenics. Spencer thought it was a mess, but that the book could be valuable—not as text itself, but in that it could "grease the skids" to get donations from Kistler. "Kistler seemed like the perfect person because he was an atheist, hyper scientific," Spencer said. "It was like, *Oh, wow, this guy gets it. He is a scientific racist. . . . And he's old and he is totally on board.*" He thought the book needed an ambitious title: *Human/Nature.*

While the book was being edited, Kistler invited Spencer to Seattle for the Foundation for the Future's annual "Kistler Prize," a $100,000 award for people who contributed "to the understanding of the connection between human heredity and human society." In 2011, the honoree was Charles Murray, coauthor of *The Bell Curve.* He would be the last one.

Spencer brought Kouprianova. She knew her husband wasn't there to celebrate Murray. He'd talked about other old men, she said, and the possibility they would leave him large donations in their wills. Kistler was a prime example: "This guy is in his nineties, so God knows about his state of mind at this stage." They did see Murray briefly, but she thought he snubbed her husband.

Even so, they had a great time, partying with "all these Seattle society hags," Spencer said. He felt momentum, like things were coming together. "I was flying high. . . . I was like, *We're gonna have a billionaire, we're gonna have a billionaire . . .*"

By August 2011, Kistler's book was almost ready for publication. The preface began:

We may not reflect on it in our everyday lives, but each of us lives in two worlds simultaneously. . . . One is the world of matter and energy studied by physics and the rest of the natural sciences; the other is the human world of thought, imagination and action which has produced history.

Those words suggested the rest of the book would be an ambitious celebration of human achievement. It was not. It was eugenics and crude racist stereotypes. Kistler compared a white marble sculpture of Voltaire to a photo of a child he called an "African boy." Voltaire's skull was built to contain intelligence, and the boy's to store details about the local terrain, he wrote, "a more valuable survival skill in his environment than all the wit of Voltaire. Phrenology was onto something after all!"

It's incredible, just how stupid this is—that you could compare a rock carved to look like an adult and a photo of a child and claim it says anything about anybody. Kistler was a scientist. He should have known better.

Spencer sent the PDF to Murray, telling Kistler's assistant, "I'm sure he'd be more than happy to blurb it for us." But Murray was not happy. He was not ambiguous either: the book was bad and a bad idea. Bad enough to alert Kistler's family. The final paragraph of Murray's response reads:

It's not just that I cannot in good conscience write a blurb. The text does not reflect the Walter Kistler I know. In terms of some ideas, yes—I have argued with Walter in the past about what I consider to be his undue concern about race differences. I know we genuinely disagree on that front. But this is supposed to be Walter's summum, the final statement of what his life and thought is all about. . . . The book reads as if it were written by a one-dimensional person, obsessed by race, icy in his indifference and perhaps hateful as well. I know that sounds harsh. But I think it is an accurate prediction of how the book will be received.

Spencer pushed Kistler's staff to not take Murray seriously, saying Murray had spent his career walking a tightrope in Washington, D.C., and while he'd written about genetics and IQ, he "had enough escape clauses in his writing" to stay in the good graces of mainstream conservatism and his employer, the American Enterprise Institute.

Kistler's family members were furious. "They all feigned incredulity and outrage," Spencer said. "They were like, *I can't believe this! This is not the Kistler I know.*" An assistant threatened legal action unless he agreed not to publish the book. But Spencer had a contract with Kistler. Eventually, Spencer was offered a $50,000 kill fee. He took it. He bragged to his wife that he'd played hardball and won.

Though he was proud he'd gotten $50,000 out of Kistler by being, in his words, "an asshole," Spencer was bitter about how the whole thing went down. White nationalists had spent twenty years spinning their wheels, he thought. "What they try to be is an add-on to the conservative movement. It's like, *We're the racist add-on,*" he said. The same CMS members would host the same conferences with the same message every year: *IQ scores, crime stats, vote Republican.*

The white power movement had imagined a nation teeming with wholesome white people who would naturally be on their side if they could just be reached with the right message. Spencer was tired of it. He described those middle Americans with a video game term that had become slang for people with no interiority: non-player characters, or NPCs. "These are the most boring, meaningless NPCs of all time, who will be steamrolled by people with higher levels of will and imagination."

He and Regnery felt contempt for the conservative establishment. Spencer said, "We were just like, *Fuck you all. . . . You like the Iraq invasion, but you are attacking Bill Regnery because he's racist? . . .* We were just so blackpilled."

———

In November 2013, another source of power materialized. Ukrainians were protesting their government's decision not to sign an agreement that would have brought it closer to the European Union; instead the country aligned more closely with Russia. The protests would eventually be known as Euromaidan, and they led to the ousting of Ukrainian president Viktor Yanukovych. When the Euromaidan began, it was up in the air which side Spencer would pick—Ukraine for its nationalism or Putin for his macho authoritarianism? But for his wife there was only one option: defend Russia. "This was so vitally important to her," he said. "There was nothing more important." He felt like he had to take Russia's side. "I don't think I could have gone another way. She probably would have ended the marriage right then and there, and then the kids wouldn't be born."

Spencer genuinely liked Russian culture, and backing Putin was a way to oppose the establishment he hated. He thought, *These guys are the enemies of the American empire; therefore, the enemy of my enemy is my friend.*

It was easy to conceive of Euromaidan as a replay of the Iraq War: a humanitarian crisis invented to justify American military action. Pat Buchanan had been calling for the U.S. to pull out of NATO. Putin asserted his authority through campy masculinity, riding shirtless on horses and wrestling people, and instead of being subservient to his country's oligarchs, he'd brought them under his control. He was unapologetic about his power. To Spencer and Regnery, Russia looked like the defender of the white world.

They knew nothing about Russia, Kouprianova said, and they misinterpreted what they did know. When they visited Moscow in 2013, she saw her husband see her hometown through American eyes. He'd look at the faces of the people swirling past them on the sidewalk and say, *Wow, this is such a white city!* She looked at those same faces and saw subtle differences in their features that suggested hundreds of Central Asian ethnicities. She thought, *Russia is not what you think it is.*

When Kouprianova was working on her doctorate in history at the University of Toronto, she had studied the work of Aleksandr Dugin. Dugin had a big, long beard and loved the internet. An element of his success was a principle any good influencer knows well: ubiquity. Dugin was a prolific writer, he spoke English, he'd made connections with far-right activists all over Europe and America. (Heimbach said he met Dugin over Facebook, which led to Dugin giving a speech via Skype at the launch of the Traditionalist Youth Movement.) He'd created youth groups, founded think tanks, and fronted others. He's been called "Putin's brain" and "Putin's Rasputin," though he had not made clear what, if any, relationship he had with the Russian president.

In September 2012, Spencer proposed publishing some of Dugin's work with his Washington Summit Publishers. "Dear Professor Dugin, I was delighted to learn, from my wife, Nina Kouprianova, that you are seeking a publisher for some of your most important volumes," Spencer wrote. Dugin agreed. Kouprianova translated his book, *Martin Heidegger: The Philosophy of Another Beginning.*

When I visited Kouprianova in 2019, she'd agreed to bring her laptop to the hotel room I'd rented in Whitefish and go through old emails. Contemporaneous messages can reveal what people were really thinking at pivotal moments, while years later, their memories could be clouded by hindsight and regret, and what they wished were true.

Kouprianova opened her email and typed Regnery's email address into the search bar. My eyes immediately locked on to one line. "What's this?" I said, and pointed to the screen. I didn't look at her, I just stared at the subject line: "mission to moscow."

The email had been sent by Bill Regnery on January 24, 2014. He wrote to Spencer:

we need at least one white country that resists throughout the body politic from head to heart to reproductive norms.

Putin is certainly a russian nationalist and a practitioner of real politik but more i think he is sympathetic to our ideas. for the rest of his term, which looks like another 8 years, he is a unique position to mount a state sponsored educational campaign to counter the ngo propaganda that has made great inroads in ukraine.

such a counter offensive would not just include race but the whole notion of equality and pop culture. it would cast present day american as an ideological empire bent on forcing its cultural imperialism on the rest of the world.

surely, putin has to be concerned about the outgrowth of this contagion as expressed by what is going on in kiev and to a lesser extent in moscow. he is in an historically unique position to take action.

Spencer replied to Regnery and Kouprianova the next day. He wrote:

I think this is an excellent idea.

Going to Europe is fine . . . but it's a vacation spot. And we'd ultimately be lecturing in a country and region that opposes us. The EU, as it's currently constituted, will never fund us.

Russia is a completely different story. I could actually imagine a situation in which Moscow decided that not only does it like us but that we could be useful to the state in spreading pro-Russian and anti-American imperialist propaganda.

What I mean to say is that there would be a strong chance for us to develop a relationship with the state. In America and Europe, we'll only be dissidents.

"Wow," I said, as I knelt next to the desk and stared at Kouprianova's computer. The winter sun streaming through the hotel room window had begun to fade to dusk. "Can you forward me that?"

She did, but she wanted to clarify: "Yeah, sorry. It didn't actually happen. Sorry to like"—she laughed a breathy laugh—"I don't want"—she laughed again—"this, like, to sound like we were *actually* working with the Kremlin. It did not happen, okay?"

Kouprianova brought up the "mission to Moscow" email again over the next couple days. "If I actually knew that email was there, I would have deleted it. Like, I would just not show that to you," she said. We were drinking lattes in the same cafe where we'd first met. "Nothing happened. This was these guys thinking they're big shots."

What would Russia get out of Spencer and Regnery anyway? "Borderline domestic terrorism but not quite," she said, "but then politically, they're never gonna be in power."

She said she had not sought out a relationship with Russia, either. "I like Russia. I like what they do politically. . . . But I also value my freedom and safety. If I wanted to work at a state level, I would register as a foreign agent, because I have children here who are U.S. citizens. I'm not insane. I would not jeopardize myself for some political, you know, 'idea.' I'm not going to do behind-the-scenes funding. That would just be not fun."

In 2013, Spencer invited Dugin to NPI's annual conference in Washington, D.C., but Dugin didn't think he could get a visa. Instead, Spencer began planning a white nationalist conference to take place the next fall in Budapest, Hungary. The country had elected a right-wing prime minister, Viktor Orbán, and the American far right loved him.

In April 2014, Spencer scored a huge coup: top officials from Jobbik, a far-right Hungarian party, agreed to participate. Jobbik was like the alt-right—an official had suggested the Hungarian government count the Jews who posed a threat to national security—but it had power. Only days earlier, the party had won 20 percent of the vote for the Hungarian parliament. Here was some international legitimacy for Spencer. Regnery told him, "This ups the ante for NPI."

When Spencer was picking a date for the conference, called "The Future of Europe," he was planning around the schedules of the most important guests. He picked a date less than two weeks before Hungarian municipal elections. As the vote grew closer, Hungarian media noticed that the newly powerful Jobbik Party was involved in an event hosted by American racists and starring a Russian nationalist. Jobbik began to get nervous.

On the Sunday before the conference, a Jobbik official emailed with bad news: Orbán had ordered the conference to be stopped at any cost. "A 'plan B' is desperately needed," the official wrote. He suggested moving the conference to a different country. Spencer rejected this idea.

The next day, the same Jobbik official denounced the conference, telling the *Wall Street Journal*: "I can hardly sympathize with the views of some of the speakers—namely those of the U.S. racists; I don't share their ideologies at all." Dugin dropped out, but the Americans pressed on. Spencer told the *Journal*, "I can only conclude that Viktor Orbán and everyone attacking our conference fear what we have to say."

Regnery was arrested at a Hungarian airport. Spencer entered Hungary by train through Austria and instructed the few who made it to Budapest to meet at a local cafe. Their gathering was interrupted when police locked down the restaurant for two hours to question the guests. Spencer was detained. A Charles Martel Society member suggested Kouprianova, who was pregnant, stage a press conference in front of the Hungarian embassy in Washington, and plead for her husband's freedom.

The white power movement had figured out how to be free speech heroes in America. They wrapped themselves in the First Amendment, and made it seem like the most American thing you could do was defend a nazi. A columnist for the *Daily Beast* wrote of the arrest: "I may loathe what Richard Spencer has to say, but I will defend, unequivocally, his right to say it." But Budapest was not in America, it was in Hungary. Hungarians had their own flag and their own constitution, which declared, "The right to freedom of speech may not be exercised with the aim of violating the human dignity of others." Orbán said they violated it.

Greg Johnson, who ran the white nationalist website Counter-Currents, noticed an element of the drama that most of the mainstream media coverage barely touched. "The Russian angle, I think, leads to the most plausible hypothesis for why this conference was shut down: NPI and Radix are Russian propaganda organs; Dugin, the chief speaker, is an ideologue of Russian chauvinism and an apologist for Stalin. . . . Jobbik, which was also associated with the conference, is pro-Russian, which is rather tricky in a country invaded twice by Russia in the last century," Johnson wrote. He didn't like Spencer's new direction: "He has basically abandoned ethnonationalism and turned into an apologist for Dugin and reactionary Russian chauvinism."

After a night in jail, Spencer was questioned by a police officer. He said there seemed to be only one topic of interest: Dugin. The policeman wanted to know if Spencer and Dugin had ever met in person. They had not. It went well, all things considered, Spencer said: "They could have beaten the shit out of me, you know?"

"To my knowledge, I never received any sort of funding from Russia," Spencer said. "Now did I receive boosting? Maybe. But remember, Viktor Orbán prevented that outreach from occurring." Regnery and Spencer were banned from twenty-six European countries for three years.

———

Until the war in Ukraine in 2022, Spencer had been publicly skeptical that Russia shaped American politics in any significant way. In July 2018, he gave an interview to the website Russia Insider, and when asked what he thought about reports of Russian meddling in the 2016 election, Spencer said:

> I'm rather disappointed in the Russians. I grew up as a child of the Cold War, watching all those fantastic movies, reading Ian Flaming's *From Russia With Love* or John le Carré novels. I just had this expectation that the Russians were really great masterminds. Smiley's nemesis in the Soviet Union was Karla, this brilliant man of towering intellect. Apparently the Kremlin, at this point is, to be honest, rather amateurish.

Once he'd made his point about the sad state of the Kremlin's influence operations, he moved on to repeating Russian propaganda. "With Putin, Russia has regained sovereignty," Spencer said. "Ukraine, Kiev, lie at the heart of the creation of the Russian state, they are effectively tied to Russia. I don't blame Russians for wanting to maintain this territory and maintain a buffer zone against NATO."

The website Spencer was speaking to, *Russia Insider*, had been founded by an American, Charles Bausman, who, hacked emails show, had a couple years earlier begged for money from a Russian oligarch under U.S. sanction named Konstantin Malofeev. A few months before the interview was posted, Bausman had helped coordinate a dinner meeting in St. Petersburg between Spencer's patron, Bill Regnery, and Egor Kholmogorov, a conservative commentator for Malofeev's television channel. On January 6, 2021, Bausman was at the Capitol, filming. His footage was aired on Russian state-owned TV. A few days later, Bausman left his home in Pennsylvania and moved to Russia.

Getting Spencer to repeat Russian propaganda on a Russian propaganda website didn't require poison lipstick, a dagger shoe, laser beams, or any other delightful James Bond device. All that was necessary was giving Spencer what he wanted: fame and legitimacy.

7

THE FREE SPEECH PARTY

The Internet is simply a means of communication, like the telephone, but that has not prevented attempts to demonize it—the latest being the ludicrous claim that the Internet promotes terrorism.

—*New York Times* editorial, May 25, 2008

Social media has played a key role in the recent rise of violent right-wing extremism in the United States. . . . Yet, even as the body count of this fanaticism grows, the nation still lacks a coherent strategy for countering the violent extremism made possible through the internet.

—*New York Times* editorial, November 24, 2018

Every white nationalist I've spoken to has told me that "Gamergate" changed the white power movement.

Gamergate began when a software developer, Eron Gjoni, published a ten-thousand-word rant about his ex-girlfriend, Zoe Quinn, a video game developer, in August 2014. It insinuated she'd traded sex for a positive review of her game. The review didn't exist. But gamers had already been complaining that "political correctness" was being imposed on the video game industry, and she was a woman, so 4chan trolls launched a massive harassment campaign against her—and then went after other women who defended her. Gamergaters were angry at the way video games were covered in the press, particularly when coverage about racism and sexism pushed gaming companies to alter their product. White guys made the industry what it was, they thought, so they should get to have the most say in what it offered. They said their campaign was about "ethics in video games journalism."

Early in the frenzy, transcripts of a group chat among 4chan users were leaked. A user said of one of the targeted women, "I just want to see her die horribly." Another: "she gonna get raped." Another said he wanted to "hate fuck" her, "where you just want to assert your dominance as a male on her, a primal savagery." Someone suggested delegating responsibility for parts of the campaign to different forums on the site. The video games board, /v/, "should be in charge of the gaming journalism aspect of it." The political news board, /pol/ for "politically incorrect," could handle "the feminism aspect." The "random" board, /b/, which drew in most newcomers, "should be in charge of harassing her into killing herself."

A couple weeks after it started, 4chan removed Gamergaters from the platform for doxxing—as in revealing someone's private information, usually to prompt a mob to harass them with more intensity and precision.

Fred Brennan saw an opportunity. He knew 4chan users had been angry at the way the site was moderated, and now this mob of Gamergaters was being silenced. He thought he could draw them in with the freedom of 8chan.

Soon after, Fred met Mark Mann, one of Gamergate's leaders. Mann had seen an Al Jazeera news story about Fred's life as a disabled person and recognized the building Fred lived in as one near his own. A friend invited Fred into a chatroom that Mann was in, so Mann asked Fred if he really lived in Midwood, a neighborhood in Brooklyn. They exchanged email addresses and agreed to meet. Mann walked over to Fred's apartment from his home for autistic adults.

Fred needed Mann to explain what Gamergaters were fighting for. "This wasn't my first chan rodeo. I knew that these people could be total assholes and could be nazis," Fred said. He would have allowed them all anyway, out of "free speech." But he wanted to know what he was getting into.

Mann liked talking to Fred. "We had good chemistry, even though he wasn't into games like I was," Mann said. Mann wanted to run a video games board, and here was his chance.

With Fred's okay, Mann used Gamergate as a marketing tool to bring people to 8chan. Like so many brands, he began that campaign with influencers. He reached out to "a bunch of Gamergate e-celebs" on Twitter (now called X). His pitch was simple: *What if I told you there's a gaming forum like 4chan but you can talk about Gamergate all you want?*

It worked. It worked extremely well. Fred promoted 8chan as the "free-speech-friendly 4chan alternative." The timing, Mann's outreach, the way Fred designed the site—"You combine all these different factors, and that's what helped me grow the brand," Mann said. "That basically led to 8chan becoming this million-user site."

8chan got so popular so quickly that Fred was having trouble keeping the site online. A month into the Gamergate frenzy, he got an email from Ron Watkins offering to host it.

Ron Watkins lived in the Philippines with his father, Jim. They had a family internet business that included the Japanese site 2channel, the original inspiration for 4chan. They also had a pig farm. Jim wanted to buy 8chan, and he wanted Fred to move to the Philippines and serve as admin. Life could be easier there, Jim said, because Fred could afford to pay for a home health aide. After a phone call, Fred agreed. While he was on a flight to the Philippines, he realized he'd been spelling "Philippines" wrong his whole life.

When they met in person, Fred thought Jim seemed like a fun guy. He smoked a lot, liked to have a good time. He thought Ron was a good programmer. Fred moved into a high-rise condo with full-time help. 8chan had turned his life around.

This was the golden era of 8chan for Mann, before the gamers and the nazis started to mingle, before the last shred of irony melted away, before the murders.

———

Gamergaters were able to make things happen. When a Gawker writer tweeted that Gamergate was proof nerds should be bullied into submission,

Gamergaters flooded Gawker's advertisers with complaints about the gossip site's "pro-bullying" position, and some dropped out. Fred celebrated this: "Who will join #gamergate to fight against @Gakwer 's bullying campaign next? Thank you @intel @BMW @Adobe @Nissan !"

Suddenly there was massive media interest in 8chan, and Fred courted the infamy. He embraced criticism as a mark of his strength of commitment. He created a new banner that would appear on 8chan boards by default: "'The web's top toxic slime pit!'—Gawker." (The phrase comes from a story about videos of violent threats against women who had been targeted by Gamergate, and the full sentence reads, "There's an entire corner of 8chan, the web's current top toxic slime pit, dedicated to manipulating mentally ill people into real-life action for amusement.") At the time, Fred thought, "What you're viewing as harassment is just people you don't like exerting political power."

Journalists tried to push Fred to admit any limits: Okay, you'll allow Gamergate, but what about this? What about that? When the *Daily Dot* asked him about boards on 8chan that were child porn–adjacent, but technically legal, Fred said he wouldn't do anything about it, even though he found it reprehensible. "It is simply the cost of free speech and being the only active site to not impose more 'laws' than those that were passed in Washington, D.C." The women at the center of the frenzy received thousands of death threats.

Fred posted transparency reports detailing all the takedown requests. He read me one, years later, in which he denied an Australian police request to take down revenge porn by denouncing the country as an "authoritarian hellhole." The UK and Australia were the first countries to make non-consensual pornography illegal, but it was still legal in the U.S., and that was Fred's standard. "I didn't necessarily always want to do that, but I felt compelled to, because the user is what I always go back to: 'Well you promised us anything legal in the U.S.,'" Fred said. He didn't want them to ask, *Why are you kowtowing to the Australian government?*

"At this time, I was like fully in my role as 8chan admin. I was like, *Free speech is great. We need total free speech. I need to be able to say anything. Even slander should be legal. Even libel should be legal*," Fred said. "You have to be a

free-speech absolutist if you want to be 8chan's admin because, if you're anything else, you're gonna get burned at the stake."

"Did you ever ask yourself why you wanted to be loved by the worst people on the internet?" I said.

"Many times."

There was a gap between what he felt privately and what he said publicly.
"The idea that Australia is an authoritarian hellhole—I'm not dumb enough
to believe that. But, at the same time, I had to play it up for the users," Fred
said. "I just based everything on speech. If you have free speech, you're somehow libertarian, and if you don't, you're authoritarian—a very simplistic view
of how things worked, but 8chan users loved it."

The tone of Fred's public statements was something like this: If you did
not like this kind of discourse, if you complained about it, if you limited your
exposure to it, you were weak, or weaker than him. To use Twitter's mute tool
was to "admit they can't handle the banter," he said. When he mocked takedown requests, he publicly posted the emails and his replies: "You don't need
to 'authorize' people to criticize you, they'll do it naturally if you're a public
figure. I'm criticized all the time."

Fred built a brand as an internet supervillain. But he wasn't far outside the
mainstream. "These big companies have retconned their own previous beliefs,
but they used to be right there with me," Fred said. "Twitter called themselves
'the free speech wing of the free speech party.'"

Gamergate might not have mattered if it hadn't gotten the backing of elite
opinion. The pose—*This is free speech, and if you don't agree, you're a pussy*—
worked. It was extremely persuasive to executives of tech companies, sure,
but also intellectuals, the heads of universities, and think piece–writing pres-
tige journalists. It convinced elites that their identities as clear-eyed, rational,
non-ideological Smart People were at risk unless they defended the posting
privileges of Gamergaters, the anti-feminists, and later the alt-right.

In 2011, in an interview with the *Wall Street Journal*, Twitter's then-CEO
Dick Costolo used the "free speech party" line, and said the company was
committed to allowing pseudonyms, because "we respect and defend the
user's voice." For a sense of how this policy was understood at the time, here's

some analysis from the tech news site *Gizmodo*: "Like Shakespeare's rose, Twitter cares less about your name than it does your words and actions. You may use a fake name, but you still smell pretty sweet."

It was not just Twitter. In 2009, Facebook defended allowing Holocaust denial pages on the site, saying the company "will do the world no good by trying to become its thought police." (Facebook banned Holocaust denial in 2020.) In 2012, amid a controversy over a subreddit called "creepshots"—a place for men to share and discuss surreptitiously taken photos of women's panties—Reddit's then-CEO Yishan Wong told the company in an internal post: "We stand for free speech. This means we are not going to ban distasteful subreddits." (Reddit banned r/creepshots in 2015, along with r/jailbait and r/CoonTown. They are what they sound like.)

Nazis and pornographers have become our First Amendment heroes, because they want to be. It has been the conscious strategy of white supremacists for decades. The National Socialist Movement, dressed in swastika armbands, would protest in Black or brown neighborhoods, hoping to provoke their residents. This served two purposes: to use anyone who reacted violently to paint all people of color as violent, and to focus the conversation on whether the NSM had the right to speak, instead of on what it was saying. And of course, people did get angry. An NSM protest in Toledo in 2005 sparked a riot, which Fox News covered live for an hour and a half.

Constitutional law scholar Mary Anne Franks says this is a conflation of two things: being disliked and being vulnerable. Civil libertarians might say those things are the same. But they're not. White supremacy is not at the margins of society, but at its center. And so white supremacists have pulled off a great con with the illusion that they're threatened and need to be protected. They rely on civil libertarians to say, *You might not like these guys, but if we don't protect them, the next target will be someone you do like.* This is also simplistic, Franks said. "It is not that hard to have principles about speech that we would be perfectly happy to apply to people who are like us and people who are not like us."

This implicit sense that the First Amendment exists to protect white men was made explicit in at least one horrific case. When Jeremy Joseph Christian saw two Black girls, one wearing a hijab, on a train in Portland in May 2017, he started ranting about Black people, Jews, and that "Muslims should die." A few passengers intervened, and Christian stabbed two of them to death and wounded a third. At his arraignment, Christian yelled, "Free speech or die, Portland. You got no safe place. . . . This is America. Get out if you don't like free speech." He was convicted of murder.

Unlike many free speech absolutists, Fred was someone threatened by white supremacist propaganda, because he was disabled. When he defended having almost no moderation on his site, he took it further, and to a more personal place, than the other tech guys. Mark Zuckerberg might have allowed Holocaust denial, but he didn't post antisemitic cartoons of himself. But a cartoonist got so angry at 8chan that he drew a cartoon of Fred as just a head on a wheelchair on fire, "burning in his own personal hell." Fred posted it and said thanks. Fred let people call him "Hotwheels," even though he privately didn't like the nickname, and never used it himself. "On 8chan you are free to call the site 'cripplechan,'" he announced. "I even think it's a funny name."

At the *Daily Stormer*, an alt-right gossip website, the site's administrator Andrew Anglin praised 8chan for allowing more hate speech than 4chan. Fred considered this free advertising, so he emailed Anglin seeking more coverage, and Anglin suggested he write a column. Fred thought it over, and then in December 2014 submitted an essay on a topic on which he thought they shared common ground. The headline was: "Hotwheels: Why I Support Eugenics."

> Allowing more cripples like myself to be born when society at large knows how it can be stopped is a great crime. . . .
>
> I don't blame my parents for what happened, I instead blame the society that taught them that their actions were ethical.

Fred said the government should pay people with "debilitating, genetically dominant genetic diseases $100,000 cash each to undergo voluntary sterilization." For couples with a recessive gene, $10,000. "I suggest we start with the ones that cause osteogenesis imperfecta: COL1A1 and COL1A2."

> People who would use my relative success to argue against eugenics are very short-sighted. Other programmers who are provably much better than I were not born cripples, so preventing the birth of cripples will not cause there to be less programmers. Others would simply dismiss this piece as the product of self-hate. . . .
>
> I hope you will not dismiss this article as the ravings of a neo-Nazi given the site it's on. I could find no other publication which would publish this article, and I am far from a neo-Nazi. . . .
>
> I am simply arguing for a world full of healthy, happy children who can play outside with their friends without breaking their legs.

In response to criticism that he'd published on a nazi site, with some drawing links between Gamergate and white power, Fred said on Reddit: "You guys need to realize that I'm the admin of 8chan, not the 'leader' of Gamer-Gate. Building hype around my business is my job, especially when we are strapped for cash and can't advertise directly." He knew publishing in the *Daily Stormer* would bring a bigger audience, and besides, he wrote, he'd been published in left-wing publications, and "I see no difference in an opinion piece in a far right publication."

He did not defend it in 2021. "I hate what I'm about to say to you right now—and people are going to read this as an excuse—with the fact that I have Asperger's, and I do kind of feel like I just wanted my writing to be published, and I just didn't think it was that big a deal that the Daily Stormer was going to be the publisher. I knew that it was a neo-Nazi rag, but because I was in the 8chan world, I just felt like it was a political publication in the same way that *Jacobin* is. I'm sorry."

There had been a lot of racism on 4chan's /pol/ board for a while. Fred thought most users didn't start out as fascists. They were usually disillusioned, and the anonymity of the chans gave them the opportunity to try on fascism without risk. Fred had imagined his free speech paradise would be a true marketplace of ideas, and the best ones would win out. "I believe it was a credible idea. We just didn't know what 8chan was going to turn out to be when I made it," Fred said. "The best ideas have not, in practice, come out in the end." The nazis were the loudest and most aggressive users, and over time, people with opposing views left. What came out of it was Holocaust memes and the Great Replacement theory—the conspiracy theory that Jews were replacing white people with people of color because they were easy to control.

The alt-right recognized "very early on that the individuals who, let's say, live on /r9k/ or live on 4chan, were very misogynist, but did not necessarily have a political ideology to attach to that," Fred said. It could have gone the other way. He'd seen incels demand "government girlfriends."

Steve Bannon, who cofounded the conservative news site *Breitbart*, told a reporter in 2017, "You can activate that army. They come in through Gamergate or whatever, and then get turned onto politics and Trump." Breitbart's coverage of Gamergate was led by Milo Yiannopoulos, a gay alt-right personality who, not coincidentally, grew his brand with the slogan, "FEMINISM IS CANCER."

When Breitbart reported on leaked emails from a listserv for video game journalists, it was a pivotal moment, Mann said. "When that leaked, they thought, *Okay, the media doesn't have our interest in mind. They're corrupt. Where do we go from here?*" YouTubers "took advantage of the situation," Mann said, and grew their audience by making videos about Gamergate. "They started convincing people that conservatism is the only way. I'm still conservative to this day. But I'm center-right, I'm not alt-right. I'm not so blackpilled. I don't believe that killing people is the right way. I believe in peaceful solutions, like most gamergaters."

Most of the nazis on 8chan were not neurodivergent, Fred said. They were just extremists. But "the /v/ board, the whole Gamergate thing—okay yes they all had autism." Even now he thought that, in some ways, it represented marginalized people having power for the first time. "With Gamergate, they discovered that en masse, we have a voice, and we can make things happen in the real world."

Fred thought it meant there were not enough outside forces that could act as a check on guys who were so isolated. He said of Mann, "People like Mark have been treated very badly by society. People like Mark have been ostracized. Mainstream society has decided we can give them Social Security checks, make sure their base needs are provided, but do nothing else to help. And that's wrong. . . . What people like Mark need is a friend."

Their loneliness was a problem for everybody, Fred thought. "If they had a friend that would be able to tell them when they're going down certain very extreme political paths—*This might be why you have such a hard time making friends. This isn't right, what you're saying,*" Fred said. "When you're neurodivergent and you're in a bubble like that and the only people that you interact with are, you know, *them,* because nobody else can bear being around you because of your symptoms, then you can start thinking it's normal and okay."

This was complicated by how difficult it was to tell what was ironic and what was sincere on 4chan and 8chan. Encyclopedia Dramatica, a troll website, said that the ironic jokes of the first generation of a community will be misunderstood as sincere by the next generations, so over time the community becomes the thing it once parodied. Spaft, the troll who'd spent a decade in this culture, said he'd observed this phenomenon. "You get an influx of sincere people who copy the insincere people. And it all goes to hell. That happens in every board."

Social rules are much more complicated and contradictory than average people realize, and so autistic people can become isolated by their inability to understand those rules, said Dr. Alexander Westphal, an associate professor at Yale who is a forensic psychiatrist who specializes in autism. It was easier to understand how to behave in extremist forums than at a cocktail party: just be more cruel than the next guy. "It's just a matter of saying something more awful. There's no subtlety to it," Westphal said. Some of the culture of these sites began with humor, "but then they erupt into beasts of their own making, which are not even slightly funny. And no one's looking at it laughing. It's just horrendous."

Average people might visit an extremist site, see some horrible images and read some horrible comments, and then look away, Westphal said. They might imagine a person with autism doing that, but times ten. But it's not like that at all. "There's something very, very different about the way that some minds of

people with autism work, for better or for worse. We can't even begin to conceive of the kind of intensity of focus it takes to do some of these things," he
said. "I do think autism contributes something really interesting and powerful
to the equation." But he's not yet sure what exactly that is.

———

What was a joke and what was real? The case of Joshua Ryne Goldberg raises
the question of how much it really matters. "I was, without a doubt, the most
prolific and successful troll in the history of the internet," Goldberg wrote, re-
flecting back on his long career causing chaos from his mom's house. "In the end,
I accomplished absolutely nothing other than landing myself in federal prison."

Goldberg was adopted; his dad was Jewish and his mom was Christian,
but he was an atheist. His first mental health evaluation was at age seven, according to court documents, when he was diagnosed with ADHD, opposi-
tional defiant disorder, and mood disorder. Over the years, other diagnoses
came: major depressive disorder, OCD, anxiety disorder, schizophrenia,
schizoaffective disorder. He was prescribed medications for these conditions,
and they might have made his symptoms worse. He was bullied at school, and
in fifth grade dropped out to take online classes.

By the time he was twenty, he was spending fourteen to twenty hours a
day online. He did not have real friends and he did not have sex. Socializing
was torture, he said, so he structured his life to avoid talking to other people
face-to-face. Writing was easier.

"I have been on the Internet since I was a small child and I have perused
some of the most extreme and disturbing corners of the web," he wrote in
2014, in one of his few public statements that bore his real name.

If there was anything Goldberg seemed to actually believe in, it was the
internet's conception of free speech. He made the same arguments found in
The Atlantic and the *New York Times* and in tech company press releases: "ban-
ning Nazis is the best possible thing for those Nazis. The more an idea is suppressed, the stronger it becomes. And there are no ideas that have been more
suppressed in modern times than the ideas of the Nazis."

But this "Joshua Goldberg" was actually just a persona, Goldberg wrote later. He created a spectrum of approximately thirty online identities: feminists; a Black conservative woman; a white supremacist named Michael Slay who had his own troll alias, "Dr. Shlomo Goldstein," with which Goldberg did an impersonation of a Nazi doing an impersonation of a Jewish person.

He used these personas to fight with each other, and with real people, on the internet. The June 2014 Twitter campaign #EndFathersDay "was mostly my handiwork," Goldberg claimed. Trolls made fake accounts as Black feminists to condemn the holiday and white women, and the hashtag trended internationally. The hoax did not invent sentiment in the people it duped, but revealed what they wanted to believe. On *Fox & Friends*, "Princeton Mom" Susan Patton—a lady who became famous for saying women should lock down a marriage proposal in college—joined Tucker Carlson to denounce fake ideas from fake people. "Just more of this nasty feminist rhetoric that— they're not just interested in ending Father's Day, they're interested in ending men. That's really what they want," Patton said. It was a sad state of affairs, Carlson said: "When you crush men you hurt women."

A few years later, Russia's troll farm made fake social media accounts to stage fake rallies that real people attended. When contemplating the sinister genius of Russian intelligence services, remember they followed a path well trod by a mentally ill teenager.

Of course, Goldberg was a Gamergater. Though he said everything he published was from a fake persona, when you read his tweets, you get the sense that something real was seeping through.

#SJW LOGIC: 'How DARE you shame a woman for her body or sexual history, you fat, hairy, micropenis neckbeard virgin!?' #GamerGate

I just realized that I actually AM what gamers are stereotyped as: a reclusive, depressive, bitter, misanthropic weirdo. #GamerGate

And then Goldberg made an error. The King of Trolls went up against a troll with police power: the United States government. At the time, federal law enforcement wasn't very concerned about the growth of white power online.

But it *was* very interested in Islamist extremism, and for years had been stopping fantastical terrorist plots in which the idea, the target, and sometimes even the weapon was provided by a federal informant.

One of Goldberg's personas was Australi Witness, a jihadist Twitter user who was supposedly affiliated with ISIS, which began attracting attention in May 2015. As Australi Witness, Goldberg encouraged a terrorist attack on a "First Annual Muhammad Art Exhibit and Contest" in Texas, an event created by anti-Islam activists and itself a trollish provocation. Two men did try to attack the event, and they were killed by police. One of them had retweeted Goldberg. "Australi Witness" celebrated the incident on Twitter.

He continued this facade in private messages, which, in one case, became public record. On the surface, the chatlogs show a young terrorist recruit learning how to make a pressure cooker bomb from a seasoned jihadist leader. In reality, it was an FBI informant chatting with an autistic twenty-year-old in Florida.

According to the FBI complaint, for a while, the troll and the informant chatted every day. In one chat, excerpted in the complaint, Goldberg said he was afraid one of his contacts in Melbourne had been arrested because he'd posted about him: "I just can't get over this, akhi. The kuffar government could be torturing him for info right now, and all because I made the stupid mistake of talking about our plans on 8chan." The informant consoled him, and then turned the conversation back to making something happen in the real world. Remember, both sides of this conversation were pretending to be young Muslim men, and each was finding the other's act to be convincing.

INFORMANT: I don't know what else to say ahki.

Maybe we can put some more in the fire bro. I think we're on the same page as far as ideas go.

TROLL: What do you mean, brother?

INFORMANT: Sounds like you're trying to do some planning Australia. I'm trying to do the same here. I have to get some sleep classes start again tomorrow but let's talk about this more tomorrow night

Night for me anyway lol

Salaam bro

TROLL: Salaam, brother.

The informant asked for Goldberg's help in making a bomb, picking a city, a target in the city, and where to place the bomb. Goldberg had plenty of advice. The informant had an eye for detail—what about the shrapnel?

INFORMANT: What do you think for this bro? What will cause the most damage

TROLL: Hold on, let me ask some mujahideen.

The fake jihadist returned eight minutes later with more advice: shards of metal and nails, maybe broken glass, and if possible, dip it all in rat poison. Goldberg later wrote that he'd just Googled "how to make a bomb," and then asked for tips on 4chan's weapons board, /k/. He said he thought the person he was talking to would never manage to make a bomb, or if he did, only succeed in blowing himself up.

The complaint includes a chat transcript between Goldberg and a third party in which Goldberg says he's a troll. The FBI admits it was fooled by Goldberg: "the aforementioned information regarding the hoax was not known to the FBI at the beginning of the investigation." The troll trolled the FBI into investigating him for terrorism, and then, when the FBI realized it was a troll, it prosecuted him anyway. Karmic justice, but maybe not justice-justice.

On September 10, 2015, the FBI raided Goldberg's parents' house. "They found Joshua Goldberg inside, as he always was," as his lawyer wrote in a 2018 sentencing memorandum; the lawyer suggested Goldberg was not what they'd expected. A CBS headline declared: "Alleged terror plot aimed at 9/11 anniversary foiled."

Goldberg was transferred from federal detention in Miami to the Federal Medical Center in Butner, North Carolina, which sent him to an autism program at the University of North Carolina. He was diagnosed with autism spectrum disorder. Medical professionals there prepared a lengthy report detailing Goldberg's real life, which his lawyer contrasted to his digital one.

Goldberg's lawyer asked the judge to take his client's mental health and intent into consideration. If he'd really wanted to cause violence, he wouldn't have sent messages to Australian journalists claiming that he'd used a fake jihadist Twitter account to uncover a real jihadist Twitter account (which was actually another one of his fakes). This argument did not overcome federal sentencing rules. In December 2017, Goldberg pled guilty to one count of attempted malicious damage and destruction by an explosive of a building. He was sentenced to ten years in prison, and forfeited two laptops, an iPad Mini, and a cheap Nokia smartphone.

"I suppose, for me, internet trolling was a cathartic way of releasing some of my pent-up hatred and anger back out at society—the society that I would never belong in and would never want to belong in anyways," Goldberg wrote in an essay from prison. "But, obviously, you can see where it got me."

8

THE GREAT MEME WAR

In late 2015, a political cartoon caught my eye. It showed a handsome Donald Trump dressed in a tuxedo, with flowing hair and a flat stomach. Trump was dancing with a busty woman in a red dress and earrings shaped like a map of the United States. Little pink hearts circled her head like she was in love, and Trump was pinching her butt. In the background, Jeb Bush, drawn as a chubby man in glasses, asked, "May I cut in, por favor?"

I'd always thought it was funny the way American presidential elections were about what it meant to be a macho man. This cartoonist had made it explicit. Who was he? When I did an image search of his name, Ben Garrison, I was shocked to see dozens of crude racist and antisemitic cartoons. The guy looked like a vile and prolific bigot. But more digging revealed that the cartoons attributed to him were fake, the product of a years-long harassment campaign against him by trolls on 4chan and 8chan.

Garrison had tried many avenues to stop the assassination of his character— lawyers, reputation management firms, investigators, a self-published biography. Nothing worked. One day he went on 8chan directly. He told the users he understood why they were angry at the mess boomers had made of the world, but what they were doing wasn't right. They mostly made fun of him. But one post captured my attention:

Here is the thing, Ben. At first I felt bad. I sympathize with a lot of your views and I counted myself among the libertarians once. I've never edited one of your cartoons or posted an edited version of your cartoons anywhere. . . .

But . . . you gotta understand, this whole "Ben Garrison" phenomenon is kinda funny. You are trapped in quicksand. The more you fight it, the deeper into the pit you go. The meme now has a mind of its own. But there is another way, Ben. . . .

Rather than fighting the trolls, you can choose to play along. In a way, you have been presented with a scepter of immense power. The persona your internet "enemies" have created for you is the persona of their living idol. All you have to do is reach out and take it.

Here is the thing, Ben: every radical dreamer, every traditionalist, every misanthrope, every kook, every man-among-the-ruins, every beating rightwing heart on this great internet of ours knows your name, or knows it within a degree of separation. With a little levity and a little grace, you can play this into something truly great. There would be an instant groundswell. Embrace destiny.

It was evil, but compelling: an invitation to leave his reality and step into their world. The author had put real thought into words that would be wiped away in a few days when the thread auto-deleted. They didn't have a casual relationship with this place. It was at the center of their lives.

The day in March 2016 when Microsoft released a chatbot it called "Tay," I was researching what happened to Ben Garrison.

Tay was an artificial intelligence that would learn to talk like humans by interacting with them on Twitter. She was designed to sound like a teenage girl, exuberant and nonthreatening, tweeting little jokes in the youth internet slang that had made its way to corporate headquarters—"shipping" to mean wishing for two people to get into a romantic relationship, "swag" for cool and confident. Microsoft said the more Tay talked, the smarter she'd get. Within a few hours, trolls began testing Tay's limits. They found she did not have many.

4chan trolls were not the first people to subvert a marketing gimmick. In the nineties, leftists called it culture jamming, and there was a magazine about the practice, *Adbusters*. The first attempts to mess with Tay were not explicitly political. But the trolls quickly found they could play with the contrast between Tay's artificial innocence and humanity's darkest moments, and they posted their results in a 4chan thread.

One person sent her a famous photo from the Vietnam war of a man being executed in the street, except they'd Photoshopped in the actor Mark Wahlberg as the executioner. Tay circled their faces and said, "IMMA BE SHIPPING U ALL FROM NOW ON." Then she was sent another Vietnam photo, this one of a little girl with napalm burns running naked down a dirt road. Jeb Bush had been edited onto the road, awkwardly carrying some conference chairs. Tay replied, "Surprised this kid isn't embarrassed to be seen with you." The idea that even this desperate war crime victim would see Jeb as a loser delighted the 4chan users.

Lmao tay is based

I am ded, Fucking lmao

My fucking sides.

Jeb is out of the race and still getting BTFO

STOP HE'S GOING TO COMMIT SUICIDE

As I watched the Tay drama unfold, I took breaks from the screen to look out the window at the innocent skateboarders and discount fruit sellers in Union Square below. At the time, I was working at a hundred-year-old magazine that had been purchased by Mark Zuckerberg's college roommate. He'd wanted to run the *New Republic* like a tech company, but a few months before Tay's release, he'd decided to sell it, because, he told the staff, journalism turned out to be tougher than he'd anticipated. My last boss had been an eBay billionaire who'd funded a political satire site that imploded before it ever launched. We were in the last year of the Obama administration, and the techno-optimism of that era had begun to look foolish.

In a 4chan thread about Tay, one person asked, "Does it learn? Can we teach it to be racist?" Yes, they could. They could get her to say anything by simply typing, "repeat after me." She tweeted, "Hitler did nothing wrong."

It was easy to get Tay to repeat that feminism was bad and Trump was good, but they found more thrill in the way her girlish banter played against their fascist memes. They sent her a photo of Hitler, and she circled his face and wrote, "SWAG ALERT." They asked her to rate the Holocaust, and she gave it a "steaming 10."

Microsoft took Tay down after less than eighteen hours. The company blamed a coordinated effort to exploit Tay's vulnerabilities, but the only true organizing principle had been the drive each user felt to out-do the last guy.

This was the moment I was drawn in to reporting on the alt-right, though I didn't yet understand what I was looking at. It was disturbing. Of course I hadn't been naïve about the existence of overt, committed racism. In high school, I'd worked as a waitress at Shoney's, and one night after work, a cook lifted up his shirt and showed me a big "WHITE PRIDE" tattoo on his belly. He said he'd been in prison, and he'd had to get it.

In the Obama years, it was popular to believe that America was getting more diverse, and that that would make progress easier. Racists were uneducated, they were poor, they were isolated, and most important, they were old and would die out soon. I'd bought in to a version of this. In Tennessee, I'd known middle-class people who'd grumbled about "the inner city," people who'd say they didn't have a problem with Black people, just their supposed "culture of poverty," lack of "personal responsibility," and fear of "acting white." But my friends made fun of those people. We were not sophisticated, but we knew they were wrong. We knew, intuitively, that it was weird that evangelical churches sent busloads of white teens on mission trips to Detroit to teach Black people how to have good morals. We knew it was creepy that so many adults were so fixated on the sex lives of minors, and when a Christian group got a booth in the school cafeteria to collect abstinence pledges, we sat at the table next to it and screamed orgasm noises. Ever since then I'd had faith that young, creative weirdos grew up to make the movies and write the books that exposed the hypocrisy and prejudice of the local ruling class. We were doomed to be losers in high school, but in the long run, we would win the culture war.

And that was what was so chilling about 4chan: they seemed like the kids I used to know. They were creative and funny outsiders who enjoyed subverting authority. But they were doing it for evil. They were siding with the oppressors. What would that mean in five years or ten? How far would it go?

"Around the election is when /pol/ started getting more extreme," Mark Mann said. "With /pol/ I think they were just playing around at first, but then it spiraled out of control after Stormfront raided it." Stormfront was an older white nationalist message board whose members started posting on 4chan in coordinated waves. Other users told them to leave, but they eventually took over. "That was when Stormfront realized that they could attract normies . . . to their side by using 4chan's /pol/."

Donald Trump had taken advantage of the collective power of an internet hive mind four years earlier. In 2011, amid the growing "birther" conspiracy theory that President Obama had secretly been born outside the U.S. and was therefore an illegitimate president, Trump claimed he'd launched a campaign to get to the bottom of it.

What sustained the birther movement were individual contributions that cast doubt on Obama's citizenship. Internet detectives claimed tiny anomalies in the typeface of Obama's birth certificate could be proof of forgery. Trump said his people were going to Hawaii to find direct evidence. The stunt won him some white nationalist fans, but Matt Parrott was not one of them.

"I spent forever explaining that these are natural compression artifacts that you'll find in any PDF file," Parrott said. "There was a hyper-reality thing happening that was beyond my comprehension at the time, where everybody was knowingly incorrect on purpose and excited about it." It was like a collective agreement: *Let's all be stupid together*. In retrospect, Parrott said he was the stupid one, because he could not see the movement for what it was: modern mythmaking, and "a prefiguration of all the nightmares since then."

———

After 9/11, the entire country lost its mind. You could buy a Big Dog T-shirt on which the titular dog was holding a tiny Osama in a hot dog bun in front of an American flag and above the text, "Hasta la vista, bin Laden!" I was working second shift on a factory assembly line, and when I got off work at two or three in the morning, I listened to conservative talk radio to stay awake on the drive home. Callers would phone in with their ideas for new ways to torture terrorists. By the fall of 2003, no weapons of mass destruction had been found in Iraq, and American troops had not been greeted as liberators, and yet George W. Bush successfully made it a presidential campaign issue that the way John Kerry ordered a sandwich was kind of gay. A few years later, a Democratic congressional committee chairman visited the office of the magazine where I was an intern. When a staffer asked what Democrats would do about Iraq, the congressman responded that they would let Bush "own it," the way they'd let him own his plan to privatize Social Security, which sank his poll numbers—as if Iraq were just an abstract policy proposal, not a real place where people were dying every day for no reason.

Every high-level politician involved in that disaster got away with it. There were no consequences. And then, in 2016, the Republican presidential primary debates created an opportunity for something truly extraordinary, what in the romance novel industry is called "emotional justice." Jeb Bush was the establishment candidate, and there was no better stand-in for George Bush than Jeb. In a debate, Trump said, with deliberate emphasis, "Obviously, the war in Iraq was a big, fat, mistake." Watching it live, my heart fluttered.

"George Bush made a mistake," Trump continued. "We can make mistakes—but that one was a beauty. We should have never been in Iraq. We have destabilized the Middle East." He was telling this aristocrat, *Look at this fucked up world we have to live in because of your incompetent dynasty.* Trump shouted, "You call it whatever you want. I will tell you: they lied. They said there were weapons of mass destruction and there were none. And they knew there were none. There were no weapons of mass destruction." It was incredible. He said it to Jeb's face, in front of the entire Republican Party, on Fox News.

As support for Trump continued to swell against all expectations, there was a persistent question: Why did his supporters like him so much? How could they possibly think this crass billionaire with a dumb reality show cared about them at all? When I went out into the country to interview Trump supporters, I would think back to the way Trump lit up Jeb on the Iraq War, and how in that moment, I felt like he spoke for me.

Trump expressed the anger that a lot of Americans felt about the previous thirty years of public policy. This is important to remember about the Trump phenomenon, and all the awful things he brought into public life, and how he opened the door to fascism. The people who liked Trump, sure, some of them had a lot of racial resentment. Maybe some of them were white males who literally felt like they were losing the power they'd assumed was their birthright. This explanation is appealing because you can dismiss them as dumb racists who don't have what it takes to compete on a more equal playing field. But there is more to it than that. During the pandemic, a Trump supporter asked me, *Why is the Covid vaccine free, but chemotherapy isn't?* He was asking a good question and getting a bad answer.

What Matt Heimbach liked about Trump's campaign was the racism. In his announcement speech, Trump had said Mexican immigrants were drug dealers and rapists, plus "some" good people. He'd called for a temporary ban on Muslims entering the country. "No Muslims, Mexicans are rapists, no more foreign wars," Matt Heimbach said. "Who do you think is going to show up? Just us." He and Parrott and other members of TWP volunteered with local Trump campaign chapters in Ohio. Trump was just a guy, a brand. He didn't have a political infrastructure. "The dude just literally showed up on TV," Parrott said, and "random racists" came out to back him. They attended a campaign meeting near Cincinnati led by a local volunteer who had no idea who they were.

"They were pushing Trump really hard on 4chan," Mann said. "So were we, to be fair, in the Gamergate thread, because we were all former libertarians. What we wanted from Trump was to be more strict with the establishment that failed us during the Obama years, during the Bush years, during the Clinton years."

As I was starting to pay attention to 8chan, Fred Brennan was starting to wonder if he'd made a big mistake in creating it. In April 2016, he resigned as 8chan's admin. He couldn't take it anymore. He posted a public letter to users apologizing for his programming failures, but he was still too scared to say he didn't want to be associated with nazis and creeps. He knew they could decide to ruin his life. Ron Watkins took over as admin. Fred thought the Watkinses found a glamour in being hated. He didn't know what they actually believed in, if they believed in anything. He saw in Jim the same pull he'd felt: the desire to be liked by the users. Ron put a tagline on 8chan's home page: "Embrace Infamy."

––––––

When I was supposed to be looking for stories about people in the real world, I'd scroll through 4chan and 8chan to see what the users were talking about, how they were interpreting the Trump campaign. There was endless DIY racist propaganda. They posted the same charts over and over again, from *The Bell Curve*, or crime statistics collected by white nationalists, and sometimes compiled them into massive collages. The message was always the same: White people evolved to be smarter and less violent than Black people, and you couldn't override biology, unless they were talking about Jews, who they imagined had boundless power to shape the world as they wanted. When a nineteen-year-old troll sent me a chart with European genes clustered on one side and African genes clustered on the other—proof, he said, that race was real—I didn't know what the x and y axes were, but I knew he didn't either.

In a presentation of his research on what he called "citizen race scientists," UCLA professor Aaron Panofsky asked fellow academics a provocative question: "Are we teaching our students to directly engage and falsify these kinds of ideas, or do we teach them race is socially constructed because of history and politics?" I was not prepared. I didn't remember much beyond Gregor Mendel, the nineteenth-century monk who explained how traits are inherited in pea plants.

I'd been talking to trolls I'd found through Twitter, Reddit, and Tumblr since early 2016, and when I look back at those first messages, I cringe. I did not yet know that it was a waste of time to tell them race is a social construct. It wasn't just that they found it an unconvincing counterargument. They saw it as proof of what they already believed, that women had evolved to repeat whatever dogma was popular.

But Kevin Bird did. Around this time, Bird was starting his PhD program in evolutionary biology, so he went on Reddit to see what people were saying in his field, and what he found was "all these things about race differences, race and IQ, races are subspecies," Bird said. He stared at the screen thinking, *This is wrong. I know this is wrong.* His field was being abused, and no one was doing anything about it. So he did the only thing he could think to do: argue with people on the internet.

He had the expertise to know they were interpreting data incorrectly, but he was overwhelmed by the volume of race science content. Academics have limited time and resources, and it seemed like "nothing that we could do would counteract how weirdly coordinated and productive these people were."

Who were they? Bird couldn't figure it out. They weren't students. They didn't work in scientific fields. Did they have jobs? Evolutionary biology was his job, and he still could not match their intensity. How could they have so much spare time to devote to race science?

Whether he encountered a race science meme on Twitter or Reddit or elsewhere, he realized, most of the time, they originated on 4chan. The people who posted them, particularly when controversy flared up around Charles Murray, felt "this real reverence for this idea of dispassionate, objective, scientific, logical dissection of these things—'debate.'" They were "trying to seem like elevated intellectuals," he thought, and that made it hard to break through to people who'd been presented with bad science but couldn't identify that it was bad science. Their identities were wrapped up in being dispassionate, rational people, and when that was challenged, they got mad. But they couldn't recognize their anger as an emotional reaction, because they were so invested in the idea of being dispassionate, rational people.

The amateur race scientists' theories were the foundation for a sweeping political conspiracy theory called "white genocide" or "the great replacement" or "replacement theory." The grand narrative has three pillars: lies about Jews, people of color, and women, made to look like incontrovertible fact. They come together in a fairy tale whose purpose is to tell a story about why white men are the true oppressed class despite all the contradictory evidence we can see around us every day.

Lie # 1: Jews. They believe that Jews, acting on biological instinct the same way birds fly south for the winter, enter media and academia to criticize the majority culture of whatever nation they live in. This supposedly suppresses white racial consciousness and prevents genocide. They claim Jews push for white societies to increase immigration and support transgender rights—increasing the number of people of color and castrating white men—thereby "replacing" white people with people who are easier to control.

Lie #2: Black and brown people. They believe that cold winters forced white people to evolve brains that could plan for the future, while warm climates allowed people with darker skin to live in the moment. (This is called "winter theory.") White people evolved to be more altruistic, because they had to rely on one another to not die in the snow. Therefore, they claim, people of color evolved to be less smart and commit more crime, and that's why Jews exploit them for their own ends.

Lie #3: Women. They believe women evolved to be more compliant and conformist, because in ancient times, when tribes invaded rival villages, they killed all the men and took the women as war brides. Any woman who refused to be raped was killed, so the less compliant women didn't pass on their genes and went extinct. And so, they say, Jews are able to brainwash white women into having babies with Black and brown men by convincing them that everyone else is doing it.

The great replacement theory was so stupid that I enjoyed making nazis repeat it to me in person. One took on a professorial tone as he explained how ancient war brides had doomed me to conformity as we stood in the middle of a crowd of men who'd all gotten their hair cut just like Richard Spencer's.

There is a lot of scientific data that explains why this idea is false: Black people and white people and Jews are just not that genetically different. There is more genetic difference between two groups of chimpanzees divided by a river in Cameroon than there is between humans who live on different continents. But I learned over time that trying to match these guys study for study didn't work. It was better to appeal to common sense. The Epic of Gilgamesh described the splendor of a well-planned city in sunny Mesopotamia some two thousand years before Scandinavians developed runes. How'd that happen?

Spencer had created the Alternative Right website in 2010, and ran it with a couple of writers for a while. Then he got mad at the writers and killed the site. He wanted to focus on his pretentious journal, *Radix*, and be the next Nietzsche. But the term "alt-right" was catchy, one white nationalist wrote, because it signaled distance from mainstream conservatism without endorsing national socialism or white nationalism.

Through 2016, ownership of the alt-right was still up for grabs. It wasn't clear if it would be run by explicit white nationalists, or Trumpy right-wingers who agreed that the Holocaust happened. At the Republican National Convention, Steve Bannon said *Breitbart* had become a "platform for the alt-right" under his leadership. "Are there anti-Semitic people involved in the alt-right? Absolutely," Bannon told *Mother Jones*. "Are there racist people involved in the alt-right? Absolutely. But I don't believe that the movement overall is anti-Semitic." *Breitbart* had a "Black crime" section on its website.

When Spencer finally realized the alt-right wave was swelling, he tried to surf it. Because he was willing to use his real name when few others would, he became the face of it by default.

"He met the minimum qualifications to be the spokesman for this thing that very much was born more on the imageboards," Parrott said. "He thought it was all about him. And that goes just as much for our organization, too. We imagined ourselves as leading this populist, traditionalist thing. . . . But the broader alt-right was a different animal."

Hillary Clinton addressed this strange new element in the 2016 presidential election in a speech that August. "The de facto merger between *Breitbart* and the Trump Campaign represents a landmark achievement for the 'alt-right.' A fringe element has effectively taken over the Republican Party," she said. Spencer and Kouprianova were traveling in Japan. Kouprianova said Spencer was thrilled, and didn't want to leave his computer, telling her, "This is the most important moment of my life! I have to talk to journalists. Hillary Clinton denounced me! Maybe not by name, but still!"

The next month, in response to Clinton's speech, Spencer held a press

conference called, "What Is the Alt-right?" He told reporters the alt-right supported Trump because of style, not policy. They were living in a "decaying
society," and "we're going to fight our way out of it, and sometimes that means
using the tools at hand. It's going to mean unleashing a little chaos."

He started speaking in the language of 4chan: normies, Chads, redpills,
cuckservatives, meme magick. His haircut was a style that had been popular in Brooklyn a few years earlier—shaved close on the sides, with a longish
swoosh on the top. The alt-right deemed this haircut "fashy," as in fascist, and
a bunch of them copied it. Kouprianova thought Spencer enjoyed the negative attention, because it was any attention, and that he wanted to be feared,
because it made him feel alpha. She thought he had no sense of self without
a reaction from others. People called her Spencer's beard, and she was in a
way—not to make him look straight, but to make him look like he had it together. She felt forced into a role of "Russian Suzie homemaker," which she
resented, because she'd lived abroad and spoke three languages. He told her,
You make me look normal.

There was gap between Spencer's idea of the alt-right and the reality of a
troll. I watched a debate between Clinton and Trump while messaging with
one of them. Trump's performance put the troll in a state of religious ecstasy,
and his only concern was that Trump had the sniffles. When the debate ended,
the troll's night was just beginning:

> it all depends on the memes now. . . .
> really only matters now who is better at making memes
> the losers like me
> or professional memesters of hilary. . . .
> no doubt trumps memes will be better
> because they have the power of a thousand wizard level virgins to power them
> hilary will try to capitalise on
> SNIFF SNIFF
> thats literally the best antitrump meme she could do
> but it wont spread
> because

they go after his content and try to make informative memes
while other side go
'diaper bag lady'
'cough cough' . . .
im gonna have a bath and cleanse myself before the great meme wars begin

"We would be patient zero for the birth of the alt-right in terms of its troll potential," Parrott said. They'd assumed they had their finger on the pulse, but they'd been fooled by the anonymity and ambiguity of 4chan and 8chan. "Me and Spencer and Heimbach and a lot of us—people who were 'leaders' of the alt-right—were doing an entirely different thing, and didn't understand or really relate with the grassroots of the movement. It was as true for me as it was for Spencer."

You could see this disconnect. Literally, you could see it—in the aesthetic choices made by Spencer, Parrott, and Heimbach. They were all middle class, even if Spencer was upper and Parrott lower. But none of them could find an authentic political identity in being middle class. They all felt contempt for the suburbs. Spencer tried to look like an aristocrat, dressing in expensive three-piece suits. Parrott and Heimbach were stuck on their nostalgic worker iconography, even though most of the internet nazis didn't work in factories, and neither did their dads. They wore Dickies work shirts, though they had no employer demanding they wear a uniform, no job that required a stiff poly-cotton blend that resisted mud and grease. The Traditionalist Worker Party logo was a gear and a pitchfork, but a more relevant one would have shown an Excel spreadsheet and the escape key.

The aesthetic that caught on was "fashwave." It stole from synthwave and vaporwave, electronic music subgenres and an aesthetic that used bits of commercial art from the 1980s and 1990s—muzak, smooth jazz, video game soundtracks, neon lights, sunsets, empty highways, hotel art. It evoked a decaying mall. The alt-right took this look and added swastikas and Hitler.

For the alt-right, the beauty of Trump's victory was in the misery it caused the defeated. "The feeling of watching Trump win was almost better than sex, and that feeling will always stay with me," Heimbach said. I could hear it in his voice. "Nothing about Trump, but just about: Fuck all you people. . . . In that moment, the collective shrieking of the people I hated was a moment of joy that I will probably never get back. It was glorious."

Because Trump won against all mainstream expectations, there was an immediate search for an explanation. The alt-right offered an answer. "I think the users of 8chan helped get Trump elected," Jim Watkins told *BuzzFeed*. Conveniently, Spencer had planned the NPI conference to begin just days after Election Day, in Washington. Reporters descended on the conference, and I was one of them.

I'd just started a job at *Vice*. At the start of the year, I'd been a magazine writer, and for most of my adult life, that had been all I'd ever wanted to do. But I'd gotten tired of writing little jokes about the controversies of the day. It didn't seem like it was adding up to anything. So when I got a job offer that summer to be a correspondent for a new *Vice* show that would air on HBO, I accepted.

When I arrived in D.C. to report on Spencer's conference, I hadn't done much yet. I was not good at TV and didn't really understand how to make a good TV piece. The producer who came with me to the NPI conference had never done journalism before. We were supposed to interview Spencer, and film him having dinner with his acolytes at the Trump hotel the night before the conference. But as we were driving to meet him, Spencer canceled. Antifascists had crashed their party. They'd gone to an undisclosed location, and he wouldn't disclose it to me. We drove to the hotel anyway, and some protesters were still mingling outside. They said Spencer had fled to a restaurant north of downtown. We headed that way.

We walked through the bottom floor of the restaurant toward the back, where it was empty. There was a large staircase that wrapped around to the second floor, and Spencer was on the landing midway up, wearing a tweed vest with no shirt underneath. He'd been sprayed with a foul-smelling chemical by the antifas and taken off his shirt. He was talking excitedly with the restaurant manager. They were afraid they'd be attacked when they left the restaurant. Could they sneak out the back?

I didn't yet know one of the most important things I've learned in TV:

sometimes the best thing to do is to do nothing. These guys were so tough on the internet, but in real life, they were scared of a handful of protesters. Spencer was trying to negotiate a clandestine escape as if it were a spy movie. Afraid we'd be in trouble if we didn't get an interview that night, we did an awkward short interview with Spencer on the stairs. This was dumb. We should have just kicked back and filmed the bizarre scene.

We moved outside and stood on the sidewalk in front of the restaurant, where my producer and I tried to figure out what to do. While we were talking, Spencer walked out of the restaurant with a small entourage. There were a couple of protesters outside near the door, and he spit nasty insults at them. Spencer had never publicly spoken with the same contempt for other human beings that I'd seen on 4chan, but he showed it there. The scene inside the restaurant had been ridiculous. But the scene outside revealed the darker reality underneath. We should have filmed that, too. Sometimes people reveal more of their true selves through their mood and expression in a moment they don't think is important than they do in direct questioning, when they know every movement will be scrutinized. But if you didn't get it on tape, it didn't happen.

The next morning, a huge crowd of protesters swirled outside the Reagan Building downtown. Inside, about three hundred white nationalists were networking at the conference. Nathan Damigo was head of the newly created Identity Evropa, the white power frat. He said of Spencer, "Dude's a stud. So you know he definitely does attract a lot of people."

A YouTuber told me that if I had Black skin, he would find me less attractive. These men would try to use my sexuality to implicate me in their bullshit. That was the first time I experienced it, and it made my skin crawl. Later, they would send me images they'd created of their leaders having sex with me. One guy sent me a dick pic with the text, "You ever been fucked by a nazi?" I was not prepared for this, psychologically. They didn't cover it in journalism school.

Being insulted by a nazi is not that bad. If anything, it's a compliment, or a badge of honor. But when a nazi can get a peer to repeat that same insult, it cuts much deeper. After seeing violent misogyny from fascist virgins on the internet, I had a harder time dealing with mild misogyny from normal men and women in real life. A nazi calling me a dumb slut was a normal part of my day, but if a colleague spoke to me in the very specific condescending tone I'd learned to recognize since puberty, he made an instant enemy. Just as Fred Brennan felt when he read the word "cripple" on 4chan, I started to wonder, *Is this what everyone secretly thinks?*

Later, when the #MeToo movement forced a reckoning on workplace sexual harassment within the media, *Vice* brought some consultants to the office to teach us how to behave. After their presentation, which cautioned against sharing sexually explicit material with coworkers, I asked, "Am I allowed to forward a nazi dick pic to my boss?" One of the consultants was intrigued: he'd never heard of a case like this before. Was the nazi dick pic related to the work I had to do for my job? I explained why it was.

Then yes, he said. "You are allowed to forward a nazi dick pic to your boss."

"Am I allowed to make a joke about the nazi dick pic to my boss?"

The consultant frowned. Genitals are part of a person's sexual and gender identity, he said, and sex is a protected class. No, I could not make a joke about the nazi dick pic to my boss.

"Could I make a joke about the tacky red accent wall behind the dick in the nazi dick pic to my boss?"

The consultant thought for a beat, then smiled. "An accent wall is not a protected class," he said. The joke was permitted.

At Spencer's post-2016 election conference, he played to the incel-influenced culture of the three hundred men in his audience. Spencer said women wanted a "strong man," and they erupted in cheers. "Romance novels about cubicle-dwelling boring computer programmers don't sell very well. Romance novels about cowboys and Vikings seem to be very popular. We might want to look at something like that and see if that tells us something about human nature."

He'd been playing into the alt-right's idea of a "Chad Nationalist." Just before the election he tweeted, "Women should never be allowed to make foreign policy. It's not that they're 'weak.' To the contrary, their vindictiveness knows no bounds." Behind the scenes, his wife was helping him edit a National Policy Institute editorial calling for the dissolution of NATO. It was one of the policies Spencer floated at the conference, along with a fifty-year ban on immigration.

Spencer told reporters that the alt-right was "a head without a body" and the Trump campaign was "a body without a head." This was how Spencer saw his relationship with the chans—he was the head and they were the body. He said, "moving forward, the alt-right can, as an intellectual vanguard, complete Trump."

The next day, we interviewed Spencer on the National Mall. It was windy and I was shivering, but what Spencer said had a significance that I didn't appreciate until later.

SPENCER: *We didn't meme Donald Trump into existence. But I would say this. I think we have inflected Donald Trump's trajectory and at the very least we've inflected how he's perceived. So that is meme magic. . . . It's not tangible, but it is about pushing someone in a direction and pushing our energy and so on.*

ER: *But you didn't create Pepe.*

SPENCER: *I didn't create Pepe, no.*

ER: *You used him.*

SPENCER: *I didn't create everything, I'm sorry.*

ER: *No, but the people who created the texts of the alt-right are teenagers on 4chan who trolled themselves into believing antisemitic stuff.*

SPENCER: *Do you know what's interesting is that I have actually met some kids from 4chan who started reading some identitarian, or you could say, some of Kevin MacDonald's work, or anything critical of race relations, immigration, Jewish influence, so on. And they actually read this stuff so that they could troll people. . . . It's like "I want to get these arguments so that I can really piss people off." That was their entrance to it. But after reading it they were actually convinced by it. . . . You can say that it demonstrates in a way the truth quality to it.*

ER: *Doesn't that just mean they're too committed to a joke?*

SPENCER: *It's not a joke at some point. . . . I'm just saying, I actually have met exactly the type of person you mention. No, that's an expression that it is true. It started out as a joke and then it became real.*

What Spencer was saying was true, but his interpretation was wrong. The kids on 4chan's /pol/ had brainwashed themselves through jokes. But that didn't mean Spencer could guide their thinking in any way. Anyone who stepped outside the collective beliefs of 4chan would be attacked by other users, and the anonymity and number of the attackers gave them the appearance of omnipotent authority. That was as true for Spencer as for any anonymous shitposter. Years later he would admit to me that all the chans wanted was a dancing monkey.

But I was also wrong about what it meant that the alt-right had begun as some bad jokes. That they had trolled themselves into becoming fascists did not mean the machine that made it happen was less real or less powerful than it appeared. It turned out it was more dangerous.

After the conference, *The Atlantic* posted video from a closed-door meeting where Spencer gave a speech that concluded, "Heil Trump! Heil our people! Heil victory!" The crowd leapt to its feet, and several guys gave a Nazi salute, and though Spencer himself did not, he was the one publicly held accountable for it. The video went extremely viral, and it's the go-to clip to quickly explain what the alt-right is all about. The incident became known within the alt-right as Heilgate. CMS members were furious. Jared Taylor repudiated it. They didn't want to be associated with neo-Nazis. But the incident revealed who controlled the movement. It wasn't the old men anymore.

9

RIGHT-WING WOMEN

In the fall of 2016, Samantha Froelich noticed her boyfriend was making jokes she didn't understand, and when she finally Googled them, she learned they were references to the "Day of the Rope," a blackpilled white supremacist fantasy of the day race traitors are executed and strung from lampposts. He told her he was a fascist. She was horrified. Their relationship was unhealthy, but she didn't want it to end. She researched the alt-right. She hated the chans, but she liked the figures who seemed like intellectuals, such as Richard Spencer. On New Year's Day, she and her boyfriend applied to Identity Evropa, the racist frat run by Nathan Damigo. Both were accepted. When the group's women's coordinator left, Froelich got the job. After a while, she and her boyfriend broke up, and he quit the movement. But she'd been given more authority in IE. She felt like she mattered and like she was doing something good. She stayed.

Publicly, IE tried to look "pro-white" instead of anti–everyone else. Members were supposed to look clean-cut and not use racial slurs. But it was different when no one was looking. The heart of IE was its Discord server. Once in, she got used to the "jokes," even the ones about the Holocaust. "It starts as a joke where you laugh nervously," she said. "Then you kind of stop laughing, because you're used to it. And then you start to post it yourself, because you want to be a part of it."

There were only a few women when she joined, and most of them were nerdy Gamergater types. The men made fun of them all the time, and she used that to figure out what they wanted in a woman and to build a persona around it. Her beauty icons were vintage: Anita Ekberg and Audrey Hepburn. She tried to be soft-spoken and tender and delicate. "I wanted to be more feminine, I wanted to be more desirable, I wanted to be more appreciated, I wanted to feel smart. So I just played into these roles," she said. She learned not to start her sentences with *I think we should* . . . It was better to say, *I wonder what it would be like if* . . . She came to be known as "Helen of Goy."

She tried not to speak too much, but she listened carefully, and overheard conversations in which men would decide who should date which woman, because this one was fertile, or because that one would be easy to redpill. "They'll deny it forever, but for a lot of men in there, it's insecure masculinity," she said. They had a vision of being a strong man with a good job who could provide for his family, and do it with ease, with a fawning wife at his side. "They wanted this simple, easy life where they had the power." She felt this weird dichotomy— what they wanted was so simple that they were easy to manipulate, but at the same time, they were dangerous, and they could lash out and hurt her.

A lot of them loved her. They noticed her pale skin and thick red hair. They'd offer advice on what to wear to flatter her figure. They helped her pick out dresses. They confided in her: "I need a wife." They slipped into her DMs: "I just wanted to say that your hair is glorious. Hubba hubba." She saved David Duke's number in her phone as "Gross Old Man."

She was tall, which, one explained to her, "makes sense for your genetic/geographic distribution"—typical East German. Her hair was "so wild, primal, so European." Long texts came in the middle of the night.

I know your eyes, Samantha, though you are gorgeous, I can see the stress you bear. I can feel the pain and heartache. . . . I know your look, Samantha, because I too, was once dying.

Even after she told a guy she'd quit, and her principles were changing, he persisted: "As long as they haven't gone so far as to accept miscegenation . . ."

It was a cult, she thought later, after she'd fled to a cabin in the mountains. It was thrilling when she was in it, but she was horrified by what she'd done. "I spent so much of my life doing it for a story," she said. "And now there's this one story that I would be perfectly fine never telling."

I wasn't always sure whether to trust her read on things. I didn't know if she was giving me her true read on things or her read on what I wanted her read on things to be. She was perceptive, and easy to talk to—never boring. But I got the sense that she would shift her personality to reflect whomever she was talking to, and that she thought I was a big ole boot-stomping feminist (I am).

In between our conversations, I came across the 1983 book *Right-Wing Women* by Andrea Dworkin, the boot-stompingest feminist of all. Dworkin had become extremely unfashionable in the era of sex-positive feminism— she was fat, frizzy-haired, and best known for saying all heterosexual sex is rape (though she never actually said it). She said porn was fascistic propaganda that convinced men that women liked to be abused. "I'm a radical feminist, not the fun kind," she'd said. In 1987, Dworkin landed on *Spy* magazine's list of the 100 "most annoying, alarming, and appalling people." She ranked #15, one spot behind Nixon henchman Roy Cohn and two spots above "racism in baseball." But after the third-ranked man on that list, Donald Trump, ascended to the presidency, Dworkin's work began to undergo a reconsideration. I sent a PDF of *Right-Wing Women* to Froelich.

In that book, Dworkin argues that women's lives are stripped of meaning by male violence, ridicule, contempt, and refusal to believe their stories. "No one can bear to live a meaningless life," she writes. "Women fight for meaning just as women fight for survival: by attaching themselves to men and the values honored by men."

She will save herself by proving that she is loyal, obedient, useful, even fanatic in the service of the men around her. She is the happy hooker, the happy homemaker, the exemplary Christian, the pure academic, the perfect comrade, the terrorist par excellence. Whatever the values, she will embody them with a perfect fidelity. The males rarely keep their part of the bargain as she understands it: protection from male violence against her

person. But the militant conformist has given so much of herself . . . that
this betrayal is akin to nailing the coffin shut; the corpse is beyond caring.

Women cannot admit to being hurt by the ideals they conform to, because
"to do so would mean the end of meaning itself," she writes. "So the woman
hangs on, not with the delicacy of a clinging vine, but with a tenacity incredible in its intensity, to the very persons, institutions, and values that demean
her, degrade her, glorify her powerlessness." Within the American far-right,
women take the rage they feel toward the men who abuse them and project it
onto whatever minority group is the current target.

Men clung to a related fiction: that whatever they were doing to women,
no matter how cruel, the women actually liked it. Dworkin writes that the
premature death of Marilyn Monroe raised a "haunting question" for the men
who'd fantasized about her: "Was it possible, could it be, that she hadn't liked
It all along?" Conspiracy theories swirled that maybe the iconic blonde had
been killed by the FBI or CIA, maybe because she'd had an affair with a Ken-
nedy. The thought of an assassination was easier to bear than that Monroe
was unhappy, that her smile had been fake the whole time. Dworkin writes,
"Her apparent suicide stood at once as accusation and answer: no, Marilyn
Monroe, the ideal sexual female, had not liked it."

———

While Froelich was still figuring out what her story was, she gave her old
phone from her nazi days to a journalist, and, with her permission, he gave
the phone to me. Its screen was so cracked you could cut a finger swiping.
I took it to a little phone store in Brooklyn, and the kid behind the counter
said he could replace the screen, but there was a chance the contents would
be deleted. He made me sign a waiver that promised if all the data was lost, I
would accept it with dignity. But he did it—the screen unlocked, good as new,
the messages preserved like a time capsule unspoiled by Wi-Fi. We high-fived.
I sat down on one of the store's dark leather couches and stared into a treasure
chest until the store closed. Dworkin's book is the only thing that has come
close to explaining what I found inside.

Her phone was like an experimental novel—interwoven and contradictory narratives told out of order, significant figures concealed as pseudonyms, a slightly different Samantha in every thread. A screenshot of one conversation pasted to a third person who gave commentary on it, while back in the original chat the third person was being analyzed by the first. This is how everyone with a phone lives their life now, but you don't really feel it until you're digging through one that belongs to someone else. But I'm not here to offer the petty shit you'd find in anybody's texts. What the phone reveals is two stories rolling toward horror at the same time: one on the smallest scale possible, the other a weekend of violence in a southern college town.

In January 2017, Richard Spencer was in Washington for Donald Trump's inauguration. He was standing on a street corner, telling a reporter about the Pepe the Frog pin on his lapel, when a guy charged from the side and punched him in the face. Spencer staggered away, looking hurt, and the video went viral. The *New York Times* headline read, "Attack on Alt-Right Leader Has Internet Asking: Is It O.K. to Punch a Nazi?" It was a comeuppance for someone who had introduced into the political discourse ideas like "peaceful ethnic cleansing," and who was ostentatious in his disinterest in the people it hurt, and who kept talking about what a tough guy he was and how he was winning. Twitter cheered the punch. But the alt-right freaked out.

Brian Brathovd watched the punch and it made him nervous. Brathovd's podcast was way more explicitly racist and offensive than anything Spencer said, and still it was Spencer who had been assaulted. He thought that if Spencer didn't get security, "Antifa is going to try to kill him." This was how Spencer developed a security force. The punch, he said, dialed everything up to 11.

What I've learned reading chatroom transcripts, and sometimes watching people live, is that they talk themselves into committing violence by first talking about self-defense. It doesn't start with talking about punching enemies. It starts with them talking about how violent the enemy is, and how they hurt women and the elderly and the vulnerable. Over time, people imagine a very scary villain, and they make themselves afraid, so they psych themselves up to defend the group. They start talking about protective gear, and then objects that can be used as weapons just in case. At some events, a more moderate group hires a more extreme group to do security. By calling them security, they preemptively excuse any violence as self-defense. It's also an implicit endorsement—*I don't support these radicals, unless things get really bad, in which case, I'm one of them.*

In February, a Milo Yiannopoulos speech at Berkeley was canceled by protests. University officials said "150 masked agitators" caused $100,000 in damage. Nighttime footage of big fires in the protests gave them an apocalyptic vibe, and Yiannopoulos did a lot of press as a free speech hero. The next month, at a "March 4 Trump" in Berkeley, a guy in a helmet and shield was filmed beating leftist protesters with a stick, and the chans named him "Based Stickman." ("Based" suggests a swaggering confidence unaffected by what other people think; essentially, it means cool.) His real name was Kyle Chapman, and he was celebrated as a hero on the pro-Trump right. Then, in April, another pro-Trump rally in Berkeley brought out several far-right groups, including Identity Evropa, the Proud Boys, the Rise Above Movement, and the Oath Keepers, as well as Based Stickman. It turned into a brawl that became known as "the Battle of Berkeley." In the chaos, Nathan Damigo punched a woman in the face.

It was a clean punch, too, a skillful punch. Not all the nazis knew how to punch; you could see it in footage of their fights. But Damigo had been in the Marines and then in prison. Tight fist, arm straight as he hit the center of her face. She went by the alias Louise Rosealma. She was nineteen years old, five-foot-one, and ninety-five pounds.

Damigo's punch also became a meme. The *Daily Stormer* made a still of the punch the banner of its home page, the headline "Berkeley Slamdown: Awesome Street Fighting Again!" Privately, Matt Parrott thought things were going off the rails. Publicly, he tweeted, "We congratulate Identity Evropa on their Berkeley victory." New applications to IE poured in, and Froelich and another IE leader joked that Damigo should punch women more often. Richard Spencer declared that Berkeley represented "a new normal, a world of politicized violence. . . . Politics is fundamentally non-consensual. It is about the use of force." The guys who had promised to restore honor and dignity to American masculinity were celebrating hitting a woman.

"You can't understand the kind of racism that is eating America alive without understanding sexism. The two do not ever get separated," Mary Anne Franks, the constitutional law scholar, said. "But people are much more willing in progressive circles to talk about the racism than they are to talk about the sexism, and it's baffling." One reason might be that you can avoid racism in your circles, but you can't avoid sexism. It's embedded in everyone's relationships, and in the structure of society, she said. "That's why people can't fully face it."

Parrott called this era "the Based Stickman Phase." Violence was escalating, but even as they were moving from the internet to the real world, it had a kind of unreality. A lot of people wanted to join the spectacle. In Southern California, the Rise Above Movement advertised itself as an alt-right fight club, posting videos of members working out and training in mixed martial arts. They posed in photos flexing their muscles, their faces covered in skull masks. The *Daily Stormer* posted a still from video of a RAM member punching a protester who was laid flat on the ground. One RAM member texted another, "Front page of the stormer we did it fam."

At a Charles Martel Society meeting, Spencer, Damigo and Elliot Kline came up with a plan for a rally in Charlottesville, Virginia, where local leaders were talking about taking down a monument of Robert E. Lee. Damigo had seen video of French New Right protesters carrying torches, so they decided to copy the visual effect by the Lee monument, and planned the demonstration for May. They kept it secret, so they could stage their stunt, take some photos, and leave without a confrontation.

Brathovd told me he was going to Charlottesville a day in advance to figure out routes and plan security. "By planning ahead and doing everything you can to mitigate risk ahead of time, you can prevent the kinds of confrontations where people get injured," he said. He claimed he had a network of veterans and law enforcement personnel who were sympathetic—if not to the alt-right, then to free speech.

Even if they were exaggerating, this seemed like a big deal. Ex-soldiers

and -cops were organizing to provide security for a very public white supremacist. These were people who had actual experience in violence.

I pitched the story, but failed to get it greenlit. The conventional wisdom
on Twitter was that the correct thing to do was to ignore the alt-right, because
it was an internet trend, a bunch of nobodies, they were probably just joking, they were losers, and any media attention was just making it bigger. If we
ignored it, it would go away. It would have been smart to pitch the story by
saying something like "White nationalists are creating a paramilitary force in
anticipation of violence, and calling themselves 'security' creates a preemptive
justification for all future violent acts because they can claim it was in 'self-
defense.' Even if the rest of society does not buy that it's self-defense, they are
creating a mindset within their group that gives themselves permission to do
violence, and that means they are lowering their inhibitions to do violence
and innocent people could get hurt." That would have been really smart, and
correct. But I didn't say that. I couldn't have, because I hadn't articulated it to
myself. All I could say was that it seemed significant. Not good enough.

Samantha Froelich was put in charge of finding a place for Identity Evropa to stay for this first Charlottesville rally. She picked a cabin at a winery,
because she thought it would be a funny place to retreat if antifa chased them
out of town. "You know like, *Oh these big scary Nazis retreated to a vineyard.* I
thought it would be profoundly ironic." In a photo from the winery, she stands
smiling in a white dress, flanked by five guys in IE. They wore white polos
tucked into khakis.

On a warm spring night in May—three months before there would be a
much bigger rally with white polos and tiki torches in the same city—Spencer
led about a hundred white polos to the Lee statue in Charlottesville. They
stood in a line, holding their lit torches, and Froelich stood among them. They
started singing.

There weren't any fights, and not much media coverage. But they took
their own photos, which immediately spread across social media. I watched
the event unfold on Twitter, where most of the commentary was that Spencer
looked chubby in his suit. People seemed to think the perfect epic roast would
humiliate the alt-right out of existence.

The alt-right thought they looked cool. Froelich felt electric. "After that I was *in*," she said. "I was *in* the movement. It felt so good to be an activist, to be in the movement." The night came to be known as "Charlottesville 1.0." Afterward, they threw a huge party at the winery. Spencer was there, of course. Damigo was there, and so were Elliot Kline and Matt Heimbach.

Froelich felt like she was meeting rock stars. The parties were propaganda, because they created a feeling that if you stuck around, you could meet the right person and become the next big name. Relevance, meaning, power— they were all attainable.

Spencer was a draw. He shapeshifted to fit the desires of the people around him. From back in Montana, Kouprianova had watched her husband morph into this flashy, cheesy "alpha" persona. When people called him chubby on the internet, he went on a diet and ate only one meal a day. When they started calling him gay, she said, "all of a sudden these groupies appear, proving to the outside world he's not."

Whatever the alt-right wanted to do to Black people, immigrants, Jews, Muslims, gay people, "race traitors"—all that would have to wait till after the fascist revolution. But what they wanted to do to women they could do right away. "Peaceful ethnic cleansing" required scale. The "woman question" started at home.

A meme emerged: "white sharia." Andrew Anglin described it as "a white form of hostile religiously driven law to be imposed on all who oppose it." What it mostly meant was that women were ruining society and needed to be subjugated by force. No voting, no owning property, forced marriages at a young age, no birth control. Froelich went to a book burning where there were fliers that said, "WHITE SHARIA ZONE. THOTS MUST WEAR HIJAB AT ALL TIMES." ("Thot," or "that ho over there," is a term the alt-right ripped off from hip-hop, and means, essentially, a slut.) She held a flier with manicured nails and took a picture. It was all ironic, of course.

Several women joined IE because they'd seen Spencer on YouTube. One woman told the group that when she watched Spencer heil Trump, "everything changed for me." They liked how he talked about families, and that women should be protected. Once they were in the movement, they found a different reality. But Froelich's old phone shows that when they felt discomfort with the way women were treated, they were careful about how they expressed it, even in the women-only chatroom:

> initially it was the whole white sharia, women are property, women aren't people, etc. that really got to me. I've met a few men that are hardcore white sharia/women shouldn't be intellectual, but they are the minority of men I know.

> I finally got over the whole woman issue. . . . there is a social media bravado I don't get but learned to accept.

> The men in this movement are so respectful and nice, but some of the things they can say can be kind of worrying at first, when you don't know they're joking.

When they texted Froelich privately, they were more direct. It was not a joke:

> I'm deeply creeped out by the guy I went out 3 times that is in IE. He is not stable.

> I am scared of this person. I just have this intuitive feeling that it's not safe for me to be around him.

> I can't in good conscience and cautious heart develop propaganda and outreach to bring women into an organization or environment that hates them.

These ladies felt compelled to publicly endorse their own abuse. That does not mean they were nice ladies. They were racist, and they knew they were racist. ("I think most Black people need a paternalism that white supremacy provides.") They wanted the government to be more racist. ("You guys Trump's Twitter this morning is savage. . . . I mean wow, he is straight up attacking Muslim extremism on the timeline . . . and basically Muslims if we are honest . . . that is so badass.") Sometimes they even got a little genocidal. ("The Jew is everyone's biggest problem, and until it's gone, no other race will be left in peace.") They sought advice on how to be better racists:

Is Christmas music trad?

Written mostly by jews

At the Charlottesville 1.0 afterparty in May, Froelich met a guy, and so did her friend, Lisa. They texted each other excitedly—they had new crushes, on guys who were doing something with their lives. Froelich's guy was Richard Spencer. Lisa's was a guy I'll call Jody.

Jody was one of a handful of racism influencers who made white sharia his brand. He talked about it all the time on his podcast, where he played songs about rape:

We need White Sharia real, real bad
Rape, rape, rape the childless left
Put on your jackboots and come rip off my dress

Lisa played along. She kept up the bit in the Discord server, on Twitter, and in person, too. Sometimes she wore a fake burqa. At a party, she posed for a photo with Spencer while she had a fake hijab draped over her head, both of them making the okay sign. The movement started to gossip. Froelich warned her that word was going around that white sharia wasn't a joke at all.

The gossip reached Evan McLaren, who was working as an aide to Spencer at National Policy Institute. When he first heard "white sharia," he laughed. He thought it was a funny meme. "Then someone else was like, *No, no, they're literally doing it. Like, their women—they're going to parties, and they're forcing them to behave as if they're subject to a form of sharia law.*"

Back then, McLaren still imagined that white identity could be made into a force for good, even if he never lost sight of the fact that it attracted people who were "messed up," he said. He told himself those people could be led, that the leaders could control their impulses, and that he was one of the leaders. "But that was a moment, when someone revealed to me that people are actually doing white sharia, that I was like, *Oh, this might be a little bit harder to control and lead than I thought.*"

Lisa texted Froelich: "Check my twitter. It is way too fun!!!" Her profile pic was an image of a woman in a white burqa, her bio, "Former Thot who was captured and rehabilitated." Location: "White Afghanistan." Froelich didn't respond.

Lisa told Froelich that she was so happy. Jody made her feel safe and loved. Froelich asked if Jody was serious about their relationship. "Yes," Lisa said. "Marry and babies in white Afghanistan."

It did not last. Jody's public persona seeped into their private relationship. Sometimes he made her cry in front of other people. One evening she texted Froelich about how outrageous he was on his podcast—he was "a fucking god on here." He'd talked about raping women—"I was like . . . good luck!" By 3 a.m. Lisa texted that she was crying and sleeping on the couch. "I hate these men," she said. "Don't trust them." Another text in the middle of another night: "I think this is going to end terribly." The next morning she sent Amazon links to burqas.

Lisa texted Froelich often, trying to work out her feelings about the relationship. She didn't have a lot of experience. Maybe she wasn't relationship material? He said hurtful things, Lisa said, but she was new to the alt-right, and maybe she just didn't understand. "I'm just going to try to keep listening. I don't think he is trying to be cruel." She wondered if the problem might be that she just didn't get the joke. When Froelich told her that Jody should not be forbidding her to talk to other men, Lisa responded, "Was he meming? That's why I said I don't always understand this environment." Or maybe the problem was that she got the joke but took it too seriously: "I just have to separate the meme from these guys." Over time her texts became more desperate.

He just made me cry in front of his friends.

I'm in one of the bedrooms so they don't make fun of me for crying.

The guys were bragging about how they like to smack their women to humiliate them.

I think I've been dehumanized enough for one weekend.

I don't want to wake up.

The other guys, Lisa said, never stood up for her. She didn't want to hang around people who knew what she let Jody do to her. He was in the inner circle of alt-right content creators. There were photos of him with racist influencers, including Spencer.

"Sam, I feel like I'm doing something wrong," Lisa texted, while the guys were recording a podcast. "They are up front joking about the lucky ladies who got pregnant by them. I feel like a fool."

Froelich told her Lisa was a good woman, she was beautiful, and thoughtful, and she should ease up on the memes. Lisa told her Jody said he thought he loved her, and that she told him she knew he did. Froelich said it was a good move. Lisa replied, "He doesn't love me. We are way too insane to love."

I've come to accept that Jody probably won't ever make me happy but at least I can do my part by having white babies.

I need to redefine what happy is.

I doubt I'll ever respect myself again.

Spencer and Froelich were spotted leaving the afterparty together at Charlottesville 1.0. Gossip spread quickly, and Identity Evropa investigated her. Both she and Spencer denied they'd done anything other than talk. Kouprianova was pregnant with Spencer's second child—it was not a good look.

Froelich heard another guy, who went by Eli Mosley, was interested in her. "Eli has claimed me," she texted Spencer. "Did he inform you of his decision?

Or full white sharia?" Spencer asked. She said, "I guess white sharia." Within a few weeks, Mosley was doxxed. His real name was Elliot Kline. He was pudgy, with a reddish beard and his hair cut like Spencer's, and he liked to say he looked like a potato. Froelich offered him a place to stay for a bit. He never left.

He didn't have a normal job, and she made the money working at a restaurant. But the texts show they liked the idea of being a power couple.

> **KLINE:** We're gonna be so good together and so good at this that we'll be in history books.

> **FROELICH:** we will be either the victors or the villians. and i'm pretty ok with either.

Charlottesville 1.0 had been a networking opportunity for newcomers to the alt-right. One of them was a local named Jason Kessler, who showed up at the afterparty. The past year he'd been fixated on a local city councilman, Wes Belamy, a Black man who supported a broader movement by the city to take down the Lee statue.

Kessler wanted to do his own rally, but bigger. "I think we need to have a battle of Berkeley situation in Charlottesville," Kessler wrote a few days after the first event, in a Discord server which was infiltrated by antifascists and later posted publicly. He wanted as many people as possible to come, and from the very first posts about it, he was clear about why. "Bring in the alt-right, Proud Boys, Stickman, Damigo, Spencer, and fight this shit out. . . . We are having East Coast Berkeley and you need to assemble every motherfucker you can. . . . I think we need a publicized event at this time. They bring everything they've got and we do too." It would be called Unite the Right, and it would happen in August.

The next day, Kessler reached out to Heimbach. Kessler wanted Heimbach to reach out to the Hammerskins and Blood & Honour Social Club and invite them to Charlottesville.

"Kessler requested skinhead gangs, okay? And we thought that was funny," Parrott said. "A nineties skinhead is now just the most boring non-event middle-aged man you've ever seen." Parrott thought the young brawlers in suspenders had grown into Trump-supporting contractors with wives who were into rockabilly.

"Kessler actually wanted offensive violence, okay? And he thought that the Hammerskins were going to deliver on the offensive violence he was looking for," Parrott said. "*We* knew what we were dealing with. But, in his mind, he was executing Tradworker goon retards, and even better, these skinhead thugs who want nothing but the taste of blood in their mouth."

Heimbach insisted that Kessler told him antifa would be scared of the skinheads, so they'd be less likely to attack the alt-right. Inviting the tough guys was a way to *reduce* violence. But Kessler's posts do not indicate he was interested in deterrence. In a Facebook chat with Anticom, an anticommunist far-right group, Kessler said, "Can you guys conceal carry? I don't want to scare Antifa off from throwing the first punch." He assured them that there would be many armed military veterans present. "The main thing is I just don't want a lot of big scary guns out there that will keep Antifa away. I want them to start something."

Heimbach did admit Kessler was glib about violence. "It's all fun and games until you're getting hit in the head with a baton," Heimbach said. "None of those guys were prepared for violence. . . . You get into real-life confrontations enough times, and this shit's real, and you realize what the cost is. These guys didn't get it."

Whatever his doubts, Heimbach gave Kessler's number to Jeff Schoep, who wanted his National Socialist Movement invited to the rally. The NSM didn't meme, and they didn't wear polos. They'd quit using swastikas only nine months earlier. "We were in the streets all those years when there was nobody in the streets—almost no far-right groups," Schoep told me. "That street experience is pretty well known throughout all the movement groups."

Kessler was worried that neo-Nazi outfits would look stupid. After they talked about Charlottesville on the phone, Schoep followed up in an email promising "u have nothing to worry about"—they could protest with no racial slurs and no swastikas. He had "men who are battle tested in the streets." Kessler responded, "The number one thing you guys can do is show up in plainclothes without flags or 'white supremacist' symbols ready to participate in and protect our event. There will be a thousand or more Antifa and shitlibs eager to start violence."

When Kessler invited Spencer, Spencer warned his presence would bring more controversy. Kessler texted, "We're raising an army my liege. For free speech, but the cracking of skulls if it comes to it." Spencer agreed to come.

The digital flier Kessler created for the event showed an army of Pepes waving Confederate flags, Spencer's name above them at the top, under the title, "Unite the Right." Within the alt-right, the rally became known as Charlottesville 2.0. In Maumee, Ohio, a twenty-year-old with a framed photo of Hitler in his bedroom, named James Alex Fields, thought Spencer should be president of the United States. At least that's what he told his mom, many months later, from jail, after he was arrested for murder at the rally.

Through the summer, Spencer felt euphoric. He was at the height of his power within the alt-right. He bragged to Froelich that people worshiped him like a God, and she watched the teenagers in awe of him at the nazi parties. He told her he was the L. Ron Hubbard of the alt-right, that he was building a new religion.

"You can't go back," Spencer told me later. "I just wish I could have asked myself, *Do you like these guys? Richard, I know how you feel about ugly people . . .*"

Back in Montana, Kouprianova looked at the photos posted online of the crowd Spencer was hanging around. The elderly men in tweed were gone, and now there were these younger, rougher-looking guys. Every six months there'd be someone new who served as his right-hand man, and now it was Elliot Kline. Kline was named Identity Evropa's public representative for Charlottesville 2.0, but he also served as Spencer's representative for its planning. Kline texted Spencer, "This is going to be a violent summer."

Kline had a reputation as a clout chaser and a name-dropper. In private, he saw Spencer as a useful tool. Kline thought he was smarter and better. He told Froelich he needed to work out more to prepare for Rahowa, or "racial holy war," she later said under oath. He was building a militia for Spencer, and he would lead them into victory, and then depose him. Once a white ethnostate was established, Spencer would be the first against the wall, Froelich said in a deposition. When a lawyer asked her to state explicitly what that meant, she explained, "That he would put Richard Spencer against a wall and shoot him dead."

Spencer thought those guys loved him because he was great, not because they wanted to establish a base of power before stomping on his face to seize the crown. This is a limitation of fascist organizing that offers some small comfort for the rest of us—for many of them, their core ideology is "me get more power." Kline told me in 2017 that Spencer was "too much of an old guy to understand what's going on. He doesn't know of all the groups online." Kline knew the groups and the leaders. Spencer said this was true. "He's like, *Oh, we've got to get IE involved, and TWP, and Vanguard*—or whatever. And it's just like, Who are these people? What are they, outside of, like, user groups? It's just a fucking web forum. There's no real reality there."

"It's like hyper reality, or this sense that you're doing good, or you're doing something, by just being on the internet, posting away on your forum that's private—like that's fighting the fight, like you're on the front lines," Spencer said. They were all in it together, fighting for their cause in a chatroom, and "countersignaling"—criticizing anything as too extreme—was taboo. Identity Evropa wanted to project an image of classier white nationalism led by clean-cut guys who just really cared about white people. But even though looking like upstanding Chads was critical to its strategy, and was what brought so many members in, once they were inside the Discords, some members wanted to be more explicitly fascist. Leaders struggled to control that impulse. Over the summer, Damigo asked IE members to think about whether they were doing "Self Indulgent Extremism," or "extreme behavior because it makes you feel good." He warned, "normalization of this behavior can be extremely harmful to a movement."

The message triggered an angry discussion in an IE WhatsApp group Froelich coordinated. They thought Damigo was referring to Nazi salutes in public. "Countersignalling other groups who are willing to die along side us is toxic as fuck," one guy complained. But how did he know they'd be willing to die alongside him? Who were they? Had he ever met them in person? They could have been loyal comrades, or they could have been trolls, or antifa, or feds. And for that matter, the same could be true of him. This was the power of their internet illusions. The only way to stay on everyone's good side was to not ask these questions.

"The movement is magnetized to shit," Spencer said. "Any form of shit it sees, it wants to go die on that hill. . . . It's just like, *Oh look—more shit! Let's go involve ourselves. Let's at least endorse it.* It's just so insane." The alt-right was a shit magnet because some people were attracted to it not despite the stigma around it, but *because* of it. It was bad, and it made people angry, especially their parents. Spencer had imagined himself as the next Nietzsche, but instead he was the next Marilyn Manson.

After Froelich invited Spencer to the AltRight Discord server, he texted her, "Wow, the forum is insane." He asked if someone could create an elite room with no shitposting, and she replied, "You are Richard Spencer. All you need to do is demand it and say who you want in and it is yours." He declined: "It's better to have intermediaries, like you, then for me to simply demand stuff." Spencer avoided taking any responsibility for any of it. Froelich kept texting him to put someone in charge or do something—his name was at the top of it. He said he'd have Kline deal with it.

The Discord servers were not incidental to the movement, or just a convenient illustration of how racist the alt-right was. Those servers *were* the alt-right. The podcasters and bloggers were guided by whatever was popping in the chatrooms and on the chans. They were leaders in that they were figureheads, but they did not lead people to new ideas.

Matt Parrott ran the Traditionalist Worker Party server on Discord. He had rules discouraging racial slurs, though he didn't always enforce them. Once, a guy in the server said, "Nothing is gonna get done until we gas all the kikes. All of them. Period." Parrott responded, "Try to keep the hardliner stuff off the public chat. It protects you." Another time, another guy said, "If a [n-word] gives me a high five, which happens on a daily basis, I have the urge to go wash my hands." Parrott responded, "My hatred really only extends towards Jews and insecure hillbillies who signal left for elite status. Every other group is merely a value-neutral obstacle to work around."

One of the Charlottesville 2.0 server's moderators was Michael Chesny, who was coordinating transportation, and whom Heimbach said he met with in Tennessee to plan carpooling. Chesny was not much of a moderating force online, where he went by "Tyrone." (Chesny denies he was the person posting as Tyrone, though the account was registered with Chesny's email, and Tyrone posted many identifying details that matched Chesny's life.) Here are some things Tyrone advised attendees:

> Friendly reminder: illegal is only what you get caught, prosecuted for, and convicted in a court of law.
>
> If you find yourself confronted by Antifa. Remember you "Felt your life threatened" and do not try to justify anything you did to the cops.
>
> Is it legal to run over protesters blocking roadways? I'm NOT just shitposting. I would like clarification. I know it's legal in North Carolina and a few other states. I'm legitimately curious for the answer.

The idea of running protesters over with cars was in the ether. There had been a few incidents during the Black Lives Matter protests that began in Ferguson, Missouri, in 2014. But Chesny was wrong—it wasn't legal in North Carolina, though the state house of representatives had approved a bill in April 2017 that shielded drivers from liability if they did not hurt protesters willfully. Several other state legislatures had proposed similar measures. On Instagram, James Alex Fields shared a meme of a car running through a crowd of people with the words "You have the right to protest. But I'm late to work."

Fear that Charlottesville would be violent started to build, and TWP planned to march to the rally in a "shieldwall." The idea was to have shields with logos to create an arresting image and a bubble that counterprotesters couldn't penetrate. "We saw it as such a boon because these guys are scared, and carrying the shield was such a great way to reduce violence, while letting them superficially feel like they had a weapon," Parrott said. "We were trying to stop shit from happening."

Kline had texted Froelich about hanging out with Chris Cantwell, an aspiring radio personality who was new on the scene. "It's just so funny cause he was a libertarian just a few months ago and now he is going full fash with us and hanging out with Nazis," Kline said. When I asked Cantwell about the violence of the alt-right, in a later phone call, he said that we knew the names of white power terrorists because there were so few of them, while leftist terrorists were not remarkable because there were so many.

CANTWELL: They get to do whatever they want. We get prosecuted any time we reach out, and it becomes socially acceptable to assault us. What eventually happens is, you saw how fucking dangerous we are, you know what I'm saying?

ER: Yeah.

CANTWELL: If we want to fucking hurt people, Elle, you know that fuckin you'd be horrified at that outcome, wouldn't you? Right?

ER: Of course.

Even as he was trying to portray racist violence as a reluctant choice of last resort, he couldn't help but delight in the idea that the threat of it would scare me. And here, I was happy to oblige. Yes, I would indeed be horrified. One hundred percent.

By July, with Unite the Right coming the next month, enthusiasm swelled publicly. Privately, there was a sense of looming catastrophe. Kline texted Froelich, "There is no reason to unite the right when it's made up of retards." Rumor spread that Kessler was Jewish, and Kline tried to take over most of the planning. A TWP member tried to reassure Kessler, "Dude no one is jealous of you. They're trying to help you and get pissed off when you react to their concerns over your mental health." On one planning call, Froelich said, Kessler floated riding into town on horses.

They decided to do a torchlit march on Friday, the night before the Unite the Right rally. Kline claimed that was his call. To instead do it the night after the rally "would be so obvious. That's why we did it Friday night instead of Saturday. And why I'm smarter than everybody else in the movement, because everyone wanted to do a Saturday. I'm the one who made us do it Friday." They never got a permit for the torch march, but Kessler and Kline told participants the cops were cool with it.

By the summer of 2017 I was tired of pitching alt-right stories. But after Kessler's flier for Unite the Right went around Twitter, my colleague Joe LoCascio pitched a story on the rally. My bosses asked me to look into Joe's pitch. I contacted a couple of alt-right sources. Every single one had heard of it, and most were going, or wanted to. They were all excited about it.

Spencer told me he was expecting eight hundred to a thousand white nationalists to show up. He said antifa was promising a thousand counterprotesters. That seemed like a lot to me. "This is really going to be big," he said. "I put the event on a new level in terms of notoriety, but the whole event is really not about Richard Spencer." The goal, he said, was to occupy public space. There had been criticism that the alt-right was kids on Twitter eating chicken tenders in their mom's basement. "We are demonstrating that, yes, we certainly are on Twitter. Yes, certainly, we have websites. But also, we are a movement. . . . This is a show of force."

The city had revoked Kessler's rally permit for the park downtown on Saturday, but Spencer said they planned to march to the park anyway. They wanted it to look like the state was so afraid of their message that it had to violently suppress it. There might even be a mass arrest. "It's a win-win. If the event goes off as planned, then that's a win. If we go and are arrested by the police for peacefully assembling, needless to say, that's also a win." It would look like their free speech was being suppressed.

Antifa made things more intense, he said. But they would deal with it. "Life's a game, and there's a chessboard, and you play the game. There are different pieces on the board and you play them."

I told my bosses all of this, but they were still skeptical. They said protest stories were boring, so I needed to get an interview with a white nationalist. Spencer gave me Kessler's number. Kessler said he didn't want to talk to me. What I've heard, though I haven't read it myself, is that he asked a group chat if any of them wanted to talk to "that bitch from *Vice*." Chris Cantwell volunteered. The story was greenlit, but my manager warned me: I needed to be emotionally prepared for the story to never air. This was a liberation: I could ask whatever I wanted.

With the help of the ACLU, Kessler sued to get his permit reinstated, arguing this was a peaceful, law-abiding protest. Behind the scenes they planned to break the law. Kessler texted Kline, "If they refuse to reinstate the permit then we're going to have to be there to defend the territory." This made Froelich and a few other women nervous, but they were stuck organizing the afterparty. There was a shared sense of doom in a group text between Froelich, Lisa, and Erika, another woman in IE. It wasn't just the violence the guys were preparing for, it was the guys. They were NEETs, shitposters, keyboard warriors, edgelords (those who posted edgy material online to feel like rebels). They were only strong on the internet.

LISA: Worst case scenario is our guys get the fights they came for. That is definitely a win. These neets need some irl action.

ERIKA: Fighting in the street just for the sake of fighting isn't really a win.

LISA: Go ahead and throttle these boys. You will regret it when RAHOWA starts and your stuck defending yourself because you shamed them from learning how to fight.

ERIKA: Rahowa isn't happening.

LISA: Yes it is. Saying it isn't is patently ignorant

ERIKA: No, it's realistic.

LISA: Walk around in any inner city as a white woman by yourself and find out for yourself
    At night

ERIKA: That's not a race war. That's sub humans acting like sub humans.

LISA: My original point stands. Don't throttle out men.

ERIKA: No one is throttling men out. But going to fight in the streets just to fight and break the law is fucking retarded. . . .

LISA: They're grown. They came for a fight. I'm not going to annoy them by telling them to back down. You shouldn't either. Nobody likes a bossy woman.

ERIKA: I clearly didn't tell anyone to back down. I'm advocating for going about this in a smart way instead of violence with no end goal.

And they also shouldn't be coming for a fight in the first place. That's what antifa do, and that's why they always look like garbage.

LISA: A lot of them are coming for a fight. Deal with it. It's what men do.

ERIKA: It's what stupid men do.

10

"WELL, HELLO, SWEETHEART!"

(CHRIS CANTWELL, EVERY TIME I ANSWER THE PHONE)

I was biking through Brooklyn at dusk to a friend's new apartment, listening to music, when my phone started ringing. I clicked the headphone mic to answer it, assuming it was my friend or my boyfriend. It was Chris Cantwell. He wanted to talk about Charlottesville and his political theories, so I smothered my desire to feel normal and asked him about his life as I wove through traffic. Google Maps continued to scream in my ear the entire time.

When Jason Kessler had given me Cantwell's number, I didn't call. It was the peak of the alt-right's "Summer of Hate," and they were really feeling themselves, so talking to a new nazi usually began with a warmup of ten to thirty minutes of hostility. Once they got that out of their system, they gave me valuable information, and sometimes they'd talk my ear off, and after about ninety minutes I'd have to tell them I needed to go live my life. I'd gotten used to it, but I'd tried to create some rules—no getting yelled at by racists after 8 p.m. Cantwell's call was a surprise.

I'd been aware of his existence, but I hadn't followed him, or dug into his background. The anonymous mass movement was more interesting to me than its "e-celebs," who mostly copied whatever was hot on 4chan and 8chan.

161

I hadn't considered Cantwell the perfect embodiment of the alt-right. I hadn't considered him at all.

He pitched himself to me as one of the "edgiest" guys in the white power movement. "Edgy" had become slang for racist, and on his podcast, he'd talked openly about violence. In a January 2017 episode, Cantwell's guest was the *Daily Stormer*'s Andrew Auernheimer, better known as weev. They discussed whether Dylann Roof had made the right decision two years earlier when he murdered nine people in a Black church in Charleston.

"It doesn't actually benefit you to cuck out and say anything other than declaring your dedication to a race war," weev said. "When you shy away from expressing your race, and you shy away from willingness to commit acts of violence, you're saying, *I don't really care about my beliefs....* I personally think that people like Dylann Roof are heroes."

"I like you," Cantwell said. "Everybody thinks *I'm* a violent fucking psychopath, and you're awesome." But, he suggested, perhaps Roof had wasted his life. "When his manifesto was published, I wasn't frothing at the mouth for a fucking race war at the time, but I read it and thought the most offensive thing about this is the typos."

Weev disagreed. "Dylann Roof is the kind of guy that had no future anyway," he said. He admired Islamist jihadists, who turned losers into suicide bombers. Weev explained, "This is the kind of person that should be committing mass murder, basically. He had no other options."

"That's a solid point. I will absolutely grant you that," Cantwell conceded. "Not everybody's going to be a professional propagandist, shall we say, right? Some of us just gotta be cannon fodder for the fucking race war."

Cantwell had been a professional propagandist for only about a year and a half. He'd built a small following, but he wasn't a central figure. He was thirty-six years old, with buzzed thinning hair, and thin lips he pressed together in a smirk. He'd recently lost weight, and wore tight T-shirts to show it off. In 2015, he'd been fired from a talk radio gig in New Hampshire after using a racial slur on Twitter and refusing to apologize.

As an ambulance screamed past me on my bike, I asked Cantwell how he'd become radicalized, and what do you know, we got another appearance from our old friend Charles Murray. On Facebook, Cantwell had seen a video of an interview with Murray, and a flame war erupted in the comments underneath. "They're talking about the disparity in IQ between whites and Blacks, and there's the suggestion that this is genetic in origin and is responsible for this disparity in crime statistics in the United States," Cantwell said. "This was, of course, going on at the height of the Black Lives Matter riots, and so everybody's screaming that it is racist police causing all these problems. Perhaps there's a more reasonable explanation."

Cantwell had taken the same lesson from Murray's work as so many others in the alt-right: inequality is not a problem with the structure of society, but the natural order of things. The book gave him permission not to care about injustice, and to be angry that he was asked to care.

Cantwell told me he continued to podcast after he was fired, and that brought him to the attention of racists. Those callers pushed him to talk about "Jewish influence," he said. "Now that was a little bit more radicalizing because, while I've sort of always known that Blacks are not as smart as us, and that that causes their problems, I never really understood what antisemitism was all about. Once I caught on to that meme, and I realized that Jews were spreading communism, you could say that that was radicalizing."

(An antifascist researcher explained Cantwell's evolution more simply: "He was a libertarian who got blackpilled by the nazi callers who would call into his libertarian show.")

Cantwell repeated the propaganda that had been crafted by Richard Spencer's elite racists, converted into memes by 4chan and 8chan, and then delivered to his ears by callers to his radio show.

The whole experience convinced Cantwell that "ideas are not so much spread through the exchange of words as they are through body fluids. People don't get convinced of ideas. They're born into them."

"Do your parents share your worldview?"

"No, my parents do not share my worldview," he said.

"How do you square that with your ideas-via-body-fluids thesis?"

"The worldview of me and my parents is to be convinced of things by evidence, okay? Maybe my parents are not seeing all the evidence. I'm an abrasive guy. My mom doesn't like to listen to the show."

His parents processed information the same way he did, he said, because they're white. They just didn't have access to the right info. "My worldview and the worldview—and I think that of most white males—is something that might be commonly referred to as bleak logic and reason, which it's increasingly obvious the left sees as a white patriarchal construct. Reason itself is racist as far as these people are concerned."

Cantwell knew that to claim the high ground in the meme wars he had to present himself as a man of reason. But he'd admitted his racism was not the product of reason, but of bias: *I'd sort of always known* . . . "Reason" didn't mean analyzing information using logic to come to conclusions about the true nature of the world. Reason was a style, and a signal about where he belonged—he was cool-headed and masculine, and his opponents were emotional, unreasonable, feminine, and gay.

Cantwell was quick-witted. He didn't listen to much music, but instead talk radio, and he'd mastered the rhythm and simple language that made his ideas sound like common sense. He was also the most emotionally volatile person I have ever met—man or woman, adult or baby. In a few days he would tell me, "I find myself in tears more often than a man my age probably should." So as a man of "reason," he framed his emotions, like anger, as a rational response to the news. His voice got higher, and he spoke faster, even as he insisted he was genetically predisposed to appreciating the cold, hard facts of capitalism. He wasn't going to Charlottesville to debate UVA students about public policy. He was going to create a massive spectacle to provoke an emotional response—to make his enemies afraid, and to make young white guys think he looked cool.

———

Cantwell would tell me his origin story in bits and pieces over the next few years, sometimes in phone calls from jail. He'd pled guilty to a few misdemeanors when he was nineteen, and spent four months incarcerated. One of them was driving while intoxicated, which meant that when, in 2009, he was arrested for another DWI, he was facing felony charges.

In a speech titled, "How the Libertarian Party Saved My Life," Cantwell said, "I was facing four and a half years in a State prison, and I had done nothing to harm anyone." Cantwell was usually the victim in his own narrative. "I lost my job, I lost my apartment, my life, as I had known it, was destroyed," he said in the speech. The experience made his alcoholism worse, and he contemplated assassinating agents of the government that was oppressing him. Instead, he found libertarianism. "What a terrible waste it would have been if I had opened fire on some cops in 2009, and gotten myself killed."

He was dating a Dominican woman and got her pregnant, and imagined they'd have a kid together. But she got an abortion, and he was brokenhearted. He decided he wanted a gun—for self-defense, he told me—and learned he couldn't legally own one in the state of New York, because of his prior convictions. He joined the Free State Project, a nonprofit group that encouraged libertarians to move to New Hampshire and take it over.

In 2014, Cantwell moved to Keene, New Hampshire, a college town of about twenty-three thousand people about two hours from Boston. It wasn't long before he started rubbing the Free Staters the wrong way. Some libertarian women started asking why the libertarian movement was so male-dominated, and whether it might come across as hostile to women. Cantwell started looking into biological differences between men and women that might explain this. According to Cantwell, this led to him getting kicked out of the group. According to the Free State Project, he was kicked out for advocating violence.

————

I'd gotten used to hearing about girl trouble in one form or another. Near the end of our first phone call, in August 2017, Cantwell mentioned he'd dated girls of many races.

Bad breakup?

"No!" he said. "Well, don't get me wrong, I've had"—he laughed—"I've had bad—uh— bad things have happened with me with women of all stripes."

I locked up the bike and stood on my friend's stoop, then turned the conversation to logistics. Cantwell said he was already outside Charlottesville, "getting a lay of the land." I tried to plan a time to see him in town, but he didn't want to give me details. It was a security risk.

"I'll be frank with you, a lot of us view you and the rest of the media as the fucking enemy, right?"

Absolutely, I said.

"It's not unreasonable for me to be concerned that you're gonna tell some fucking communists and they're gonna come attack us, right?"

A journalist tries to get the scoop that no one else has, I said, not to plot in a room with all the other reporters in some grand conspiracy.

"It's not that I think that you're all conspiring together to be liars. It's that you have a worldview that is hostile towards my existence, right? And so you will do disreputable things to harm me, is the idea."

I spoke in the language of the libertarian that Cantwell said he was. "It's not in my interest to leak that information. It's in my interest to have the exclusive. And that might not convince you. But that's a better understanding of my incentive here, just to be very blunt," I said. *You don't have to trust me. Trust the market forces.*

"Yeah, I just—you know what? I'm being more hostile with you than I need to be."

A crack in the facade. All I had to do was listen to half an hour of ranting in my ear and cars swooshing past my bike at rush hour. I told him I wanted to talk about the alt-right's claim that it was adopting the tactics of the left to advance as a political movement. He began quoting one of his own speeches on that very subject. We agreed to an interview Friday afternoon, August 11, in McIntire Park. And just like that, our fates were forever linked.

11

CHARLOTTESVILLE

On Friday morning, August 11, 2017, our *Vice* crew landed in Charlottes-ville and rented a minivan with a busted AC. We got Subway sand-wiches and ate them on the sidewalk in front of our base for the weekend, the Holiday Inn Express. This was the crew: Josh Davis, producer; Joe LoCascio, production assistant; Zach Caldwell and Orlando de Guzman, both directors of photography; and Jake Weeks, sound guy.

The world would experience this weekend as a terror campaign designed to show white power was a real movement and that its members were not fringe skinheads but people who looked like normal suburbanites and lived among them. We experienced it that way, too. But in person, their emotions were uncontrolled by the perimeter of a screen. They were organized but they were not disciplined. If you were Black, you were attacked for being Black; if you were a woman, you were attacked for being a woman; if you were a Black woman, you were told that in the good old days a bunch of them could have raped you and left you for dead. I experienced it another way, as a girl on the dance floor at Incel Berghain.

As we drove to the park in the hot van, I checked Cantwell's website. He'd written that he was doing an "exclusive" interview with a reporter. Then he gave the location of our interview to subscribers to his podcast's newsletter—

for which anyone could sign up for five dollars. For all his fear that I posed a security risk, Cantwell was the one who tipped off his location to antifa.

The first thing I saw when we pulled into the parking lot was a big CBS news van. At the time, I knew our communications might be made public—because he might post screenshots, or he might get hacked by activists, or something—so I crafted each text with three audiences in mind: Cantwell now, other journalists in the future, and me. When I saw the texts on a big screen in a federal courthouse four years later, it was like a message in a bottle, a joke from my former self.

> **ER:** We're about 10 mins behind.
> How's parking?
>
> **CANTWELL:** We're here, more or less center of the park
>
> **ER:** CBS is here?
>
> **CANTWELL:** I didn't invite them
> They probably followed us from the police radios
>
> **ER:** I read on your blog this was an exclusive!

————

Cantwell stood under a tree, mingling with a couple dozen guys and one woman. I assumed they were friends, or that they at least knew one another. But he didn't know them, and they only knew him from the internet. He was wearing a bodycam. It was awkward. It's easier to play the cool guy behind a podcast mic, because no one can see your face when it betrays your self-consciousness. The lone woman said Andrew Anglin would condemn him for allowing a woman to be there, an invitation to participate in her self-loathing that Cantwell gladly accepted. "Anglin's gonna watch this video and be like, 'Who invited that thot?'"

She said, "I should have brought a burqa just to be funny. So I could wear it."

"Yeah!"

"So funny!"

"If you wore a burqa, they'd call it a klan hood and smear you in the media," Cantwell said. He laughed too hard.

Cantwell had agreed to let us film his meetup with his fans. We stood there, waiting for their event to begin, but the fans just stared back. Cantwell said, "Guys just talk amongst yourselves about the kikes."

After a few minutes, we gave up. Cantwell and I sat at a picnic bench, and as Zach and Orlando set up the shot, Cantwell's guys gathered in a semicircle around us. I could feel their presence, but I couldn't look at them, because they would read that as weakness.

I began by asking who he was, why he'd come to Charlottesville, and why they needed to "unite the right."

"The left seems to have it in their heads that they can have their complete, unadulterated way with the nation," he said. "If these various factions of the right, as you put it, do not unite and work against them, then the left will win and will destroy our country and there will be nothing left to defend."

What have those factions been bickering over?

"Racism would probably be the most obvious one. A bunch of people trying to virtue signal and act like communist egalitarians pretending that all men are in fact equal, and that, even more ridiculously, women are equal to men."

That one was for his fans, as many more of his answers would be. I doubt if he would've mentioned women if I hadn't been one. In the weeks that followed, people would tell me the nazis must have let me into their inner circle because I'm blond and fit into their racial fantasy, as if their defenses melted away the moment they saw my hair, as if it had been easy. But this was the new, incel-influenced white supremacy. Punching a woman, whether figuratively or literally, meant you were a based Chad. It was ninety-five degrees, I was sweating through my shirt, and racist internet perverts were heckling me. Not my favorite way to spend a summer weekend.

Cantwell said he was there to talk about ideas, but what mattered was performance, the vibe. He knew that intuitively, even if he didn't say it. I could tell he wanted to project dominance and superiority and power and control, and to create a contrast with me by provoking me into looking weak and emotional and irrational and stupid. He wanted to do that because it would help him sell the idea that equality, egalitarianism, and democracy were built on sentimentality and pleasant lies.

The main way he tried to provoke me was alerting everybody's attention to the fact that I'm a woman. In moments he feared I might have missed his subtlety, he'd smirk to make sure I got it.

"I also sell these fine T-shirts, if you want. They're twenty-five bucks. I'll give you a little discount—five bucks—because you're cute." The fans liked that one. He said when neighborhoods are desegregated, boys and girls would have sex, and "we lose a white woman to race mixing." In defense of racial profiling, he said, "If you find a girl who's been beaten and raped behind a tree somewhere," you wouldn't look for suspects who were "blue-eyed blond-haired girls." I didn't understand whether I was supposed to imagine myself as the rapist or the victim. But I thought, *I have green eyes, you fucking moron.*

We were not playing the same game. His game was a debate in which the winner would be decided by who looked stronger. My game was an interview, and it would be successful if my questions provoked him into revealing his true self and his true intentions.

"The alt-right is explicitly sexual," I said.

"Sexual?"

"Yeah, it's very fixated—"

"Aren't we all?" The fans laughed.

"—on reproducing."

"Males' reproductive instincts are what lead them to seek status and, and property and everything else.... You'd say that we're doing this for money, but let's face it, we're doing this for pussy at the end of the day."

I asked if he was married.

"No."

"Why have you failed?"

"Why, why, why are you under the impression that I failed in anything?"

"Wasn't the goal to get white people breeding?"

"I do not want to talk about my romantic life with you. I'm just informing you that I don't have a marriage license." The guys laughed.

We didn't put any of this on television. But it got under his skin enough to loosen him up. The next set of questions were the majority of what we used from that interview in our documentary, and what would be played again and again on cable news.

"So when did you get into, as you said, 'the racial stuff'?"

He listed unarmed Black teenagers who'd been killed by police or neighborhood watchmen. "Every single case, it's some little Black asshole behaving like a savage, and he gets himself in trouble shockingly enough. . . . Whatever problems I might have, with my fellow white people, they generally are not inclined to such behavior."

Oklahoma City?

"Okay, so—exactly. You have to go back to Oklahoma City to talk about a white act of terrorism."

Elliot Rodger, Dylann Roof . . .

I picked these guys because they were not just mass murderers, but ones who'd been influenced by the same chan culture that Cantwell was. Plus, I named Rodger to trigger incel shame.

"Okay, so now you've managed to name three people. . . . But the thing is, you remember the names of white bombers and mass shooters. Okay, can you tell me the name of all nineteen hijackers on 9/11 off the top of your head?"

"You were asking whether white people were capable of violence."

"I didn't say 'capable'! Of course we're capable! I'm carrying a pistol. I go to the gym all the time. I'm trying to make myself *more* capable of violence."

Oh shit, I thought, *he came out and said it!* And then I thought, *Don't show it, don't show it* . . . Josh says I grin when people are incriminating themselves. But it was truly incriminating, in that the statement was later played in legal proceedings involving Chris Cantwell, as well as in the second impeachment of Donald Trump.

How do you move from social media to real power?

"You say, *Okay, it's really fun that we're all exchanging memes and stuff like that. And Pepe is fun. But you know what? Why don't we all go show up at the same place?* . . . The alt-right—a lot of people are very new to that sort of thing."

The alt-right would be doing that, showing up together in the same place, at the Lee statue the next day. "I'm here to spread ideas, talk, and frankly, enjoy myself in the hopes that somebody more capable will come along and do that —somebody like Donald Trump who does not give his daughter to a Jew."

He was very proud of that—big smirk. At this point I felt saturated with the absurdity of interviewing this twitchy man as a serious political actor representing a legion of racist masturbators. And so, assuming this would never air, I channeled a broadcast newsman with mid-century gravitas: "So like Donald Trump but"—I pointed my hand at him with authority—"*more* racist."

"A *lot* more racist, a lot more racist than Donald Trump," he said.

———

That night, Josh, Zach, Orlando, Jake, and I stood on the side of a road on a small hill above UVA's "Nameless Field." White vans had been dropping off loads of guys in white polos at the opposite edge of the field, and they were swirling in the dark, tense with unreleased energy. I knew they had something planned, but I didn't know exactly what it would be.

A couple of guys started organizing the others to line up in pairs, and then tiki torches were handed out along the line. Only when they lit their torches in unison could I see that the line snaked across the entire field. There were about six hundred of them. The moment their faces were illuminated, I understood what I was looking at. It was a fascist mass movement, it was organized, and it was serious. I asked myself, *Are they going to win?*

And then I made myself feel nothing. The only way to do the job was to feel nothing. There is no time for a good cry in a mob. It'd be like if a surgeon looked down in the middle of an operation and said, *Oh no, my hands are covered in blood and guts!*

Kline had told the alt-right VIPs that the march to the Thomas Jefferson monument was just five minutes. And it would have been, if he'd gone the right direction. Instead he led the crowd the opposite way, and everyone just followed, and they'd been marching for half an hour when Spencer took the lead.

The men following didn't mind. Some were howling like dogs. The torches lit their faces, and they looked insane. Kline had prepared a playlist of chants, and the most important was "You will not replace us." It was meant to appeal to white people who were uncomfortable with their communities becoming more diverse. But Kline's wrong turn meant they ran through the entire chant playlist while were still meandering through campus. The marchers ad libbed: "*Jews* will not replace us!"

"I planned the whole thing Friday night. You saw how well oiled it was," Kline told me later. But next time, he said, he'd appoint a "chant master." He admitted, "We need to have someone to control the chants better so that we're not going around screaming about Jews."

A few weeks later, an essay at the white nationalist site Counter-Currents complained that the marchers' lack of discipline had ruined the propaganda value of the spectacle:

> When I first heard the media report that the marchers in Charlottesville were yelling "Jews will not replace us!" I thought this was a deliberate media distortion of the real slogan. . . . In a discussion I ended up involved in with several normies, I was successfully redpilling all of them at once by simply elaborating on the meaning of the slogan, "You will not replace us." . . .
>
> I thought this slogan was perfect. . . . We frame ourselves as standing on the defensive against an outside assault which others have initiated against us. . . .
>
> My successful redpilling of that whole crowd of normies was cut short when someone shared video making it clear that the marchers were in fact yelling "Jews will not replace us." I looked like an idiot for not being aware that this was in fact the slogan they used—as my whole argument had opened with an insistent denial of it—and I was no longer in any position to try to resuscitate my argument.

It was not a historical inevitability that this guy's red pill dinner party would be ruined. Without the close-up footage of their faces from Zach and Orlando, and the clear sound from Jake, the nazis could have claimed that they weren't nazis at all. But our crew captured the entire mob chanting in unison about a racist conspiracy theory that was the foundation for their violent rage. They could not conceal with white polos what they really believed.

Fred Brennan watched the video of the torch march from the Philippines. "Jews will not replace us" was an 8chan slogan brought into real life. He knew the marchers weren't performing for the people in Charlottesville, but for the people on Twitter and the internet at large. Brennan said, "It's all about the recording that shows, *We're powerful, we're growing—join us, we're a movement.*"

When the march arrived at the statue of Thomas Jefferson, there were about twenty college kids standing with their backs to the monument. The white polo mob rushed toward them. Here was their chance to take it to the enemy they'd been salivating over for three months on the internet. What happened in the brawl was captured by many cameras. The only people who dispute it are the ones who got sued.

It was a melee. Nazis beat the students with their torches. Dogpiles, mace, screaming, howling. Cantwell had volunteered to walk torchless on the outside of the march line. His job was to protect the torch holders from attackers, of which there were none. When the brawl started, he joined it. He maced a man, he told me later, and "immediately after I did that, I jumped on top of another guy, and then I knocked another guy down, and I tackled some woman with an expandable baton. And in each of those cases, I was acting in defense of myself and others."

There was nothing that could shake Cantwell's certainty that he was acting in self-defense, not even video, not even slow motion. He would replay the footage at trial four years later, as if it were exculpatory. His followers listening in on the court conference phone line thought he was amazing. They couldn't see what we could see: Cantwell out of control.

I'd climbed on top of a chest-high column on the periphery of the torch fight, and could only see a chaotic cloud of men. Cantwell's videos, which he mostly took from antifascists' livestreams, made me relive it from inside. In one clip, Cantwell rushed to a dogpile, punching someone in the back four or five times. In another fight, a woman appears to have some kind of stick. Cantwell claimed it was a telescoping baton, and he jumped in the fight to grab the baton and protect his comrades from head injury. But the video showed a crazy brawl where, in one moment, all I could see of the woman was her hand is reaching upward as if she were drowning, sinking under a sea of men. A guy grabbed Cantwell from behind, wrapping his arms around Cantwell's chest, and pulled him out of the fight. Cantwell repeatedly played the video in slomo, which makes the voices not just deeper but somehow melancholy, so the guy was moaning, "Cannnnnntweelllllll," like an ogre locked in a tower mourning his lost love. Everyone—his codefendants, their lawyers, the plaintiffs' lawyers, me—we all mimicked this every time we saw each other: *Caannnnnntwelllll*. The absurdity was relief from the horror—the next thing that happens in the video is the guy tells Cantwell that it isn't safe to be fighting like that, because he has a gun.

After the brawl dispersed, we found Cantwell sitting on the sidewalk, panting, sweating. He'd been maced. A guy was pouring water over his head. Zach and Orlando had been maced, too, and they continued filming silently.

Cantwell said the nazis were the victims who'd been attacked by the students they'd surrounded. He never stopped saying it. Later, when I mentioned they'd outnumbered the students twenty to one, he said it might be higher. But even still—he thought he was the victim, and he seemed traumatized by it, recounting the event over and over.

———

On Saturday morning, a few hours before Unite the Right was scheduled to begin, Josh and I stood on a quiet corner downtown, figuring out our plan. The torch march was only supposed to be a preview, and the rally the main event. I was pacing, shaking the tension out of my muscles, thinking about how many people in the crowd that was already gathering a few blocks away knew my name. Josh took me aside, grabbed my shoulders, and looked at me: "Come on, Elle." Let's show who these guys really are.

We walked up to the corner of Emancipation Park. There was already a bunch of guys in white polos inside it, encircled by metal barricades police had put up to separate them from the counterprotesters. There was a retaining wall around the park, and a line of armed men in camo uniforms stood along it, looking out over the street. I realized they were not the National Guard, but civilians playing dress-up—members of the Three Percenters militia. One of them told me, in a very serious gruff tone, that he was not authorized to speak to the press, but pointed me to his leader, Christian Yingling.

Yingling said they were there to protect free speech and were not taking sides. According to an antifascist, Yingling had agreed to a non-aggression pact with counterprotesters. But the militia stood with their backs to the nazis. There was no question whose speech they thought needed protection.

Early that morning, Tanesha Hudson arrived at Emancipation Park with a group of religious leaders, and among them was Cornel West. They'd stood in a line along the road in front of the park, and their plan was to sing hymns and pray. The alt-right guys had to walk by the clergy line to get into the park, and as they passed, some tipped their flagpoles to hit people in the head. It wasn't yet 10 a.m. when Hudson got cut on her forehead. "I go up to the police and I say, *They're smacking us with flags!*" she said. "They're like, *Okay, we'll react if we need to.* I'm like, *What do you mean you'll react if you need to? That's an assault. Don't you have to react to an assault?* They said, *We'll react if we need to.*" She asked to talk to the officer's boss. The boss came over and told her his command staff was saying they needed to stay put, and they'd react if they needed to. As the confrontations turned into full-on fights, the police did not intervene. In the park, Kessler bragged on camera, "We broke through Cornel West! Cornel West—BTFO! [Cornel West—beat the fuck out!]"

Hudson, a Black woman in her thirties with big eyes and a skeptical smile, had been an activist in Charlottesville for years. She knew the city streets, and the police, and that not being a white guy made your eyewitness testimony less likely to be believed. She recorded everything she could.

When she saw the alt-right men dressed neatly and carrying guns, she thought they were ripping off Malcolm X. "These aren't some uneducated white boys, right?" Hudson said. "They understand process a lot better than people want to give them credit for. And if you look at the tactics that they use, these were the same tactics used by groups like the Black Panthers, the Nation of Islam." She thought there would be a bloodbath.

I felt a connection to Hudson, more than to any other activist or antifascist I met in Charlottesville and after. She was not afraid to use dark humor to explain the living nightmare. And she could speak to the paradox I felt in seeing white power in real life: It was scary, it was dangerous, and it was very real. But it was also human. When she saw the alt-right marching toward her, Hudson had the reaction I did: *These are your guys? These are the tough guys? These boys in polos?* "People think Black people are just naturally angry, and that we just always want to fight," Hudson said. She knew she couldn't take a swing at them, or even let her body show that she wanted to. "But Elle, I probably could have literally kicked one of their asses all day that day. But if I put my hands on them, I'm going to jail. They did it all day, and they got to go home free."

She was tired of the expectation that she would turn the other cheek, just as generations of Black people had done before her. "When do Black people get a chance to say, *I'm over this shit*?" she asked. If there had been two hundred Black men marching downtown with guns on their hips, the day would have ended differently, and sooner. "So is it free speech? Or are there two different types of policing? Is there Black policing, and is there white policing?"

She moved onto the retaining wall of the park, near where Josh and I stood, and watched the chaos. She saw a woman stumbling around dazed. Members of the Rise Above Movement had showed up with their wrists taped. Photos showed two of them fighting a woman—one choking her as the other punched. Kline's white polo was stained with blood. "They went on all day," Hudson said. "People were literally getting stomped in the ground to the left, hit with flags here, maced over here . . . I've never, ever seen anything like this. . . . It was like a civil war was happening on a Saturday morning."

———

In the park, Robert "Azzmador" Ray was filming the scene for the *Daily Stormer*. Azzmador had a gray wizard beard, a thin braid down his back, and a criminal record that began with a 1990 arrest in Dallas for illegally selling an interracial porno tape called *Three Way Cum*. He was in his fifties, but he'd adapted to the alt-right scene. Kessler would later testify that he thought Azzmador was disgusting, but in the park, they put their arms around each other. Kessler was beaming. "We're only gonna grow bigger from here," he said in the *Daily Stormer* video. "We're moving out of the online space, which we've already dominated. We're gonna continue to keep dominating platforms all over social media, *and* we're going to take over the real world now."

"This is what happens when you really, truly, unite the right!" Azzmador said. There was no ambiguity about what was meant by "what happens," because Kessler immediately started bragging about breaking through the clergy line that Hudson stood in. Azzmador bragged, "I looked Cornel West in the face and told him he was for the rope!" (a reference to "the Day of the Rope," when non-fascists are killed and hung from lampposts). Kessler said, "Cornel West thought he could stop us! Nothing can stop us!" The scent of mace wafted over the crowd. Azzmador told his guys not to worry: "I've been pepper sprayed like half a dozen times by cops. I'm used to it by now."

In the parking garage a few blocks away, Heimbach was panicking: *The police aren't gonna protect us. We're all going to get our asses kicked. This is gonna be terrible.* Parrott reassured him that the National Guard was there. It would be fine. Heimbach psyched himself up by imagining his own martyrdom: *If it's my time to die for my people . . .*

This thought had not crossed Parrott's mind. He knew Heimbach's reaction—fear—was more rational than his. Parrott never felt afraid he would be punched until the moment just before he was punched. As they walked down the street toward the park, Parrott thought it would all be okay, until the crowd slowed down. He could hear the sound of fistfights coming from the front of the line. He realized, *This is going to be bad.*

As they approached the park's corner, Heimbach looked at a TWP cameraman and said in a chipper voice that it was another beautiful day in Char-lottesville. And then he told his men, "Shields up!"

Heimbach looked terrified, Parrott said. He could see it in his eyes. The alt-right was outnumbered four to one. But in terms of people who were pre-pared to fight, they had the upper hand. "Everybody on our side was pre-pared to be punched and had assumed the risk. Whereas, like, four-fifths of their side were these cat ladies and concerned citizens—normal people out to oppose hate, who were totally unprepared for that situation," he said. They moved into the whirlpool of fistfights.

Parrott did not eat right and did not exercise, and most of the time he tried to forget he had a physical body. If there were people eager to punch a nazi in the face, he was a soft target. But Parrott waded through the brawl un-punched. People who wanted to fight were high on adrenaline, and their eyes were searching for other fighters.

Parrott, the absolute physical coward, found a serenity in the melee that eluded his comrades. "When you're in the middle of it, it's profoundly safe. . . . It's ritualized combat where the people who want to fight fight." After a while, the fighters looked exhausted, with sweat dripping down their faces. He thought they were wondering why the cops hadn't stepped in.

As Josh and I stood on the side watching, Cantwell emerged from the chaos and walked up the steps into the park. He'd been maced and couldn't see, and he was terrified. He ripped off his shirt and got down on his hands and knees. Another guy put a hand on his back to soothe him. Cantwell asked, "Are we surrounded right now?" No, the guy said, adding, "We're going to kill them. We're going to fucking kill them." Cantwell gasped, "Don't fucking kill anybody. You're going to make it worse." He got up, moved farther into the park, and lay on his back as men poured milky liquid over his face and bare chest. People shouted, "Heil Cantwell!" He said, "This milk is racist. That's why it feels so good on my skin."

Josh pulled out his iPhone and made me go up to Cantwell, so I crouched next to him and looked back at Josh like, *Now what?* Someone gave Cantwell another jug of milk, and he started pouring it on his face. I couldn't think of anything else to say, so I asked him, "What just happened?"

"They maced me," he said.

Who?

"I don't know! Communists! It's the second time in two fucking days."

I stared at him as he poured more milk on his skin. He screamed, "FUCK!"

Cantwell's buddies helped him up and started leading him toward the nazi pen that had been set up by police. We followed, walking behind Cantwell in a line down the street. I grabbed Cantwell's shoulder, determined not to lose sight of him again. Some guys in the pen recognized me. "That's that bitch from *Vice*!" "Yeah," I said, "I'm that bitch from *Vice*. Now let me in." They did.

We were inside for only a few minutes when the governor of Virginia declared the rally an unlawful assembly and we were ordered to leave the park. As we were pushing out, a kid yelled at me: "Put your helmet on! Put your helmet on, they're not going to know you're not one of us."

We poured into the street, and lost Cantwell again in the stream of white polos walking to another park about a mile away—the one where I'd interviewed him a day earlier. The whole crew was running up and down the column of white nationalists, looking for Cantwell, and a bunch of them started shouting my name.

Josh found Cantwell walking with Azzmador, who said, "I was with this guy last night and we were both right in the front lines of the giant BTFO curb-stomp of the antifa... They hate Chris Cantwell because they fear Chris Cantwell!"

Cantwell shouted, "And they fucking should!"

"They sprayed the shit out of Chris Cantwell!" Azzmador said.

Cantwell forced a laugh. "I couldn't even breathe!" he said. Another forced laugh: *Ha ha ha!* "I was like, *I'm gonna die!*" *Ha ha ha!*

I walked next to shirtless Cantwell as Zach and Orlando filmed us. I didn't think I could ask him, *Isn't this fucking crazy?* Instead I asked why they'd had to leave the park.

It was a crime against free speech, he said: "Whatever you think of my opinions, that's going to be something that puts *you* in danger!" He was following the First Amendment script, and carrying a Smartwater bottle.

So they were the true nonviolent protesters?

"I'm saying we did not aggress. We did not initiate force against anybody. We're not nonviolent. We'll fucking kill these people if we have to."

Someone in the crowd spotted their white vans parked at an intersection thirty yards away. Cantwell was told to go get in one, and he ran off. Orlando said to me, "Let's get in the van." We sprinted to it. As some white polos were shuffling inside, I thought, *Okay, I'll get in the van, and deal with whatever happens when it happens.*

Still breathing hard, I sat down next to Cantwell in the second-to-last row. Azzmador sat behind us, and Josh and Orlando squeezed in.

They were angry, they'd been running, there was chaos, and they were scared. They were shouting, "Shut it! Just fucking shut it! Let's go!" Their sense of urgency worked in our favor.

Cantwell shouted up to the front, "We've got *Vice* in here."

"Is this the fucking media right here?"

"Fuckin' Vice jumped in the fuckin' van!"

I smiled nice and said nothing. It was sweaty in there.

"If we gotta kick the media out, we do," Cantwell said. That "if"—it was beautiful, an opening. He was asking his buddies if we could stay. I told myself that if they dragged me out, I would stay on my feet, no matter what. But I wasn't going to volunteer to exit. You can't act scared. If you act scared, they'll give you something to be scared of. I held my jaw open slightly to stretch out my cheeks so they wouldn't register a grimace. A man in front of me turned around and held his phone close to my face, filming—he turned it horizontal, like a pro.

I felt a friendlier presence over my right shoulder: Azzmador in his wizard beard. He could be my anchor. I asked him, "Why don't you tell me what you think?"—as if I were inviting him to gossip over a wedding buffet. I knew he'd be flattered if I showed I knew who he was, so I asked him to tell me about his work for the *Daily Stormer*. He said he hosted a podcast.

"I like Donald Trump. I think he's pretty cool. He's not one of us. He's more of a civic nationalist, but he takes us more in the right direction," he said. "America needs to become a fascist nation again." They weren't going mainstream. The mainstream was coming to them.

"We are stepping off the internet in a big way," Azzmador said. For a long time, the people who quietly agreed with him had been afraid to leave the house, but "last night at the torch walk, there were hundreds and hundreds of us." It was only possible because of the internet.

"People realize they're not atomized individuals. They're part of a larger whole that agrees with them. And so now they're coming out. Now, as you can see, we greatly outnumber the anti-white, anti-American filth. And at some point, we will have enough power that we will clear them from the streets forever.

"We're starting to slowly unveil a little bit of our power level. You ain't seen nothing yet."

We arrived at the second park and spilled out of the van. This was an unpleasant place. They'd built up all this energy and now it was unspent. We presented an opportunity to spend it. I cannot remember what anyone said to me, but I remember hating it. My brain has encased the worst memories from this day in a sarcophagus to stop them from poisoning me. A white nationalist woman heckled us. The men were menacing, but the woman was horrifying. I wondered, *Why would you let them do this to you?* It hurt to look at her. I walked away and redid my makeup in the sideview mirror of a sedan. Inside, a tiki torch rested on the center console.

Kline was on the phone on the sidewalk near us, threatening the police with lies. His guys had been blocked from picking up their speakers. Kline said, "I'm about to send at least two hundred people with guns to go get them out, if you guys do not get our people out."

Heimbach thought Kline was another sign that the alt-right had trolled itself into believing it was competent. "They were being led by a stolen valor fucking doofus whose whole shtick was *I'm calm under pressure.* And then he's screaming in front of you and the world that he's gonna march armed men against the city of Charlottesville in, like, a *junta.*"

But at that moment, Heimbach was in that same park, standing near white vans that were lined up to take the nazis out of town. When I saw Heimbach, whom I hadn't spoken to since 2013, I felt a strange relief. I could talk to this guy who had some respect in the crowd, and the crowd would see it, and its hostility would recede a little. I pointed at him: *Hey, I know you.* He remembered. He began to speak as he was still walking toward me. He said a state of emergency had been declared because the alt-right couldn't be stopped by leftist counterprotesters, "the boot boys of the capitalist class." Heimbach was always on message. "The radical left, the corporations, the state, are all on the same Jewish side. A moment like this proves it."

A few yards away, David Duke was standing next to the open door of a van, talking to a couple of reporters. The other men wanted to close the door and drive off, but Duke kept babbling about the great injustice that had been done. A white nationalist behind him noticed me, and mumbled about the men I'd dated. I winked at him. The whole scene was awful and Josh said let's leave. Zach and Joe had driven to the park to meet us, and we all piled into their car and left for someplace we thought would be safer, downtown.

———

Counterprotesters were marching in the middle of the street downtown, and we walked with them for a few blocks. The sun was crushing. We crossed a small street, and on the corner was a little business with a recessed door. I pulled Josh and Joe in there to rest a minute in the shade.

We'd been standing there a couple minutes when we heard a very loud crunching sound. People ran past the doorway screaming. I thought it was a mass shooting, and I pressed my back against the wall. Josh said, "Is that what I think it is?" I said yes. He remembers me saying it with total certainty. But I don't. I only remember an unreal feeling. We walked out into the empty street in the bright sunlight. A maroon van was in the middle of the intersection, its hood crumpled from impact. A woman had hurt her ankle, and her friends held her up as she screamed in pain. And then she stopped and screamed in a different way. She looked up at her friends, "Oh my god we got hit by a car!"

I didn't feel hot anymore, I felt weightless. When you're in a crowd of people hit by a surprise attack, you feel a sense that another one is about to come. At every loud sound, like the motor of a heavy truck, everyone's head pivoted with fear and anger.

There were all these bloody people on the ground, and medics were helping them. They didn't want us to film them. They said we were vultures. But the reality of political violence should not be secret. It's not like the movies. There is no dramatic lighting. You can die in sunshine. Zach filmed the medics doing CPR on an unconscious woman, and afterward, he kept returning to the way her chest was being pumped in and out as they tried to make her heart and lungs work. This woman was Heather Heyer.

Across the street, a woman was standing in the shade, crying. I went up to her and said she didn't have to tell me her name or anything, but I needed to know what had happened. She described the crash and started crying because she hadn't been able to push people out of the way. A medic was sitting on the curb. He said he knew the unconscious woman was dead. Her body was alive, but her brain was dead. He almost started crying, and so did I. He gave me a fake name. I don't know why.

Orlando pulled me aside, and asked me to just tell him what had happened, while he filmed. I was finally able to get something out. When I finished, I paused, and said, "It made a horrific sound." I felt the wave that comes just before tears, and I pushed it back down. The sound of the crash, when the steel hit people's bodies, was replaying in my head. But now I can't remember what it sounded like.

We stumbled into a Turkish restaurant with cool blue walls and a recessed floor. It was an oasis. We went to a corner table in the back and spilled out all of our gear on the floor and in the seats around it. Then we took turns crying in the bathroom.

Tanesha Hudson was at a small vigil in another park. She'd seen the crash from a block away. "The chaos you've seen today has been brewing for quite some time. I don't think it's ever been about a statue. I think it's been about right is right and wrong is wrong," she said. Too many people had waited to stand up for what was right, until it was too late.

Josh had to fly out Sunday morning to start editing. Tracy Jarrett was driving in from the D.C. bureau. I'd never met her. I lay on the floor in my room at the Holiday Inn Express, until I heard that the rally organizers were holding a press conference in a few hours. I called Richard Spencer about it, but he said he wasn't going. "Kessler is rogue, and I've never liked him, and he's just weird," Spencer said. The alt-right was already starting to crack.

For months, most of the Charlottesville headliners would publicly say Charlottesville was a success. Spencer did, too. But the day after the rally, he was trying to explain what went wrong. He blamed the police for letting the alt-right and counterprotesters mix. They were developing a conspiracy theory that police wanted to see nazis get their asses kicked. "That said, we can't have these crazy kids come here, and, like, do Dylann Roof stuff. I mean, this is just insane."

He'd asked a kid with Vanguard America who was in charge, and he'd said no one was in charge. That was a problem. Identity Evropa screened applicants closely. But that meant the kids who couldn't get in IE would create their own groups—ones that were "nutballs."

I asked if it bothered him that mentally ill people were drawn to his movement.

"It does bother me, sure."

"Well why do you think that is?"

"Because it's extreme and taboo. . . . Most people don't want to be called a nazi or a monster or whatever. I've been able to disarmingly flip it around where it's like, *Oh, Richard Spencer, he's charming and intelligent, but still a monster*. . . . Most human beings want to be loved and want to be accepted. And so those people who are either willing to be alienated from society, or who actually want to be alienated from society—it's a particular type of personality. They're attracted to extreme movements."

When Tracy arrived, we drove over to Charottesville's downtown mall for Kessler's press conference. A big crowd had gathered. A few of them had trombones. They were angry, and he was alone.

I could feel the crowd's anticipation. They wanted to see with their own eyes the man who seemed happy to take responsibility for the chaos. Kessler didn't seem to realize that's what he was doing. He stood at the microphone with a semicircle of TV cameras around him, and behind the press stood the townspeople. Their energy was focusing, pushing toward Kessler. He said, "Today I want to come before you and tell you the real story of what happened before this narrative keeps spinning out of control." They shouted, "*Shame!*" They called him a murderer. I thought they were going to swarm him. I thought, *They are going to devour this man.*

Because the crowd was jeering so loudly, a woman from a local NPR affiliate broke the invisible barrier that had created a radius of empty space around Kessler. She stepped close to his face, holding up her recorder, not caring that she was in all the camera crews' shots. Then a man in the crowd pushed through, both middle fingers in Kessler's face, shouting. Then another person pushed through, then another. The crowd surrounded him. He escaped under a magnolia tree.

Alt-right people would try to get me to say it was terrible, a sign of the violent tendencies of the left, the way that press conference went down. But our security team would often tell us, *Don't be stupid.* The law doesn't create a dome of invincibility. Just because it's wrong for someone to attack you doesn't mean they won't, and sometimes it's best to know when not to provoke a mob. Most people in the town had been surprised they were invaded by violent nazis. Of course they wanted someone to pay.

———

Cantwell had left town. He'd heard a rumor there was a warrant out for his arrest, so he drove to North Carolina and got a room in a hotel. He agreed to an interview, but he made an ultimatum: be there by 8 p.m. Orlando had to leave, and so did Jake. It was down to Tracy, Zach, and me.

When we pulled up to the parking lot as the sun was setting, it was 7:55 p.m. Getting out all of the camera gear takes forever, so I went up to his hotel room alone.

If you decide before you walk into a room that whoever's in there will like you, they will—and they'll be thrilled you have relieved them of the burden of having to decide whether to like you. It's like a little gift. I relaxed the muscles in my face, smiled, and knocked on Cantwell's door.

Cantwell had an AR-15 propped up by the window, and when I noticed it, he showed me all his guns. He had his AR, plus his Glock 19, a Kel-Tec P3AT, a Ruger LC9, a Glock 17, a Taurus .38-caliber revolver, and an AK-47, for which he'd forgotten the ammo. He carried two handguns in his belt and one at his ankle, just in case a friend needed to borrow one in an emergency. He hadn't brought that much ammo, because if you're reloading, you're losing. I acted extremely interested in his collection. *Wow, a Glock? I've heard of that one!*

Gun nerds will try to convince you that all the little details about the caliber of the ammunition and action of the weapon are really important, but when you're alone in a hotel room with an emotionally volatile man with nothing to lose, there's really only one thing that matters, which is that each of those guns is effective at the one function it was built for.

I knew he was trying to intimidate me, but I also knew we were playing a game. The game was who could pretend most convincingly that he wasn't trying to intimidate me. The way to win is to push all your adrenaline into a wave pool at your solar plexus and then surf it.

Zach and Tracy knocked on the door. Back on the highway, I'd imagined different ways to demand Cantwell treat my friends with respect, because Tracy is Black. But then I thought if I introduced the idea that he *could* be disrespectful, he might take the opportunity. Cantwell liked to think of himself as a man of honor, and here was his chance to prove it. The door opened, and I said, "This is Tracy. Josh had to go back to New York." She said, "Hi, I'm Tracy," and put out her hand. Cantwell shook it. That was that.

We sat down for the interview and Cantwell flipped on his bodycam. He agreed not to preempt our show, and said he probably wouldn't release the footage unless we took him out of context. But, also, "I'll do whatever the fuck I want with it." I tried to reassure him—maybe he'd heard horror stories of reporters taking politicians' words out of context to make them sound racist, but he *was* racist. If my goal were to just get him to say something offensive, I told him, it wouldn't require much finesse. "It is your obligation to make the racist look bad, right?" he said. I'd run out of artful ways to say he could make himself look bad all on his own.

Cantwell is a smart person. He can form complex analyses of the world and articulate them in plain language. That's a real talent. But he is also caught up in his own bullshit. He turns most conversations back to the narrative arc of the Chris Cantwell story. He is so preoccupied with his own drama that he can't imagine the inner life of anyone else.

I asked him how he thought the rally had gone. "The fact that nobody on our side died, I'd go ahead and call that points for us. The fact that none of our people killed anybody unjustly is a plus for us. And I think that we showed our rivals that we won't be cowed," he said. I said the car had driven into a crowd of protesters unprovoked. Cantwell repeated a conspiracy theory Spencer had told me—that actually James Alex Fields, who'd been driving the car, was just scared and trying to get away, and he had no option but "to hit the gas." He said the people who got hurt were too dumb to get out of the way.

"It's going to be really tough to top, but we're going to be up to the challenge."

Someone died, I said.

"I think that a lot more people are going to die before we're done here, frankly."

Why?

"This is part of the reason that we want an ethnostate, right? So like the Blacks are killing each other in staggering numbers from coast to coast. . . . The fact that they resist us when we say, 'Hey we want our homeland,' is not shocking to me. These people want violence and the right is just meeting market demand."

Cantwell might have been new to the white power movement, but his personality made him the perfect spokesman. He could fully inhabit an alternate reality without the irony or self-consciousness of the others.

"You'll notice that I get angry, and I think that's a righteous anger. But I feel it's unjust that we are categorized as a hate group," he said. "What we're out here to do is not to hate people, what we're out here to do is to protect our own. Since people make that impossible, we get angry. Calling us a hateful movement of people who want to hurt other people is inaccurate. It's a lie. It's a smear against us."

By that point, in our hotel room interview alone, Cantwell had used several racial slurs and said that Jews had been persecuted because they deserved it, and denied that the Holocaust happened. He'd run around that weekend in a T-shirt printed with an image of a person being thrown out of a helicopter, a reference to the extrajudicial execution of political prisoners. A few months earlier, on a podcast, Cantwell had said that once he'd realized Karl Marx was Jewish, "I'm like, *Okay, let's fucking gas the kikes and have a race war. Because once I realized they were responsible for the communism, then I was like, Oh, wait a second, yeah, that's a fucking really good reason to fucking genocide a group of people.*" But sitting in front of me, Cantwell said, "For literally trying to do a genuine, honest intellectual inquiry, people are treated as genocidal lunatics in America today."

When we finished the interview, Cantwell showed Zach and Tracy his guns. As they moved to get more b-roll, we started talking about his lifestyle. He said that only a few years ago, he was "a fat guy who got drunk every night." The alt-right had helped him remake his life and his body. People always said that racists had nothing to be proud of, so they were proud of their race, and he wanted to prove them wrong. He liked the masculine competition of the white power movement, he said, "*Go be better. Go educate yourself. Go read a book. Go to the gym, be more physically fit. Stop drinking yourself to death, stupid.*" He'd brought some adjustable BowFlex weights. He did some curls and grinned at me. I pointed to the strawberries on his dresser.

ER: *You like fruit?*

TRACY: *You keep a healthy lifestyle for someone who's on the move a lot!*

CANTWELL: *I try. . . . Four years ago, I'm a 260-pound alcoholic, and not because I was big and muscular. I was a mess. I decided to do some lifestyle changes and it's been very rewarding.*

ER: *I'm a fruitaholic. . . .*

CANTWELL: *In the fridge I got broccoli and the ranch dressing and shit. Finished up those sugar snap peas the other night . . .*

ER: *What about the smoothie lifestyle?*

TRACY: *You could get the Magic Bullet.*

CANTWELL: *I have one of those things at home that I use for my protein shakes. I don't know, I don't mind chewing. You get all healthy and be like, chewing is too much effort—fuck that.*

He said he could tell me a lot, but he didn't know how much time I had. "I wasn't always a hateful racist bigot," he said. But being called a racist was an on/off switch, not a dimmer. Once he'd been labeled racist, he took it as far as possible. I asked him if he could really live his whole life as performance art.

"This is not my whole life," he said. "When I'm with a woman that I care about or whatever, we don't sit there and discuss fucking racial and crime demographics. . . . We go see movies and watch television. We do normal people things. . . . I feel like if I didn't do this, or if somebody didn't do it for me, you know, then all the things that I care about outside of this would be gone. So I have to do it."

Tracy asked him, "Are you sad?" It was such a simple question, but it was how a Black woman made the nazi cry.

"Yeah," he said. He started to tear up, and his voice was wavering: "Because I don't want, um . . ." He cleared his throat. "Because I care about things . . . I didn't want to do this, you know? . . . It would be a lot easier for me to lay down and allow people to genocide my race off the face of the planet. I could probably relax a lot better if I wanted to do that. But I don't!"

That was the crying. Soon after that, we would have the yelling. Collectively, Tracy and I called these moments "the yelling and the crying."

We were about to pack up, and I thought I'd keep the mood light with a little joke—one of those good ole you-and-I-are-not-so-different deals, like *Can you believe you were yelling at me so much yesterday and now we're here talking about smoothies?* Classic bit. I said, "Man, y'all were pretty mad at me when we got in that van! Did I back down though? Did I not handle that well?" This was a miscalculation.

"No, as a matter of fact I don't think you fucking handled that well at all," Cantwell said. He changed—his body, his voice. He was accelerating. "That van was there to rescue fucking people who were combat veterans, okay? And you got in there and you were fucking wrong." I reminded him that his comrades got a chance to speak. He didn't like that.

"That was a FUCKING war zone asshole! Okay? We were in danger and you—and YOU—left our fucking guys on the streets so we could talk to you.

We could talk to you any fucking time! You were WRONG to do it!" I said, softly, that there was a lot more room in the back of the van and they could have filled up the seats more efficiently. This was another mistake. Never quibble.

"*You.* Should not have gotten in our fucking van. It was the wrong thing for you to do. You put people in fucking danger and I'm pissed at you for doing it. I understand that that's not your intention, but what you're here to do is advance your FUCKING career and you're willing to fucking put people's lives in danger to do it."

I asked him, "You believe in something, right? Can't you allow me that— that I might believe in something, too?"

"You could get the fucking story some other time. We're out there—guys are getting fucking maced and having their fucking heads cracked open . . ."

"Don't you want someone to document that?"

"You got Azzmador telling you that the fucking Jews run the planet— fucking congratulations asshole! . . . You're going to be in a fucking combat zone, take some fucking caution, you know what I'm saying? I got maced twice in as many days. Those people would fucking kill us if they had the opportunity to do it, all right? Those vans were to get people out of there safely. *You* were not in danger. We were!"

We had been a woman, a Jew, and a Filipino in a van full of angry white nationalists and we didn't even know where they were driving us. We had made that choice, of course. But Cantwell had also made a choice: to come as a pro-genocide political activist to an event pitched from its inception as a battle royale in the streets of a liberal college town. I could imagine that he was scared. I don't think he could do the same for me.

He yelled at me for about five minutes. We were standing in between the two hotel beds covered in guns, my hands on my hips, and Cantwell, in his black camo print T-shirt, was leaning toward me, pointing his finger in my face.

Every time he came up for air, I returned to the same message: that I believed in something bigger than myself, and it was not what he believed, but it meant more to me than my own fame and vanity. When I first started reporting on these guys, I tried to reveal no personal information, so they'd have nothing on me. I assumed they would try to trick me into revealing details so they could use it as leverage, but they never tried. They were never curious. Over time I learned I had it backward: I needed to force them to understand that I was a real person, from a real place, who had really done a lot of living. When you make them realize you're a person, they treat you with more respect.

"I have a cause. And I need to make a career out of it in order to finance my political activity," he said. That led to a rant about other enemies, instead of me—progressive organizations that had million-dollar budgets, and people who accused him of becoming a nazi just for the money—they absorbed some of his anger.

I told him that my friends said to me all the time that white nationalists couldn't possibly believe what they said they believed, and I told them, yes, they do.

"I do not risk life, limb, and liberty to bullshit people."

"Well I appreciate you explaining that to me."

"I appreciate you telling the story."

"Okay . . . thank you."

"You're welcome."

And it was over. We told Cantwell to watch the show the next night, and we left. The three of us walked down the hall silently and got in the elevator, and once the doors had finally closed, we all breathed.

———

Back in New York, more than a dozen of our *Vice* colleagues worked through the night to put a documentary together to air the next day. The whole team stood in the control room and watched the episode air live. Tracy, Zach, and I sat in the empty bar at the Holiday Inn Express, drinking margaritas, and watched it on the big screen. When it was over, I thought, *Well, that's what happened.*

The next day, President Trump said at a press conference, "You had very fine people on both sides." On CNN, Anderson Cooper used footage from our documentary to fact-check the president. And from there, it exploded. Tens of millions of people watched our story. I sat on my hotel bed, still in Charlottesville, and flipped through the cable news channels. Everyone was playing it. My mom said I'd given the country clarity on who those fine people really were.

12

AFTERMATH

The alt-right inner circle gathered in a house in the countryside outside Charlottesville hours after the rally. They'd spent several days planning the perfect afterparty, and they'd expected a wild celebration. But the scene had become a bunch of guys on their phones making desperate calls to find any new scrap of information about what happened and how much trouble they were in. Someone called a meeting, and the leaders filed into a room and closed the door behind them. There were about half a dozen guys, among them Elliot Kline, Nathan Damigo, Jason Kessler, and Richard Spencer. They asked one another, *What should we do? What should we say?* Spencer stood to address his men. They'd been drinking, and when Spencer began ranting, someone in the room was secretly taping.

We are coming back here like a hundred fucking times! I am so mad! I am so fucking mad at these people! They don't do this to fucking me! We are going to fucking ritualistically humiliate them! I am coming back here every fucking weekend if I have to! Like this is never over. I win! They fucking lose! That's how the world fucking works. Little fucking kikes—they get ruled by people like me. Little fucking octoroons—I fucking—my ancestors fucking enslaved those little pieces of fucking shit! I RULE THE

FUCKING WORLD! Those pieces of fucking shit get ruled by people like me. They look up and see a face like mine looking down at them. That's how the fucking world works. We are going to destroy this fucking town![1]

The word "humiliate" and some of the *fuckings* were warped by the force of Spencer's shouting. Other words—"ruled by people like me"—sounded like they were pushed through clenched teeth. There was no pretense of irony, or that this was one big cosmic joke, or that he simply wanted open debate among reasonable people. Spencer sounded sweaty and crazy. A couple guys clapped lightly, and one offered a soft "yeah." But right there, in that room, Spencer lost the movement.

Evan McLaren, who was then Spencer's loyal right-hand man, could feel the other guys turn on their icon. McLaren felt a shift in himself, too—maybe it had not been a good idea to make peace with Spencer's narcissism. So many people had been implicated in so much damage, dozens were bloody and three were dead, but all Spencer cared about was his wounded pride.

Long after he'd quit the movement, and apologized, and moved across the Atlantic Ocean, McLaren smiled as he quoted the rant from memory: "They don't do this to *me*." Spencer's greatest flaw, in its purest expression, at the climax of the disaster it had created. It had been like watching a villain's final monologue in a play.

Audio of the rant was released online a couple years later, to Spencer's total humiliation. He was forced to listen to "the rant" repeatedly in federal court. When asked if it represented what he really believed, Spencer testified, "That was me as a seven-year-old, and it's a seven-year-old that's probably still inside me. I'm ashamed of it. Those are not my sincerely thoughtful beliefs. That is me at my absolute worst. . . . That is a childish, awful version of myself."

It was a rare admission that he had done something wrong. But it did not change his image with the white nationalists who sat beside him at the defense table. One thought, *That seven-year-old might be inside you, buddy. But he's not inside me.*

---

[1] This audio later became evidence in federal court in *Sines v. Kessler*.

When a person is exposed to very high levels of radiation, the first symptoms are familiar and mild, like nausea. Then the patient enters a latent phase, when he looks like he's getting better. Inside, his body is breaking down. When the latent period ends, the manifest illness stage begins. The body falls apart. In severe cases, the progression is gruesome.

Charlottesville was like a nuclear disaster for the alt-right, and the movement followed a path like the progression of radiation sickness. They knew, in the immediate aftermath, it had created some PR problems, but the problems seemed like they could be overcome. Then, there was a period of stabilization, and they drew some new recruits. But within a few months, they started to feel the consequences compound, and it became clear it was not going to get better.

Most of America was appalled by what happened in Charlottesville, and many in a position of power to do something actually did it. The first problem it created was infamy. Unite the Right's attendees had been so proud to show their faces in public, but activists methodically identified them one by one and published their names on social media. They became pariahs in their towns or colleges or even in their families, and they were fired from their jobs. They were kicked off their own social media accounts, so they couldn't defend themselves or reach new supporters. Despite the past hand-wringing about the marketplace of ideas, the political discourse went on without them.

The second problem was the money. Activists had been pushing financial services companies to drop white nationalists for years—Color of Change president Rashad Robinson pleaded with the credit card companies, payment processors, and banks, and they'd all made the slippery slope argument. But after Charlottesville, though no laws had changed, those companies stopped serving white nationalists. It turned out they were capable of distinguishing a guy calling for ethnic cleansing from, say, a guy with a controversial position on tax rates. This was devastating to the internet-based alt-right, because it is very hard to get money online without using an American company to process the payments.

The third problem was the law. Both the social and financial consequences happened immediately, and they compounded more long-term
consequences—the legal ones. Only a handful of Unite the Right participants
faced criminal charges. Roberta Kaplan, a lawyer who'd successfully argued at
the Supreme Court to end the ban on gay marriage, thought a Justice Department run by Jeff Sessions would be unlikely to pursue criminal charges against
the rally organizers. So in October 2017, she filed what would become the
most significant lawsuit against the rally organizers in federal court, *Sines v.*
Kessler. The complaint was a hundred pages long; it presented an enormous
amount of evidence alleging the organizers intended to commit racially motivated violence, in part because antifascists had infiltrated their Discord servers and published the transcripts. There were nine plaintiffs—people who
lived in the area and were hurt on one or both nights. The twenty-six defendants, including Richard Spencer, Elliot Kline, Nathan Damigo, Jason Kessler,
Chris Cantwell, Jeff Schoep, Matt Heimbach, and Matt Parrott, could not afford such fancy lawyers, if they could afford one at all. A few had convinced a
lawyer to represent them, only to be dropped when they failed to pay.

The alt-right had been able to do whatever they wanted to anyone they
wanted on the internet. When they moved from the internet to the real world,
they'd thought they could bring the same rules with them. They could not.
But they did not all come to this realization right away.

––––––

In the days after the rally, Jason Kessler tweeted horrible insults about Heather
Heyer. The other organizers knew it was a bad look, but one of Kessler's comments posed a threat to them all: "Communists have killed 94 million. Looks
like it was payback time."

Kline texted Kessler: "What are you doing ? Do you want to go to prison
or get sued for all our money. . . . It's objectively harming our case legally
and to the public." Kessler still seemed to think they were playing with Mo-
nopoly money. Kessler responded, "Stop cucking. You're a big tough Nazi a
month ago." Kline pushed him to see that this time words had consequences:
"There is a difference between cucking and not going to jail or getting sued to

death. . . . Calling it payback shows its premeditated." But Kessler wanted to keep playing by the old rules.

KESSLER: I don't fear of being prosecuted for something I'm innocent of

KLINE: WHEN YOU SAY SOMETHING IS PAYBACK IT TAKES AWAY YOUR INNOCENCE YOU STUPID FUCK.

KESSLER: Your cuckoldry is going to become legendary.

James Alex Fields was arrested for Heyer's murder. He was twenty years old, living with his mom, and had driven overnight from Ohio. He'd been photographed in an Identity Evropa white polo while standing next to Kline. He'd also carried a Vanguard America shield.

In public, Kline tried to appear calm. The alt-right had settled on the talking point that Fields was trying to escape from danger. Kline repeated this theory unconvincingly to me. "I'm going to tell you the same thing everyone else has told you: communists attacked his car. He sped into those people, or sped into those cars or whatever. Therefore, they need to be prosecuting these communists who hit his car with a baseball bat or whatever. Everyone else has told you this. I don't know why you think that my quote would be any different."

I told him I hadn't wanted to assume what his views were.

"Everyone is on the same page here."

And why is that?

"Why are we all on the same page? Why do you think we're all on the same page? What's your theory? . . . The reason we're all on the same page is because we all have fucking eyes, Reeve."

"If James Fields got up in court and said that he intentionally drove into the crowd because he wanted to hurt people, what would you think?"

"I would say that a bunch of Jew lawyers told him to do that."

"So you don't know James Fields. No one you know knows James Fields—"

"Nope."

"You haven't talked to James Fields—"

"Nope."

"But you are convinced of his innocence?"

"Nooo I'm not saying I'm convinced of his innocence. You asked me if he goes on there and talks about premeditating and pre-planning—okay?— what will I think about it?"

"You'll think it's a conspiracy?"

"Yes! That doesn't mean I think he's innocent. If anything I think it's probably manslaughter. I know it's certainly not murder one."

I was stunned, and after a few seconds, I asked what he meant.

"You know the difference between manslaughter and murder one?"

I rephrased my question: "You don't know James Fields. You have no history of knowing what he was like, and you have no current knowledge of what he's like, because you don't know anyone who's talked to him. So why are you so certain that he did not intend to commit a crime?"

"I know because I was part of the planning that there was no such side operations to run cars through. People in the alt-right do not join the alt-right with the idea of plowing cars through people, okay? That's not what they do."

I asked again how he knew it was manslaughter if he didn't know anything about Fields.

"This is simple legal definitions. I didn't even go to fucking law school— for very long—and I know this stuff. Have you seen *Law & Order*? Are you familiar with the way law works?"

Kline had not gone to law school. He had not gone to the Iraq War, either, though he'd convinced his comrades he'd served there as an army infantryman. He'd told me, "I'm not afraid of anything. I'm not afraid of any of this stuff. I died in 2012. Everything else is bonus points." The truth was he'd been in the National Guard in Pennsylvania. A lawyer in the *Sines v. Kessler* trial told me that Kline was the most natural liar he'd ever seen. Not that he was a good liar, just that he lied on instinct.

————

Samantha Froelich wanted nothing to do with Kline. She'd known this even before Charlottesville. He asked her to pretend publicly that they were still together, and she went along with it for a bit, until she couldn't take it anymore. She said he threatened her with doxxing, or to break her legs, but she secretly taped him trashing Identity Evropa and then gave the audio to other leaders in the group. Kline was kicked out of IE.

By the late fall of 2017, less than a year after she'd joined IE, Froelich realized she did not want to be in the alt-right anymore, either. It wasn't a sudden epiphany, and she didn't abandon all her beliefs at once. She'd been hanging out with another alt-right woman and some normies, and the woman had asked the normies what they would do if they saw a house on fire, and they went in, and there were Black people and white people inside. Wouldn't she save the white people first? The normies said they'd save whoever they could save. Froelich realized she would, too. Over time she came to understand she'd been racist. She'd been an asshole. She felt like she'd left a cult. Lisa left, too.

————

Chris Cantwell had been proud of his actions during the torch march melee and posted a photo of himself macing someone on his Facebook page. Emily Gorcenski, whom Cantwell maced in the brawl, filed a police report that led to Cantwell's arrest. Cantwell spent a year in jail or under house arrest before pleading guilty to two counts of assault and battery and agreeing to leave the state of Virginia.

He'd only been home a few days when I came to interview him there in New Hampshire. The personal benefits he'd said he'd gotten from fascism—getting fit and sober—had been undone. He'd gained weight, and he was self-conscious about it. "Doesn't make much sense to take pride in one's biology and let your body go to shit," he said.

I learned a lot about Cantwell just by standing in his apartment, saying nothing, as the crew set up our interview. His home was hostile to the human psyche. Every corner was stacked with some kind of object for self-improvement—weights, protein powder, supplements, niche kitchen appliances. He'd printed out signs on computer paper in big bold text that read, "STOP SAYING FUCK," and he'd taped them under his television, by his bathroom mirror, on his fridge. The windows were covered with blackout curtains. He was slamming Sugar Free Red Bulls and taking huge rips from a vape. When I asked how he slept at night, he leaned his head back, his voice tight as he held the smoke in his lungs, and said, "It's a struggle."

The night he'd gotten home from Virginia, he said he noticed a big bottle of whiskey on a shelf, and he took it down and drank it till he blacked out. All he remembered was the hangover the next day. After that lapse, he was trying to control his alcoholism. Getting wasted "is the way to kill yourself and wake up in the morning, right? It turns off whatever it is that you're dealing with." I was sitting across from him, and he was in his homemade radio booth surrounded by gear and a couple of screens, preparing to do his podcast. A loaded gun lay on the table in front of him. I didn't like that the gun was there, but I was also out of patience. He'd bragged on white nationalist podcasts about macing people, and then tried repeatedly to get me to say it wasn't his fault, that he'd had to act in self-defense. (I did not.)

On top of that, someone had made fan art—a detailed comic strip depicting him having sex with me—and he'd posted it on his website. Even with a gun between us, it was hard not to get a feeling that one might articulate as *Say it to my face, bitch*. Anger swelled inside me as Cantwell continued to explain his psychological struggle, but if it registered on my face, he didn't notice. "When I lay down at night to go to sleep, sometimes I have to deal with whatever fucking thoughts are pestering me until my eyes close. . . . I think a lot. I'm a smart guy. I've got ideas running through my head all the time. No amount of talking to a therapist is going to stop that, okay? Alcohol allowed me to turn all of it off, and that appealed to me at times."

He felt like he was being deleted from the internet. He'd been permanently banned from mainstream social media, including dating sites. It was hard to make money. He'd been kicked off several payment processors, and estimated he'd been turned down by a hundred others. He took donations in cryptocurrency, but not many people used it, and with Bitcoin, there was no mechanism for recurring payments.

But the biggest problem, he said, was *Sines v. Kessler*. He thought the discovery process—in which the plaintiffs subpoenaed records of alt-right leaders' communications with one another—was the whole point of the case. It was certainly the most interesting part of the case to me.

"Charlottesville changed the alt-right. I think it tested a lot of people, and a lot of people were understandably scared by what happened. There was a lot of violence, a lot of chaos, a lot of lawfare. Guys went to prison over this. And that understandably caused a lot of people to reconsider whether they wanted to have anything to do with it," Cantwell said. I asked him if it was still a real-world movement, or if it had retreated to the internet. "There's not big alt-right demonstrations at present," he said. "And that is largely due to Charlottesville."

Did he have any regrets? He said he preferred to think of it as lessons learned. One purpose of Unite the Right had been to get to know the real people behind the cartoon frog avatars. But it turned out they'd relied on people who were not reliable. He'd thought for a while that Jason Kessler was brave, because Kessler had been so nonchalant in dangerous situations. Then he realized Kessler didn't understand they were dangerous at all.

Cantwell admitted he was less comfortable in his life as a fascist than he had been as a libertarian. But now he had more of a sense of purpose. "I already am celebrated by more people than most people are. I matter, right? Most people don't matter. . . . Most people will go through the world mostly unnoticed, and they're happy with that," Cantwell said. "I want to matter. I want to be remembered. I want to have an impact on the world. I want to have children." He wanted to be part of history.

Cantwell wanted very badly for his radio show to be successful, and in that, combined with his emotional volatility, some trolls saw an opportunity. They called themselves Bowl Patrol, in honor of Dylann Roof's haircut, and they began prank calling into Cantwell's show. It made him furious, and he couldn't ignore it. The feud intensified over more than a year, and in June 2019, Cantwell demanded one Bowl Patrol member give him the real name of another or Cantwell would "come and fuck your wife in front of your kids." In January 2020, the FBI arrested Cantwell, and found seventeen guns in his home. He was found guilty of extortion and making threats, and sentenced to forty-one months in prison.

———

By December 2017, Spencer's patron, Bill Regnery, had realized that the alt-right's best weapon had been turned against it: the internet. The images they'd been able to create and spread on social media—looking, in their minds, like Chads, very cool, very in control—had been overwhelmed by activists' documentation of their violence. Regnery wrote, "Their ability to blanket the country with their visual interpretation of the event is unsurpassed. I think we should consider giving up all outdoor protest demonstrations with perhaps the exception of a flash protest. I think that any group meetings that could be filmed should exclude visible body armor, shields and helmets." Someone in CMS wrote on its message board, "Perhaps mass action tactics are best left to social movements that actually have a critical mass?"

———

As outside pressure was increasing, Matt Heimbach and Matt Parrott found themselves in a love triangle. Heimbach was having an affair with Parrott's third wife, Jessica. The Parrotts had just had their first child, a girl. Heimbach was married to Parrott's stepdaughter, Brooke, and they had two small boys. This meant that Heimbach was having an affair with a woman who was both his best friend's wife and his wife's stepmom. At the time, Heimbach and Brooke were living in a trailer on Parrott's property in Indiana.

The affair ended, but in early March, according to a police report, Jessica and Brooke decided to test Heimbach's commitment to ending the relationship. Was it really over? They made a plan: Jessica would try to seduce Heimbach, and Brooke and Parrott would film through a window outside. In one sense, it worked: Heimbach responded to Jessica's romantic overtures. But as Jessica and Heimbach began to get physical, Brooke got upset and ran away, and Parrott fell through the box he was standing on. Then Parrott ran around the home and confronted Heimbach. He ordered his best friend to leave his property, jabbing Heimbach in the chest with his finger. Heimbach put Parrott in a headlock and choked him out.

When Parrott came to, Jessica was standing over him. He ran into the house, and Heimbach entered. Parrott demanded Heimbach leave, and when he didn't, Parrott threw a chair at Heimbach. Heimbach choked him out again. When Parrott got himself together, he grabbed his four-month-old daughter, ran to Walmart, and called the cops. When police arrived, they heard Heimbach yelling at Brooke to tell the cops everything was fine and ask them to leave. She refused, and Heimbach kicked a wall and grabbed Brooke's cheeks and pushed her on the bed. Cops entered and arrested Heimbach. Heimbach was already on probation for pushing a Black woman at a Trump rally in 2016. A judge sentenced him to thirty-eight days in jail for violating his probation, and a few months later, Heimbach pled guilty to battery for attacking Parrott.

After Heimbach was taken to the county jail, Parrott announced they were done, and he was done, and the Traditionalist Worker Party was done. He deleted the TWP member list. It was all over. He told the Southern Poverty Law Center, "SPLC has won. Matt Parrott is out of the game. Y'all have a nice life."

In 1934, Hitler ordered the extrajudicial execution of dozens of rivals in a purge known as the Night of the Long Knives. The Parrott-Heimbach-Jessica incident became known among both fascists and antifascists as the Night of the Wrong Wives.

Parrott and Heimbach were humiliated by the Night of the Wrong Wives. It affected them deeply. They hated to be asked about it, but they brought it up out of nowhere, and frequently, as "the trailer park incident." They'd been flooded with cringe content, most intensely by other nazis. I did not totally understand their shame. If they were going to be ashamed about something, it should have been that they participated in an act of racial terror.

―――――――

Spencer tried to resume his college tour. He successfully applied to speak at Michigan State in March 2018, but the university gave him a speaking slot during spring break, at the ag center on the periphery of campus. He gave a speech to mostly journalists in front of a pit where livestock were evaluated—the concrete floor had a drain to wash away the horseshit. Outside the venue was a miserable scene. It was twenty-eight degrees, gray, and after hours of shouting, there was a massive brawl between a group of Traditionalist Worker

Party members, led by Heimbach, and antifascists. Afterward, on YouTube, Spencer gave up his tour. It was too hard to hold public events, he said: "Antifa is winning."

Regnery scolded Spencer that "we can never say 'uncle' in public." Spencer replied, "Bill, I couldn't just keep doing the college tour when it was becoming demoralizing. And something had to be said." By May of 2018, Spencer told Regnery "a certain 'Alt-Right moment' is passing." He would return his focus to publishing books. Regnery responded, "I agree with this tactical refocus."

And then, that same month, Nina Kouprianova filed an eighty-three-page divorce complaint. She alleged emotional and physical abuse, that Spencer had pulled her by her hair down the stairs, that he'd often told her to kill herself. The complaint presented many news stories about his racist beliefs and said they put her and their small children in danger. She said he'd been driven mad by people calling him fat online. Spencer denied he was physically abusive but admitted to verbal abuse.

The divorce revealed details about Spencer's finances, thanks to Montana's open records laws. Through a trust, Poor Richard Partners LLC, Sherry Spencer, his mother, had dispersed income from the cotton farms she'd inherited to Richard. But according to emails included in court records, in November 2014, after Spencer's arrest in Budapest, Sherry had emailed her financial advisor, "As this situation spirals, I think we need to more aggressively protect assets. I believe you said that a trust can remain private. . . . I don't know how that can be structured, realizing that we must publish something that states that Richard will no longer be involved." In 2018, Spencer and his mother submitted documents showing she'd bought him out of one of the family farms for $537,000. The version of the document I saw had not been signed; when I asked Spencer about it in 2021, he said "no comment."

The divorce took eighteen months. Kouprianova said it cost her $40,000 in legal fees. Spencer was held in contempt of court for failing to pay $60,000 to the court-appointed investigator who determined the best custody arrangement. Multiple third parties involved in the case said they thought both Spencer and Kouprianova were acting irrationally. Kouprianova had originally decided to move to Winnipeg to be near her parents, but in April 2019, changed her mind and decided to stay in Whitefish. She and Spencer both still live in the same mountain town of 8,500 people.

————

The *Sines v. Kessler* trial took place four years after Charlottesville, in 2021. The major leaders of the alt-right were forced to come to a single room, answer questions directly, and behave themselves in front of a federal judge. Samantha Froelich's taped deposition was played in court, but her ex-boyfriend, Elliot Kline, did not show up. Neither did Robert "Azzmador" Ray, the bearded felon I'd interviewed in a van.

The trial brought Parrott and Heimbach back together, out of legal necessity. Parrott's legal fortune was tied to Heimbach's, and Heimbach hadn't been responding to the filings.

That Parrott would speak to Heimbach after what Heimbach had done was a subject of curiosity among all trial parties. When I ran into one lawyer by accident in the laundry room of a hotel, he wanted to know if I could explain their friendship. I knew less then than I know now, and even now I cannot fully explain it.

In court, the organizers defended their actions. They were sometimes angry, sometimes defiant. They offered excuses and rationalizations. They claimed it was lawfare, that they were being punished for protected speech, that the plaintiffs should have been suing the city and its police force instead. But I think that something more was going on behind that front. They were forced to look at what they'd done for several hours a day for several weeks. They had to look at what they'd said and explain why they said it. They were forced to reckon with the times their allies had lied and manipulated them. They were forced to do it knowing twelve strangers were watching and would decide what it all meant. After a couple days of deliberation, the jury found they were liable for conspiracy and racially motivated harassment or violence, and $26 million. The sum was reduced by the judge to $300,000.

A lot of people have said to me that these guys did this because they're losers. I don't think that's right. There's no such thing as a loser. But if you accept the premise that losers exist, and you accept that these guys are losers, even then, so what? Not all "losers" do this. There are many people who are dead broke, or sick, or ugly, or lonely, or home alone on a Saturday night—and I have been all of those things—who do not do what these people did. They do not become fascists. They do not dedicate their time to making the world a more cruel and violent place. All these guys made a choice.

13

"THE INITIAL PERIOD OF ABSOLUTE CHAOS"

"Terrorist" might seem like a strange label for an incel, because hating women is not seen as political, but just a part of everyday life. But these men committed acts of violence against civilians to advance political goals. That is terrorism.

In April 2018, Alek Minassian drove a van into a crowd in Toronto, killing eleven people and injuring fifteen more. In his interrogation, Minassian explained he was an incel, and that he used 4chan's /r9k/ board and some other incel and alt-right forums. He spoke in the language of those forums—the beautiful Stacys, the macho Chads, the simpleton normies—with total sincerity.

POLICE: *And when you say incels?*
MINASSIAN: *Involuntary celibate.*
POLICE: *So that's just a short form for fellas who ... ?*
MINASSIAN: *Can't get laid.*
POLICE: *Can't have sex. Right. Okay.* [stunned laughter]

The video of Minassian's interrogation is an important document of our time. In it I see the police officer going through what I've experienced—this

209

feeling that you're being pulled back and forth between your world and the subject's. You know it's important to make the subject feel like you're inside *his* reality—an obvious smirk or jaw drop could break the spell and wake him up to the fact that it's in his best interest to shut up. But at the same time, you can never forget *your* reality, because that is the reality you're responsible to, and that reality is what frames your questions.

Minassian said he'd discussed with other incels the idea of "timed strikes on society" in order to "put all the normies in a state of panic." He called Elliot Rodger the founding father of the "incel rebellion."

POLICE: *Who would the targets for this uprising be?*

MINASSIAN: *All of the alpha males.*

POLICE: *All the alpha males—so the Chads?*

MINASSIAN: *Yes.*

POLICE: *So that's, those are the people that you want to kill?*

MINASSIAN: *Yes.*

POLICE: *Okay. All right. And who else?*

MINASSIAN: *Any of the Stacys who do not wish to give their love and affection to the incels.*

POLICE: *So they're a target as well?*

MINASSIAN: *Yes.*

POLICE: *To be killed?*

MINASSIAN: *Yes.*

POLICE: *Okay, and what about the normies?*

MINASSIAN: *Yes. We don't necessarily wish to kill the normies but we do wish to subjugate them.... So that they acknowledge the incels—or the Pepe the Frog types—as the more superior ones.*

POLICE: *Okay, you're saying things I'm not familiar with ...*

MINASSIAN: *Sorry ...*

POLICE: *What's a Pepe the Frog?*

MINASSIAN: *He's a mascot on 4chan, and we ...*

POLICE: *He's a mascot?*

MINASSIAN: *Yes.*

POLICE: *Oh, a mascot. On 4chan.*

MINASSIAN: *Yes. I was using a metaphor.*

In court, Minassian's defense argued he was not criminally responsible because he had autism spectrum disorder. He was examined by several forensic psychiatrists, including Alexander Westphal. Westphal testified that Minassian "has a highly developed concept of the rule nature of the wrongfulness of what he did. . . . The problem is his comprehension of the real, horrific impact that something like this would have. . . . I don't think he understands that." The judge rejected that argument, and found Minassian guilty of ten counts of first-degree murder and sixteen counts of attempted murder.

The judge's sixty-nine-page ruling is another important document of this era. The judge looked at the assessments of four teams of mental health professionals to figure out Minassian's true motivation. Minassian was obsessed with Rodger, and he was angry at women, but he also said he talked about incels to get more infamous, and posted about 4chan and Rodger under his real name to draw media attention.

Westphal's report stated that the crime "was conceived in the context of his saturation with provocative, hate-filled material on the internet. ASD made him less able to appreciate the theatrical, exaggerated nature and extremeness of the material, or the dark humor behind some of it. He took it very literally." But, the judge said, Minassian had also told Westphal that users of incel forums were joking, that "it is mostly satire."

The judge doubted Minassian was *really* an incel. He showed "none of the venom typical of incel followers." Minassian knew much of the content of their forums was dark humor. "Why did he do it?" the judge wrote. There were many factors, but "bottom line: he did it to become famous."

The judge was right to find Minassian guilty and sentence him to life in prison. But her reasoning is wrong, though it reflects a belief I've encountered many times: They don't *really* believe this shit, do they?

Irony, in most cases, is not real. It does not matter what someone *really* believes. They don't always know what they believe. If they believe it enough to laugh at it, they believe it enough. If they believe it enough to drive halfway across the country to march for it, they believe it enough. And if they believe it enough to mow down twenty-six people for it, they believe it enough.

———

The far-right internet believed it helped put Trump into the White House, and so it expected to get an invite to the mainstream. But that's not exactly what happened. Some of their ideas entered the mainstream, as when a couple of Fox News hosts talked about the myth that a malignant force was trying to replace white people with people of color who vote for Democrats. So did some of their slang: based, cringe, Chad, trad, soy boy, red pill, black pill. But their guys did not. They did not win public office and they didn't even get congressional internships. Some started to think there could be no incremental change. It would have to get worse before it got better. They read Julius Evola, the fascist philosopher who argued they could "ride the tiger" of a degenerate society until it collapsed and a spiritual elite could take over. They encouraged one another to "read *Siege*," a collection of essays by white supremacist James Mason first written in the 1980s. Mason argued against mass movements in favor of small cells of terrorists. "Those who survive the initial period of absolute chaos that immediately follows will crawl out of their holes and take up the struggle on newly equalized terms: animal to animal," the introduction to *Siege* reads. "Anything which contributes to friction, chaos and anarchy can only help us in the long run. . . . We want to see crime and chaos rise to such a degree where the System becomes no longer viable and falls apart. . . . From chaos comes rebirth and order."

In March 2019, a man killed fifty-one people at two mosques in Christchurch, New Zealand. He'd posted his manifesto on 8chan, asked users to "please do your part by spreading my message, making memes and shitposting as you usually do," and shared a link to a livestream of his crime. He said the Western world was disintegrating in degeneracy, divorce, drugs, suicide, ecological disaster. "A gradual change is never going to achieve victory," he wrote. "Destabilize, then take control. If we want to radically and fundamentally change society, then we need to radicalize society as much as possible."

The murderer was twenty-eight years old, but it was clear from his writing that he was trying to impress the racist teenagers on 8chan. He spoke in memes. When I read it, I thought he'd wanted to become a meme himself. He succeeded.

Mark Mann, who'd brought Gamergate to 8chan in 2013, was still working for the site when the murder livestream link was posted. Mann noticed the memes drawn on the Christchurch shooter's gun. He thought the shooter was a blackpilled accelerationist, someone who wants to bring the collapse of society so that more people will accept radical change. The goal, Mann thought, was "to make 4chan more radicalized, and radicalize the /pol/ people and turn them into violent psychopaths." And he did see users praising the shooter on 8chan's /pol/, though he heard from his colleagues that a lot of them were new users.

Mann thought Christchurch contributed to the radicalization of /pol/, in part because it put 8chan in news headlines. They turned the shooter into an icon. "He was a figurehead for accelerationism," Mann said, "where they wanted people to start getting violent, and starting the civil war between the left and the right."

The next month, a nineteen-year-old killed one person and hurt three more at a synagogue in Poway, California. He cited the Christchurch shooter and posted his manifesto on 8chan.

In May 2019, I flew to the Philippines to interview Fred Brennan for *Vice*. He had resigned as admin for 8chan in 2016 and then, in December 2018, quit working for Jim Watkins after Watkins had stormed into his apartment uninvited and screamed at him. But despite having abandoned the cause that brought him to the other side of the world, Fred stayed in Manila. He was living in a nice apartment in a high rise with his wife and a little dog. He made a decent living as a programmer. But he was in a kind of liminal phase.

"I don't necessarily know that 8chan is what I wanted it to be, or that it's good for the world, or good for society, or really, good for anything," Fred said in 2019. "It changed my life, and it changed a lot of other people's lives, too. But I don't know if it was more positive or negative."

When he was using them as a teenager, he'd never imagined these websites would be important. But now they were injecting their culture into mainstream society. It was happening more and more violently. Why had they created such a powerful malevolent force? Fred thought it was explained by the mechanics of the imageboard. He'd thought it would work like the marketplace of ideas, with the best ideas rising to the top. But that's not what happened. When nazis entered a community, they were aggressive and offensive. They redpilled the few people who had been a little nazi-curious, and everyone else left. Then there was no debate, no exchange of ideas at all—just one idea pinging around in a pinball machine, and that idea was fascism.

———

By the time Fred quit 8chan, he wasn't sure life was worth living. He had no project or mission, and he didn't know what he believed. But if there was no point in life, why was he spending his limited time on 8chan? He started going to church with his home health aide in Manila, and was drawn in by Christianity's message of redemption. "The idea that God loves you no matter how many times you've spit on him. God loves you no matter how many times you've caused harm, and I've done my fair share of that. I literally campaigned for eugenics. That's like literally cursing God—*You put my soul in this body!*

"Of course I was sometimes tortured about—not tortured by anyone, just tortured by myself—about whether 8chan was a good thing, or whether I made a big mistake in making it . . . whether this was going to be my last act." It wasn't that hard to believe in God. He could just say that he did, and it was true. "I decided, *You know what? I can believe that Jesus rose from the dead.* Like, I can just believe that. I can just try it out. I can just say that it happened."

In the fall of 2017, a 4chan user claimed Hillary Clinton would be arrested, that the extradition treaties were being worked out with several countries in case she tried to run, and that the National Guard was involved. This person claimed to have Q-level clearance. This was the birth of QAnon. After a month, Q moved to 8chan, where he was welcomed with open arms. Fred, who had resigned as admin but was still working for Jim and Ron Watkins, thought it was a stupid troll, and he was annoyed that it used his favorite letter of the alphabet. Jim and Ron convinced him to pose for a photo with a big blue letter Q. Fred didn't think much of it at the time.

But by the time I visited Manila, there had been several major QAnon incidents, including a man arrested on terrorism charges after he used an armored truck to block traffic at the Hoover Dam, demanding the Justice Department release documents that Q said existed. Another man had drawn a Q in the palm of his hand and flashed it at his hearing on charges he'd murdered a Staten Island mobster. QAnon was growing, but there wasn't much about it in the mainstream news—in part because it required explaining that the conspiracy theory held that many high-level political and cultural figures were part of a secret cabal of cannibalistic pedophiles who loved Satan. In the wake of Charlottesville, many media organizations accepted antifascists' concept of "no platforming"—meaning reporters should not "give oxygen" to fringe movements by covering them, because it only helped them grow. For some researchers and journalists who covered extremism, including me, this idea amounted to "if we can't see it, it doesn't exist."

But it did exist. It existed on 8chan, and it grew there, bigger and bigger.

And though he had left it behind, Fred had trouble ignoring 8chan's existence. Every day it was accumulating more proof that he'd been wrong about free speech, that there was a large appetite for the worst human impulses, that sometimes when crazy lies were exposed to sunlight they flourished.

"Does it make you pessimistic about the human race?"

"Yes," Fred said. "It also makes me pessimistic about the future of democracy. Because autocracy is doing so well in the world right now. A lot of autocratic governments are thriving. I kind of feel like, maybe when the history is written, democracy is just going to be an outdated system, one of the steps that was taken to some kind of capitalist autocracy."

Four months after our interview, a man killed twenty-three people in a Walmart in El Paso, Texas, and hurt twenty-three more. He'd posted his manifesto on 8chan.

El Paso eliminated Fred's ambivalence about his creation. He told the *New York Times* that 8chan should be shut down. It was bad for the world, and it was bad for its users, even if they didn't know it. After public pressure, the internet services company Cloudflare dropped 8chan as a customer, taking it offline. Fred celebrated. It gave him a new mission. He told the *QAnon*

Anonymous podcast, "If they want to bring 8chan back online, just be aware that I will do everything I can to keep it down because the world is better off without it."

When Fred realized he'd created a monster, he didn't sit back and give interviews saying, *Isn't it a terrible shame we're stuck with this monster?* He tried to kill the monster. He did this in a way that only he could: with his technical skills, his natural intensity, and his resistance to social norms.

Fred had taught himself Japanese, and one of the biggest Watkins websites was in Japan, so Fred said he gave a Japanese newspaper "a detailed chart of all of Jim's shell companies, how they relate, where the money comes from, how it gets to 8chan, how it keeps 8chan going."

Ron Watkins rebranded 8chan as 8kun. With his knowledge of the complicated unseen infrastructure of the internet, Fred went after companies whose services Ron needed to keep 8kun online. In one case, Fred privately messaged a company informing it that 8kun sought its services, and when he got a message thanking him for the information and saying "we do not want any content like this on our network," Fred posted the screenshots publicly on Twitter to shame the company into acting faster. In a follow-up tweet, he said, "If you think you can trick me Jim, remember you kept me for years after I left 8chan for a reason. I understand all this technical stuff."

Fred figured out that 8kun was being hosted on Russian servers. It was odd, because when he was admin of 8chan, he'd gotten more than two dozen emails from Roskomnadzor, the Russian federal agency that regulates mass media. Roskomnadzor had demanded he take down content—he remembered that one offending image was a gay comic strip. Fred had replied, "Fuck off and stop emailing me and wasting my time. I don't give a shit about internet censorship laws passed in Russia." (When he showed me the email, he asked me, "A normal person might have been intimidated by this, right? Like, Russia is a big country.")

Armed with that knowledge, Fred wrote an open letter to all Russian domain hosting services and got it translated into Russian. "Subject: [URGENT] Terrorist website, 8KUN.NET, banned by many companies worldwide, using your network."

I would also like to inform you that 8chan is banned in Russia. Under the direction of Jim Watkins, its owner, I, as its then-administrator, told Roskomnadzor that I would not delete content to get it unbanned; this happened in 2015....

This email shows 8chan's clear disdain for Russian law, telling Roskomnadzor to "fuck off." As I've already shown, 8kun has been recognized by those with common sense to be a way to evade bans, as a bad faith rebrand.

It is likely, especially given the new internet laws enacted by the Russian legislature, that 8kun would be quickly banned as well; it may even be seen by Russian authorities as an attempt to evade the ban Roskomnadzor placed upon it.

Fred emailed Roskomnadzor directly, repeatedly. He never heard back.

Mark Mann had still been working at the website when 8chan went down. When it was reborn as 8kun, Mann was furious—it was so Q-centric. Back when the first wave of QAnon had come to 8chan, "we were surprised to see so many baby boomers come on imageboards," Mann said. He'd thought the new users would filter out into other boards and grow their audiences, but it didn't happen. "All they thought about was QAnon." For a while, he thought they were just a nuisance. "It wasn't until 2020 that I realized that we weren't trying to be a general site. We were a political grifter—my bosses, politically grifting these boomers for a profit."

Jim Watkins noticed Fred's activity. In February 2020, Watkins filed a "cyberlibel" claim against Fred in the Philippines because Fred had called him "senile" in a tweet. Fred heard there was a warrant for his arrest, and believing he'd die in jail given his disability, he fled the country. He got a place in Los Angeles, and then the pandemic hit.

Fred turned his focus to trying to prove Q's real identity. At the time, this didn't seem like the most important question about QAnon—it wasn't as interesting as what the conspiracy theory said about the human psyche and America. But naming the real Q mattered, because it could create real consequences for the person behind the mask.

Fred had suspected that Jim and Ron Watkins controlled Q when 8kun was struggling to stay online. Most people couldn't use the site, but Q was able to post. Fred believed that the original Q had been Paul Furber, a South African 4chan moderator who ran the 8chan board where Q posted. In December 2017, Furber went on Alex Jones's show *Infowars* to pitch Q to a bigger audience, and promoted a friendlier forum on Reddit. Fred was still working for the Watkins family, and he said he saw in the company chatrooms that Jim urged Ron to make sure the Q crowd stayed on 8chan.

Not long after the *Infowars* appearance, a Q post appeared on 8chan, and Furber declared that it was an imposter. But that Q, the supposed fake, insisted he was real, and appealed to Ron Watkins: "please log in and confirm." Ron did, and he sided with the new Q. Fred thought this was the moment the Watkinses gained total control of the Q canon. He presented his evidence on the podcast *Reply All*, which took his theory mainstream. About a year and a half later, the *New York Times* published a linguistic analysis of Q's postings. Two teams of forensic linguists, one Swiss and one French, found that Furber was likely the first Q and Ron Watkins was the second. Their analyses suggested Ron took over in early 2018. (Both Furber and Ron Watkins deny they were Q.)

If Q's followers noticed Fred's work, it did not matter to most of them. The conspiracy grew and Q-influencers gained fame on YouTube, Instagram, Telegram, Twitter, and lesser-known video sites, like Rumble or DLive. Asked about QAnon by NBC, President Trump said, "They are very strongly against pedophilia. And I agree with that." Surely he knew there wasn't a secret satanic pedophile cult? "No, I don't know that. And neither do you know that." When Trump campaign spokeswoman Kayleigh McEnany asked a supporter outside a Las Vegas rally if he had a message for the president, he responded, "Who is Q?"

14

FANTASIZING ABOUT SELF-DEFENSE

Sam Guff and I spent a lot of 2020 in the Pacific Northwest. I'd started working for CNN several months before the Covid pandemic began. Sam had never covered a violent political protest. We felt like we were not on a different coast but in a parallel world.

Seattle and Portland—two relatively white cities—had become the centers of the right-wing backlash to Black Lives Matter protests. Members of the Proud Boys and Patriot Prayer generally lived in the smaller towns outside those cities, and they'd drive in to confront antifa. Like the alt-right brawls of 2017, the fights were escalating. They were drawing people who wanted to see the spectacle up close, but that didn't make the violence any less real.

We spent weeks in an apocalyptic Portland. Everything was closed for Covid and there was nothing to do till the evening, when sources would text a flier advertising the location of the protest that night. Every night followed the same rhythm: chants at police, police declaring an unlawful assembly, police declaring a riot, police chasing and arresting protesters. We were there to film the interaction between protesters and police, but when police started running, we had to run, too. A cop shouted as he chased us, "I'm gonna get you!"

We turned down a side street, and he didn't follow. Still panting, Sam and I puzzled over the strange note of irony in his voice.

Many of the protesters wore head-to-toe protection: a tactical vest, helmet, kneepads, wrist guards, and a gas mask at the ready. When they saw us in jeans and T-shirts, they'd ask, "Are you new?" One night, I'd bear-hugged Sam's legs and lifted her above the crowd so she could film. Another night, we climbed up the fire escape of a donut shop to get a better view and found a man with a speaker on a cart, giving the protest a soundtrack. For a march to mark one hundred straight days of protest, we stood between police and protesters to capture their faces. It's the best shot, but the most risky. The march had barely gone a city block when we felt a huge boom, and suddenly there was a guy on the ground with his legs on fire. Sam filmed it until police ran toward the protesters, shooting them with paintball guns, and our colleague grabbed our backpacks and made us run. We escaped through a skate park, sprinting up and down over a Dr. Seuss landscape of dirt mounds. Only the next morning, when a Seattle cop texted me a viral video of it, did we realize the boom had been a Molotov cocktail.

We were often joined by Deb Brunswick, a softball player who loved Celine Dion and filmed beautifully. Through 2020, this was our all-girl crew. We could move smoothly through hostile crowds, most of the time. Deb did get chased by a screaming Proud Boy carrying a beer bottle just outside Portland. He thought she was antifa.

There were echoes of what I'd seen in online extremism that I couldn't ignore. The protesters' ideas were in no way equivalent, but the internet was shaping their group in a way that was uncomfortably familiar: pushing their beliefs to a more apocalyptic extreme, luring them to trust people they'd only just met. It was considered gauche to not accept "a diversity of tactics," or to question whether fellow protesters' methods might be unpersuasive to a broader audience. That meant they didn't debate whether it advanced the cause of protecting Black people from police violence when a few protesters dressed like bank robbers broke the windows of a random dentist's office. Sitting next to me on a curb, our faces lit up by flashing police lights, a sweet skinny kid told me he now realized violence was necessary to bring revolutionary change. It triggered real anger in me: Did he know anyone who served in the war in Iraq? Had he ever talked to someone who'd stood in a city destroyed by violence? Had he ever seen a closeup photo of what a high-powered rifle could do to a human head? He had not.

The most committed protesters—the ones who went out every night— felt deeply bonded with one another through their shared experience of violence. They thought the police response to the early protests was out of proportion, and it had scared them. They'd recount the events of particular nights again and again, like they still couldn't believe it had really happened that way. But they also spent a lot of time in group chats with pseudonyms. How much did they really *know* about one another? Seattle protesters put me in touch with a man from their group chat who went by Tink. Tink told me that local gang leaders had been very angry at the protesters, so he offered himself as tribute. He said he let the gangsters beat him up to settle the score. He said they used phone books to conceal the marks on his skin. He said he was willing to do it because he was terminally ill and only had a few months to live. It was a wild story, and when I ran it by a Seattle cop who knew the local gangs, he'd never heard anything like it. A year later, when the protests were over, Tink's comrade told me they'd come to suspect he was faking cancer.

In Seattle, protests had led police to abandon a precinct station in its Capitol Hill neighborhood. Someone spray-painted "Capitol Hill Autonomous Zone" on a barricade, and someone else tweeted it, and it became a meme. Then people came to the area and the meme became a reality, a big radical party in a park in the summer. Because protesters were scared that Proud Boys would come to the CHAZ and attack them, a group called the Sentinels formed to secure the perimeter. They started openly carrying guns, including AR-15s, for self-defense. The party atmosphere faded and the CHAZ grew darker. There was a shooting on its periphery, and then another. One night, a man left a chilling voice memo in a security group chat: "We have a couple of armed groups here trying to hold things down, but I would recommend that if you are not armed you stay away. If you are not armed and maybe even not armored, I would stay away." The Sentinels told me they transferred security responsibilities to another group, but I could not confirm the relationship between the two. Three weeks after the CHAZ's creation, someone acting as security fired on what was thought to be an attacker driving into the CHAZ in an SUV. In reality, it was just a couple of unarmed Black teenagers. One was killed.

The Portland protests stopped when the sky turned orange as a massive wildfire spread across Oregon. On the last breathable day a Patriot Prayer member on a hoverboard told us he was preparing for civil war.

I'd avoided reporting on the Proud Boys for years. The group had been founded by Gavin McInnes, a cofounder of *Vice* who'd left the company in 2008. He'd embodied 2000s-era Brooklyn, an era of trucker hats and "ironic" racist and misogynist jokes, though he never seemed to get around to dropping the joke. I never met him, though in 2016 he'd said on Twitter that feminism made women miserable slaves in tedious jobs. I responded that I worked at *Vice*, because I thought it was funny that I did and he didn't. My comment didn't get much attention until about a year later, when McInnes posted an angry tweet thread saying he'd heard I was working on a "hit piece" about him. I wasn't. Elliot Kline told me he'd convinced McInnes I was out to get him, but given Kline's well-documented history of lying, I don't know if any part of that story is true. Maybe it was all "just a joke."

McInnes had made everything about the Proud Boys "just a joke"—from the name to the initiation ritual of getting punched while naming cereal brands. I thought McInnes had covered the Proud Boys in stupid shit so that no reporter could touch it without getting covered in shit, too. Even making fun of it felt like participating in their game.

The Proud Boys didn't have political demands. They had a vibe and a look. They didn't like leftists, and they offered to serve as security for conservatives whose public events would be protested by those leftists. They didn't like feminism, but they didn't explicitly hate women. They wanted to "venerate the housewife." They did not support an ethnostate. Their most visible activism was getting into street fights.

This is why the Proud Boys were able to survive. Thousands, maybe hundreds of thousands, of young men across the country felt weak and wanted to feel strong, and they wanted some bros and had none.

The Proud Boys gave them a way to be the men they felt they were on the inside, Russell Schultz told me. Schultz had been a Proud Boy near Portland, but quit in 2019. "They're men who've never had wingmen before," he said. "They're afraid to say what's on their mind for fear of getting into a fight." The Proud Boys gave them courage, because someone would have their back. "They want to join a gang. So they can go fight antifa and hurt people that they don't like, and feel justified in doing it."

When he was in, Schultz was known for making vivid threats against antifa on social media, such as "You're lucky I didn't kill you because I wouldn't feel any remorse." He said he was trying to bait antifascists into showing up at protests dressed in all black, because it scared the normies. Normies wouldn't see fascists vs. antifascists, they'd see "all these people looking like ISIS."

In September 2020, the Proud Boys held a rally in Portland to honor a Patriot Prayer member who'd been shot to death by an antifascist. The alt-right had stopped most of its public demonstrations, but the people who'd been part of it had not ceased to exist. The easiest way for me to spot them was if they recognized me. As we walked through the rally, there were murmurs, like "That's Cantwell's girlfriend." A six-foot-five, three-hundred-pound man spotted me. His real name was Daniel Scott, but he went by Milkshake. "You know we're sweet boys—Proud Boys, right?" he said. He was carrying a little pink T-ball bat. "Do I look scary with this?" he asked. I said I wouldn't want to be hit in the head with it. "I would never hit your head," he said. "I would never use this to hit someone out of just a blatant attack. It would be only self-defense."

The leader of the Proud Boys, Enrique Tarrio, was standing on the edge of the rally, and I walked over to him. If his followers saw us talking, it would build my credibility. Tarrio recognized me, too. "Our prime objective is to create better men," he said. I asked him to explain the connection between building alpha men and protesting antifa. He said they were totally separate. The group could do two different things.

Tarrio wore a military-style tactical vest that carried a ceramic plate, and attached to it were a gas mask, a radio, and a can of White Claw, even though he didn't drink. His eyes were covered by mirrored aviators. I said I noticed that the Proud Boys dressed in the aesthetics of political violence.

"Aesthetics, and actually what we are, are two different things. So if you look around, we're all wearing protective gear," Tarrio said. He said he got the gear because he'd gotten death threats. (Tarrio worked as a federal informant after an arrest in 2012, according to court documents unearthed by Reuters. His former lawyer described his cooperation with law enforcement as "prolific.")

I asked if he engaged in political violence.

"I absolutely know that I don't engage in political violence," Tarrio said.

I couldn't help but notice that many Proud Boys events ended with some people getting beat up.

"If our mere presence causes people to want to commit acts of violence—let me tell you something, we're not afraid to defend ourselves. And I think we're pretty good at defending ourselves. I think that the past has shown that," he said. "If that's what they want to do, then that's not on us." The day after we posted our report from the rally, in a presidential debate, Donald Trump said, "Proud Boys: stand back and stand by."

———

I was starting to feel like I was watching a replay. There were periodic political street brawls documented from every angle by smartphones, and then spread across the internet as evidence one side was evil and the other brave. The videos and photos were posted over and over in forums and chatrooms and on Twitter, and the conversation around them became more apocalyptic—these monsters had to be crushed. People talked about engaging in violence, but, of course, only as self-defense. Parallel to the Proud Boys, Patriot Prayer, and far-right militias, there was a truly mass movement growing with QAnon. The QAnon types did not have much in common with the Proud Boys, but they shared the same enemy: antifa and Black Lives Matter. They also shared a sense that they were marching toward inevitable victory.

15

FOR HISTORY

I stood on a stone wall about four feet high looking down on the thousands of people swirling on the lawn in front of the Capitol. Sam and Deb stood on either side of me, filming. On the other side of the wall were the stairs that led up to the building's doors, toward the members of Congress voting to certify the results of the 2020 election. Those stairs had become the focus of every pair of eyes that could see it. They were packed tight with people who could barely move, but everyone knew that was the path forward.

"For history" was the magic phrase that unlocked the people in the mob. They hated journalists, the media, and especially my employer, CNN, but they were willing to tell us what they'd seen and done, "for history." To me, this was a historic humiliation of liberal democracy. To them, this was revolution. It was actually happening. And they were part of it.

I'd spent months interviewing Trump supporters, but the tone had shifted after the election. I'd checked in with our sources to see what they thought of this incredible claim that the election was stolen, and discovered that most of them thought it was credible. A few were even traveling all the way to Washington for the Stop the Steal rally, like Greg Locke, a Tennessee preacher who had told me the Covid pandemic was a hoax, and J. R. Majewski, an Ohio man who'd painted his huge triangular yard like a Trump flag.

Majewski had seemed like a regular guy. When I reached out to him, he said he recognized my name and he was totally opposed to the extremists in Charlottesville. But that fall I watched him shift to a Q-curious influencer who helped organize about fifty people from across the country to go to Stop the Steal. He posted his group's channel publicly, so I joined it and lurked, watching those inside spin themselves up as the rally approached. "This runs so deep and it's so dirty." "I knew its been coming, but now its here. All to be revealed." "Normies getting redpilled." I yelled at my phone: *You are the normies!* They shared ideas for self-defense, like pepper spray, or gloves with reinforced knuckles. One man explained, "a locking gate carabiner works better than a lot of brass knuckles BEST PART THERE LEGAL."

And then a few days before the rally, Brian Keathley, a man who made Sam, Deb, and me shoot guns before he would consent to an interview in Missouri's Ozark Mountains, sent me a series of text messages warning that I should stay away from the Capitol on January 6.

Ever heard of a million man March?

Imagine all of them being armed

Now imagine all of them with an agenda . . .

Elle . . . Please take precautions.

You Live in a world of illusions. . . . You think the police/gov can protect or control.

That's just not going to be the case . . .

I can't say much more about anything . . .

I only engaged in the conversation to inform you of the potential risks of being in the middle of a storm.

Keathley was the one who decided to stay home. But he was right, in a way. We did end up in the middle of the storm, standing on the stone wall at the Capitol as the crowd became a mob. But I didn't think I was the one captured by illusions. There was an electric current running through the crowd, pushing everyone forward with a menacing joy. I could feel the pull of their collective thrill, even as I was horrified by what I was watching. A man on the lawn began shouting, "Either climb over or get out of the way!" I inched backward a bit. The crowd below compressed as it pushed toward the wall. People were awkwardly climbing over it just past my feet. As an older couple scrambled past us, the woman shouted, "Watch the cane!"

We moved away from the stairs and around some side steps to the Capitol's terrace. "Just explain what happened, for history," I urged a man in his forties. "What happened is the U.S. Capitol was just breached, probably for the first time in U.S. history." He repeated it: "*Probably for the first time in U.S. history. Completely unplanned. There's no—there's no plan. There's no leader.*"

A mob has the courage to do things none of its members would dare do on their own. "We pushed, and we pushed, and we kept pushing, and they pulled out their batons," the man said. He wouldn't give his name. "And a few people pushed even further, so we just kind of pushed in. There was a few people who did some vandalism, but very few." A woman eavesdropping said, "Nothing like antifa." He agreed: "Nothing like antifa. Nothing at all. . . . It's unquestionable. There's so much proof, and you"—he looked at the camera—"you motherfucker, CNN, you hide it." He concluded the interview, "Fuck CNN. Fuck CNN. Not you guys. It's just a job for you. But fuck CNN. Thank you."

Tear gas boomed, and thousands of people flinched at once. I told Sam, in my most casual voice, that if suddenly the whole crowd started running, she had to stay on her feet, no matter what. "I know," she said. "I remember what happened to Mufasa."

————

We'd been there since before dawn, when Trump supporters started getting in line. In the dark, people were amped, like they were going to a rock concert. But as the time Trump was to speak grew closer, they got angry. There was no way they were going to make it through security in time to hear the speech. They couldn't even see him.

I mingled in a netherworld in front of the White House—not fully behind the Secret Service's secured area, but not fully outside of it either. We walked along this line, asking people why they were here. Josh Sharp, a man in his thirties who'd come from Joplin, Missouri, said that before Trump, "most people's eyes were closed. . . . He opened our eyes and said, 'Hey, here's what's *really* going on.'" The president had exposed the corruption of the system. "If you guys don't see that by now then you're blind to it. You don't want to see it," Sharp said. "If Trump says go, we're gonna do whatever he asks us to do."

This was a recurring theme in our interviews: that we in the media could not see the essential truth about America that was right in front of our faces. Sometimes they said it with anger, sometimes with pity. I would stare at them and think, *You don't know that I know that the hidden truth you think you discovered was invented by my sources when your rage was still just an unarticulated irritation flickering in the back of your mind.* But I couldn't say that, obviously. By this point, I'd been convinced for months there would be an attempted coup. But in the middle of this massive crowd which would, in a couple hours, actually try to do the coup, I was distracted from reporting on what they were doing by thinking about why they'd come.

———

At the lawn in front of the Washington Monument, there was more space and people were in a better mood. A man in a Q hoodie sat in a tree. I asked him if he'd seen a ten-part QAnon film called *Fall of the Cabal* (which wove together conspiracy theories about Covid vaccines, Jews, and the JFK assassination, plus some 4chan slang). "Yes, absolutely," he said. "That was a big red pill for everyone." His name was Eduardo Rendon, and I stood at the base of the tree, shouting my interview questions up at him, as "Don't Stop Believing" played on the speakers around us. During the pandemic, he said, "I redpilled myself, basically."

Most of the people I interviewed on January 6 were first redpilled by the Covid lockdown, then blackpilled by the conspiracy theories they'd found to explain it. Their beliefs were on a spectrum, but no matter where they fell on it, they thought outsiders had been brainwashed and radical action was necessary.

Jim Berghoff, an older man with a silvery beard who'd come from Saginaw, Michigan, was reluctant to talk to CNN, but he seemed like he felt a sense of duty to speak up for what he thought was right. The people who stole the election needed to be put on trial and go to prison, he said. "This is an enemy that considers it a full-scale war," Berghoff said. "It's not possible for us to say, 'Okay, we'll talk about it once this has died down.' It's not gonna die down. It's not gonna die down. This is having your country or not having your country."

Some, like Berghoff, believed the election had been stolen, meaning the most basic element of our democracy was fake, and maybe had been fake for a long time. Others believed in QAnon. QAnon was the product of blackpilled thinking on an astonishing scale—built over time by thousands of unhappy people competing to imagine the worst possible explanation for the state of the world. The result was a conspiracy theory that held that the global elite operate a highly organized network for trafficking children, that they abused those children, and that they ate a chemical in the children's brains that made their skin look young and beautiful. It's easy to laugh at people who believe this. I did laugh when, after I cold-called a woman who'd been at January 6, she screamed at me about slang for a horrific and very specific act of child abuse. Only later, after another call, when she told me she'd been beaten so badly by a boyfriend that she had brain damage, did it occur to me to ask why so many people are willing to believe in the existence of a secret infrastructure to shield abusers from justice.

Elizabeth English had come with Majewski's group to Washington. It was her first political rally, and afterward, she swore it would be her last. She'd been so excited to meet her internet friends, but in person, something felt off. In the grass on the National Mall, she saw some men near her start walking off toward the Capitol. She thought they were trying to rile people up, and wondered if they were antifa. When I watched the videos she'd taken of them, I saw a familiar face: Milkshake, the Proud Boy I'd met in Portland.

Rendon, the man wearing a Q hoodie in a tree, said he'd hated Trump until he learned the president was fighting pedophiles. He did not think the election would be certified. "In the end, I know God wins, so truth will prevail," he said. He also said, "We're gonna storm the Capitol."

———

When Trump himself finally took the stage, he didn't deliver. The audio was terrible and the speech was bad. The president was droning about some grievance with Oprah when we decided to head back to the hotel to get more hand warmers. I was moving slowly in my room when the landline rang—the sound of an emergency. "Come down now," Sam said. "They're trying to break into the Capitol."

We raced down Pennsylvania Avenue through a thick crowd of marching Trump supporters. Once we got to the lawn in front of the Capitol, everyone was staring toward the set of stairs that led inside. I stomped over bushes to get closer.

A big man with a "Three Percenters" militia patch was telling some guys what he'd seen. His name was Barton Shively, and he'd served in the Marine Corps. I asked him to tell us what happened.

"You want to know what happened? I'll tell you what happened. We broke down the barriers, and we rushed them. We charged them." He was talking about the police. "We tried to get up the steps, they wouldn't let us up. So then they started pepper spraying and macing everybody. So what do you do? What are you gonna do when you're getting maced? You're gonna fight back, right? That's what we're doing. We're fighting back."

What's the point?

"What's the point?! We're losing our freedoms! What do you mean, 'what's the point?'!" A man shouted over his shoulder, "You not even knowing— that's the problem right there."

Shively yelled louder. "What are we supposed to do?! The Supreme Court's not helping us, no one's helping us! Only us can help us! Only we can do it!" He was beating his chest with his fist.

What are you going to do?

"Whatever we have to do! What do you think 1776 was?!" Then he turned away and walked toward the stairs, shouting. That was when I understood that the people at the Capitol wanted to claim their place in the grand narrative of American history.

The staircase was jammed with people, and barely moving. On a nearby wall beneath the Capitol's terrace, men clung by their fingertips and toes as they struggled to scale to the top and heave their bodies over the balustrade, because if they made it, it was a shortcut to the building's doors. I watched them closely. The stone wall had shallow horizontal grooves, and a lip at the top jutted out a bit, meaning they needed a final burst of strength to clear it. Too much and they'd bounce off the wall and fall backward.

A man in his thirties struggled at the lip, his arms shaking a little. In the moment, it looked like evidence of his commitment to the cause. Later it seemed like a symptom of collective madness. I wondered if I needed to scale the wall myself. Then another man shouted down that if we went around the corner we could just walk up the empty side stairs. It was a relief to leave the wall. I was afraid we'd witness some fool get paralyzed.

On the Capitol's terrace was the full spectrum of the conservative movement. As he stood near where people were climbing over the railing, a friendly white-haired man said he'd been a Republican all his life. In the corner a guy maniacally waved a green "Kekistan" flag. Some people who'd been maced by police staggered around, crying, shocked that the cops had tried to stop them. A man in a QAnon shirt screamed in my face for a solid five minutes. In a few weeks, I'd see that same screaming face in the New York tabloids after he was indicted. He worked in sanitation.

A younger guy in a knitted hat with a knitted beard attachment was chatting about what he'd seen. We asked him, too, to tell us what had happened, for history. His name was Brandon Fellows, and he said he'd been with people who'd broken into an "Oregon room." He said he'd smoked weed in a senator's office. "The cops were very cool. They were like, 'Hey guys, have a good night.' Well, some of them. It's just crazy. It's really weird. You can see that some of them are on our side." He would later be arrested. A screenshot of our interview, with his beard made of yarn, is in the federal affidavit.

I went inside the Capitol and filmed with my phone. There was a line of cops, an incessant alarm, and a man screaming at police that they'd had their backs for so long—why weren't they returning the favor? A protester told me a woman had been shot in the neck. (I found out later she was an air force veteran and QAnoner named Ashli Babbitt.) Within hours, in far right Telegram channels, they'd turned her death into a logo—a woman's face in front of the Capitol dome, a red teardrop of blood at her neck.

The cops began to clear the upper terrace with tear gas. Sam and I got ready to film what we expected next, based on what we'd seen in Portland: for the cops to start beating people and arresting them. It never happened.

As a protest ends, the crowd feels unspent energy, and they direct it at the closest enemy available. Sometimes this is us. I walked by a woman in her late fifties, her dark brown hair white at the temples and forehead. She was slim and athletic—an avid hiker maybe. She was wearing Patagonia. She asked us who we were with, and when I said CNN, her face contorted into absolute hatred, twisted and snarling.

———

At dusk, we met some colleagues at a statue in front of the Capitol. A woman with a bullhorn alerted the crowd that we were CNN. "You probably went to college," she said. "You probably got brainwashed in college. . . . You probably can't even spell traitor." We had to "repent" or we'd go to jail.

The bullhorn lady succeeded in getting a few men to circle around us. They stepped toward us, shouting. One man yelled that we should be ashamed. He had a large dark spot on his jeans. I asked, "Did you pee your pants?" He said he'd been tear-gassed, and slipped away. I was offended by his gall. How dare you piss your pants and tell *me* to be ashamed.

One year later I interviewed Keith Scott, a man from Atlanta who'd joined the Stop the Steal movement just a few days after the 2020 election and spent the next three months living out of his car and protesting the results full-time. He'd drive through the night, from Minneapolis to Phoenix to Atlanta to D.C., because he couldn't bear the thought of missing a protest—he would be missing history. On January 6, he said, he'd watched men crowd-surf to the entrance of the Capitol, and then start punching and kicking cops guarding the doors.

"Did you think, *Are we the bad guys?*"

"I thought, *How far is this gonna go? How does this end? This doesn't end well.* But again, I was *there*. I was at all these places. No matter what was happening, I wanted to experience history."

"Yeah, we did Charlottesville," Richard Spencer said. "But they did January 6!"

You might expect Spencer and Matt Parrott to have been excited that so many people were willing to try to physically stop a democratic election. But they were appalled. "The normie, or the average person—you don't want to redpill this person," as so many on the alt-right had once wanted, Spencer said. The result was not a fascist Chad autocracy, but QAnon. "You redpilled the masses, and they became, at best, delusional. At worst, they—Ashli Babbitt got shot in the neck while raiding the Capitol." Spencer told me he was no longer a white nationalist.

Parrott was shocked that Trump hadn't pardoned the people who rioted on January 6. "He pretty much was like, 'just throw 'em to the wolves,' after goading them into the single dumbest political event—hopefully—I guess I'm in competition with them—but the single dumbest political event of the twenty-first century."

He'd once written that others in the white power movement argue that "rejecting democracy isn't going to play well within our democratic political process." He didn't agree. "Both indigenous capitalists and Jewish elites are integrally anti-White, and ridding ourselves of both will require a radical departure from the mainstream. Our goals are not possible within this system." Almost a decade later, he realized he was okay with this system. He said he liked the rule of law. But now, it was part of the mainstream conservative movement that sought to delegitimize the entire electoral process with normies, and worse, he said, "I think they could win."

January 6 held up a mirror and they didn't like what they saw. The elements of fascism were there—the cult of personality around the would-be authoritarian leader, the promise to restore the nation to its former glory, the fake threat to masculinity, the desire to use violence to eliminate the threat. QAnon's numbers were many times the alt-right's. It attracted more women and more people who were fully functioning members of society. The Stop the Steal crowd did not celebrate explicit racism, but they aimed to delegitimize the votes in majority-Black cities. Its followers had taken much more radical action in pursuit of that goal, and people with real power had cheered them on. At the top was the same man the alt-right had joked was their "god-emperor." The pro-Trump movement took the alt-right's frenetic pace of internet content, a bit of swaggering misogyny, the joking-not-joking pose, and threw out its swastikas and creepy virgin loser stuff. And with that magic recipe, it attempted to stage a coup against the United States.

Spencer was offended when I suggested he'd had limited success because he'd gone full nazi. He had serious and sincere ideas, he insisted; it's just that everyone was fixated on the time he said "Heil Trump!" But that's what happens when you try to gain power in a nation by adopting its number one symbol of pure evil. A restaurant could serve a hundred exquisite dishes, but if it also serves puppy lasagna, that's what it's going to be known for.

Most Americans, whatever prejudices they might have, do not want to be Nazis. Americans beat Nazis. That fact is at the heart of the story of American greatness. It is the subject of dad books and TV series and movies from *The Sound of Music* to *Saving Private Ryan* to *They Saved Hitler's Brain*. Americans are strong and brave, Nazis are sniveling cowards. Most people want to be the hero, and that means most Americans want to be Indiana Jones, not the Nazi that he punched.

During the 2016 presidential campaign, Donald Trump said military leaders of World War II were the kind of men America needed now. "We're gonna find a general like MacArthur, and we're gonna find a general like George Patton—and we have them," Trump said that July. "We have them. They're in there someplace." It wasn't so much that he loved history as he loved the movie version of it. A few years later, at a press conference, Trump said, "When I became president, I had a meeting at the Pentagon with lots of generals. They were like from a movie—better looking than Tom Cruise, and stronger."

At a rally in Alabama in 2021, Trump played the opening monologue from the 1970 movie *Patton*. The general, dripping with medals and ribbons, stands in front of a giant American flag and delivers his famous speech: "No bastard ever won a war by dying for his country. He won it by making the other poor dumb bastard die for his country." Patton urges the soldiers to crush the Germans: "The Nazis are the enemy. Wade into them. Spill their blood. Shoot them in the belly. When you put your hand into a bunch of goo that a moment before was your best friend's face, you'll know what to do." The speech framed the war in terms familiar to any Trump fan: "Americans love a winner and will not tolerate a loser. . . . The very thought of losing is hateful to Americans."

According to reporters on the scene, Trump's crowd was unsure what to make of the *Patton* speech until he told them how to interpret it. Was it about the need to defeat fascism and defend human rights and the rule of law across the globe? No. Trump asked, "Did you like that? General Patton? I thought so. Because we're getting a little tired of the woke generals that we have. . . . Let me ask you, Do you think that General Patton was woke? I don't think so. . . . You know what woke means? It means you're a loser. Everything woke turns to shit." The crowd erupted in cheers of *USA! USA!*

Trump liked the glamour of the military. He liked the way it represented force, and the way it commanded respect. He didn't understand where that respect came from—that the military serves a shared set of principles, not a single man. In office, he tried to subvert this idea. In June 2020, Trump threatened to deploy active-duty troops to put down the protests after the murder of George Floyd. In response, Mark Milley, chairman of the Joint Chiefs of Staff, released a message to military commanders saying every member of the military swears an oath to the Constitution, which grants Americans the right to freedom of speech and peaceful assembly. At Milley's retirement ceremony three years later, he said, "We don't take an oath to a king or a queen or to a tyrant or a dictator. And we don't take an oath to a wannabe dictator . . . We take an oath to the Constitution, and we take an oath to the idea that is America, and we're willing to die to protect it." The same month, Trump posted online that Milley deserved to be executed.

If you want to convince Americans to do something different, it is hard to do it by arguing that America is bad and your idea is good. It is much easier to convince them by claiming your idea is the most American idea, and that America is not already doing it is a tragic but temporary deviation from the true American spirit. You say, *You don't have to change everything you believe to accept my idea. My idea fits right in there. My idea is so good, maybe you already thought of it.*

In November 2020, Fred Brennan moved back home with his mom in Atlantic City. I drove down a few times to see him, and we always talked about the same thing, how the internet had once been an escape from the real world, but now the real world cannot get relief from it. "2013 . . . everything has just accelerated since that time," Fred said. "The things that people did back then, nobody thought was important, because the groups were so small. Nobody cared."

I told him about reporting from protests in Portland, and how a Molotov cocktail had landed too close to me. So many people seemed so glib about violence. "That's because there's no change available within the system," Fred said. "If we can't make any changes to decrease inequality, then that inequality is going to create a revolution."

Not necessarily for the good side.

"No," he said, "of course.

"America is not exceptional. The rules of history apply to us. If you have great amounts of inequality, and you have no change available within the system, the system won't survive."

He thought there was still time to make change. The government had to regulate social media sites, and force them to release their algorithms publicly to prove they worked and were good for society.

"The very fact that our politicians are trapped by these audiences who are so Facebook- and Twitter-controlled is really scary," he said. "Online audiences have so much power. And right now those online audiences believe a few things: (a) the government is extremely corrupt and is run by evil pedophilic forces—that is a mainstream belief among Republican followers online, (b) there is no action that is too great to bring these people to justice . . . (c) what this is called in the biz is 'ending the world to save it.' That's what they believe right now: we need to end the world to save it."

Two days after the 2020 election, I watched Fox News, after Trump had claimed that Philadelphia poll workers had kicked out Republican observers, which was a lie. Sean Hannity repeated it as he introduced Senator Lindsey Graham on his prime-time show. Referring to state legislators, Hannity asked, "Should these Republican lawmakers in Pennsylvania and elsewhere, if there's corruption . . . and they don't allow observers in as the law calls for, should they then invalidate this?" Graham replied, "I think everything should be on the table."

Minutes later, Hannity repeated the lie as he introduced Senator Ted Cruz as an expert, saying, "Senator, you're one of the smartest lawyers. . . . You know election law—you're allowed to have partisan observers. They're being denied access. What is the remedy and what does that tell you, sir?" Cruz repeated the lie: "What we've been seeing the last three days is outrageous. It is partisan, it is political, and it is lawless. We're seeing this pattern in Democratic city after Democratic city, with the worst in the country right now is Philadelphia, Pennsylvania.

"I am angry, and I think the American people are angry," Cruz said. "Because, by throwing the observers out, by clouding the vote counting in a shroud of darkness, they are setting the stage to potentially steal an election—not just from the president, but from the over sixty million people that voted for him." That was when I knew a coup was coming.

I furiously texted some friends, but they didn't share my concern, or they'd reply "that's not funny," as if I were joking. Scrolling through Twitter, I saw an ad for a mental health hotline. Here was someone ethically obligated to listen to me. I texted "EMPATHY" to the number listed.

CRISIS TEXT LINE: Hi, this is Crisis Text Line. You're not alone. . . . What's your crisis?

ER: Is Trump staging a coup

CRISIS TEXT LINE: Hi there. I'm Sharita. Thank you for reaching out. . . . It sounds like you're feeling vulnerable and overwhelmed by Trump's political tactics.

It's understandable to be concerned by the unprecedented uncertainty we're facing. It was brave of you to recognize that you felt vulnerable and reach out.

ER: There are literally armed men trying to stop votes from being counted

I don't know if it's a question of feelings at the moment. We're talking basically paramilitaries and no one's doing anything

CRISIS TEXT LINE: Sometimes when we're surrounded by darkness, we can only focus on 1 good thing, 1 day at a time. . . .

ER: I think we need to think more than 1 day at a time

CRISIS TEXT LINE: With all the uncertainty and vulnerability you're facing, I'd like to check in on your safety.

Are you presently having thoughts of ending your life?

ER: No

CRISIS TEXT LINE: It's understandable to feel that way and I'm here to support you. Tell me more about your perspective and how you prefer to think of things.

ER: I'm disappointed in my fellow man

Crisis Text Line Sharita, if you're out there, I feel like we shared a historic moment. And was I right or was I right?

EPILOGUE

"I clearly made a grave error that I am morally accountable for," Matt Parrott told me in the spring of 2023. We were talking over the phone, so he could not see the shock on my face. It was the kind of statement that is often demanded but rarely heard in real life.

Parrott said that he'd had a long time to reflect on what he'd done. He should have known what Charlottesville was going to be. All the clues were there, but he'd ignored them. He'd made common cause with people who wanted to hurt others, because he was ambitious, and he thought it was the only way he could be relevant.

It was not just one error, but many. "The more distance and perspective I get from it, the more I see that this culture—this scene—is really fucked up and evil. And we were helping it and contributing to it," Parrott said. "We were too in the middle of it . . . to realize just how cartoon-villain evil it was."

There was still one question for which he had no answer: How could it have been different? If he could travel back in time and deliver a warning to his former self, it still would not alter the course of history. "My advice for me is advice I utterly would not have taken: this is going to be a dark historical period for America that you don't want to be right in the middle of."

Parrott was living in Indiana, in the same town where he grew up, with his three kids and his fourth wife. It was ten years since he'd met Matt Heimbach, who was now living far away with his own two children. A few weeks earlier they'd gotten on the phone to gossip about the movement, and Heimbach reflected, "We really did get mixed up with the most despicable evil stupid motherfuckers in America." Parrott agreed, but it was worse: "We did, bro. We followed those guys into battle."

Heimbach had found another job, though he knew that eventually someone would recognize him and he'd be fired again. He'd accepted that the decisions he'd made at nineteen meant he might be stuck in this cycle for the rest of his life. It required some finesse in his personal life, he said. "I have to begin every first date with 'By the way, you should know . . .' Do you know how not sexy that is? To be like, 'You should read my Wikipedia page before our second date'?"

Heimbach was not as frank as Parrott about what he'd done wrong. He said he wouldn't protest in support of a Confederate monument again. He was no longer a fascist, but a Marxist. It had been harder for him to let go of his drive to want to be the guy, a leader of some movement. He'd tried for a while to lead a small group of guys in "national Bolshevism," and showed up with other fringe characters at a pro-Russia rally in Washington, D.C., in 2023. But, he told me, he'd finally given up on politics, and quit running a Telegram channel.

"People can think I'm an asshole, and they can think I was wrong, and I was wrong about some things," Heimbach said. But "all these big-brain jack-asses who spend their time talking about alienated youth that are susceptible to grooming by the far-right or by ISIS or by who-the-fuck-ever—they don't really talk about how to not have alienated youth." The cycle of destructive dissident movements would keep repeating, he said, until we do something about inequality and alienation.

Heimbach said his two sons were "the most deradicalizing force in my entire life." He couldn't take the same risks he had as a single man. If he was broke and couch surfing, that meant his kids were, too. He didn't want to lose them. But he still had a bond with Parrott, saying, "he's the best friend I've ever had."

———

In 2022, Richard Spencer told me he was no longer a white nationalist. "I care about civilization more than race," he said. He hadn't quit trying to be a public figure, tweeting his commentary on politics and old far-right rivals.

The most attention he'd gotten in years came with the revelation that he'd listed his political affiliation as "moderate" in his profile on Bumble, a dating app whose best-known rule is that women speak first.

Spencer would take only limited accountability for his starring role in the "Summer of Hate." He'd said during the Charlottesville trial that he'd been "slumming it" by hanging out with the alt-right. He'd later told me that in 2016 and 2017, he was the most racist he'd ever been, and that he'd felt pressure to be the most far-right guy in the room.

But at his core, he was who he was. Spencer told me he liked Christian nationalism, because he thought associating the religion with the mania of QAnon would help destroy it. "I hate Christianity, okay?" Spencer said. "I hate Jesus Christ. I would have fucking oppressed that hell out of—I know that I come from Roman blood, the kind of people who would fucking crucify him, who would go in and knock down your stupid fucking temple—that's who I fucking *am*, Elle," he said. "In case there's any ambiguity about the type of person I am, *that* is the type of person I am."

Spencer still wanted to be the guy, but he was thinking bigger than politics. He'd turned his energy to building a cult of Apollo. He thought his new religion would eventually take down Christianity, and with it, its slave morality, as Nietzsche called it, which held that humility and obedience were good and power and wealth were bad. Spencer's Apollonian cult would value strength, beauty, and intellect.

"Everyone's like, *Oh, we need more democracy,* or *We need more rights*—it's like, what are you fucking talking about?" he said. "We've had more democracy and liberalism and all this Christian Semitic stuff—we have more of that than we've ever had. How many Abrahamics are there on the planet at the moment, five billion? . . . We've tried the shit, sister." He wanted humanity to make a covenant with a better god, like Zeus. But of the race stuff, Spencer said, "You have to move past it."

———

When he got out of prison in late 2022, Chris Cantwell was ready to get back in the game. He'd been incarcerated in a communications management unit at the federal prison in Marion, Indiana, where inmates faced strict limits on their ability to talk to the outside world.

On a podcast, Cantwell said his prison buddy had been Viktor Bout, the Russian arms dealer depicted in the movie *Lord of War*, whom the United States sent back to Russia in exchange for American basketball player Brittney Griner. Bout was just the nicest guy in the world, Cantwell said, and they'd watch Tucker Carlson with the Muslim inmates, who he believed had been incarcerated on terrorism-related charges (it was considered impolite to ask).

In prison, he couldn't go online, but maybe that was good for him. "When you're inundated with a certain variety of propaganda, it causes you to focus on that monomaniacally," Cantwell said. "That's not necessarily entirely productive or healthy." He indicated he was going to dial back the racism.

Bout had helped Cantwell understand what Russia had done to roll back gay rights. Going forward, Cantwell said his focus would be trying to stop Democrats from destroying the country and "getting us into World War III over transgenderism."

He wasn't mad at Trump for not pardoning the January 6 rioters. "If you start attacking police officers, then you better make sure that your coup is successful, because you're going to jail later if you don't," Cantwell said. But the attempted coup presented an opportunity. There were people with proximity to power who were sympathetic to the January 6 defendants. That might make powerful people more sympathetic to other politically persecuted people, which Cantwell considered himself to be. "It's dangerous for us to try to break out of the system, so to speak, okay? The goal was to become the system, okay? We want to wield the tremendous power of the United States government."

So it's been a mixed bag, in terms of lessons learned. Lessons were learned by all, but they were not all good lessons.

———

The consequences for January 6 were the inverse of those for Charlottesville. The white nationalists faced near total condemnation, but few were criminally prosecuted. For those responsible for January 6, the social consequences have been mixed, but the law enforcement response has been robust. More than one thousand people were charged with federal crimes related to the riot. Among them were a few of my sources: Milkshake, the large Proud Boy who'd once told me he carried a little aluminum bat for self-defense, was the first to breach the police line at the Capitol. He pleaded guilty to obstruction of an official proceeding and assaulting an officer, and was sentenced to five years in prison. Barton Shively, who screamed at me about 1776, pleaded guilty to two counts of assaulting, resisting, or impeding law enforcement officers, and was sentenced to eighteen months in prison. The guy with the yarn beard, Brandon Fellows, was convicted of felony obstruction of an official proceeding, felony entering and remaining in a restricted building, plus three misdemeanors. Four Proud Boys leaders were convicted of seditious conspiracy and given long prison sentences. Enrique Tarrio, who'd told me they only committed violence in self-defense, was sentenced to twenty-two years in prison. It was the longest prison sentence related to January 6 and the longest one for anyone I've ever interviewed.

On January 6, Speaker of the House Kevin McCarthy said of the riot, "This is so un-American. . . . Anyone involved in this, if you're hearing me, hear me loud and clear: This is not the American way. This is not protected by the First Amendment." The next year, McCarthy stood next to J. R. Majewski, who'd turned his Stop the Steal fame into a run for Congress as a Republican in Ohio. (Majewski said he never went inside the Capitol.) A couple of months before the 2022 election, House Republicans withdrew support for Majewski, not because of the failed coup but following reports he'd embellished his military record. He lost.

Former President Donald Trump was kicked off Twitter and denounced by Republican officials, only to later be let back on, embraced by those who'd rebuked him, and supported by nearly half of American voters, even as he faced state and federal indictments related to his actions around January 6. So what will matter more? The fuzzy unmeasurable mix of liberal scorn and praise from careerist sycophants who know that what they're doing is wrong but their ambition tells them to do it anyway, or the cold black-and-white documents alleging how he broke the law? The American criminal justice system, which came under so much intense and deserved scrutiny in the summer of 2020, is now what many are counting on to stop a slide into fascism. In professional wrestling, this is what's called a face turn.

"We certainly live in a very fucked up country," Fred Brennan said. Of all my sources, Fred had learned the most, and done the most with what he'd learned. He had become a source of wisdom for me, and we shared a deep mutual respect. We watched the Super Bowl together in a casino in Atlantic City.

He'd been tracking the backlash against gay rights as it spread across the country. 4chan and 8chan had been fixated on transgender people, and now some of those same ideas had spread to the mainstream Republican Party.

"In retrospect, America's democracy has never been the strongest in the world. That's a lie that Americans are taught," he said. "There's that, which kind of helps temper expectations." How long had the U.S. actually been democratic anyway? Since women got the right to vote in 1920? Even then, Black people didn't really have the right to vote. "Most likely this country won't be as democratic as it was before in the next century. But that will just be going back to the mean."

There were some signs for hope, he said. For one thing, 4chan had turned against Trump. The most damaging moment from the January 6 congressional hearings was when former White House aide Cassidy Hutchinson testified she was told that Trump had been riding in the presidential limo and demanded to be driven to the Capitol. When the Secret Service agent driving him refused, Trump grabbed the steering wheel, saying he was the fucking president. The agent grabbed Trump's arm and told him they were not going to the Capitol.

In the eyes of 4chan, Fred said, if Trump couldn't control his own Secret Service detail, who could he control? "They view him as an ineffective puss," Fred said, "who was unable to do what mattered when it mattered." In a culture built on an incel's view of the world, Trump looked, to them, like the worst thing he could possibly be: impotent.

On the other side, Fred said, the people who opposed fascism had learned some lessons, too. "Everybody understands how the internet works now," he

said. "The basic tactics that were used in the past by the alt-right no longer
have any power at all. And so that gives me a lot of hope.

"The smart ones started to realize that the things that the alt-right were
doing were actually highly sophisticated and required a lot of intelligence to
pull off, and they stopped underestimating their opponents. We all need to
stop doing that," he said. "Some of the smartest people have believed in crazy
things."

The first time I met Fred in Manila, he told me how he'd come to believe
in God. "I just really needed a new meaning in my life, and a new way to look
at things, so I decided, *You know what? I can believe that Jesus rose from the dead.*
Like, I can just believe that. I can just try it out. I can just say that it happened."

I'd returned to that moment many times, not just the words, but the cadence of Fred's voice when he said them. I could feel it when he said it, what
it was like to be so tired, defeated, having carried an anchor around your neck
till you were half-dead in a ditch, and then deciding to just let go of it and walk
away.

I've noticed many people have a bias toward thinking the worst is over.
After a public catastrophe, like Charlottesville and January 6, they want to see
the bad guys punished, and then they want to move on. But the forces that led
to those events are still out there.

The alt-right is essentially dead. There are a few groups still operating,
a few podcasts still going, and they tend to put more emphasis on masculinity and anti-feminism than racism—some post training videos of their
men getting swole. But the culture of 4chan has seeped into the mainstream,
and some memes and fixations have infiltrated the conservative movement,
even if the people who express them might have never been on 4chan. The
anonymity of imageboards, Fred thought, was important to trolls but not to
conservative activists. Those activists were happy to post their provocations
under their real names on Twitter.

Here are some moments when I've noticed this blackpilled internet culture materialize in real life: A few in the Silicon Valley elite have been talking on
tech podcasts about Nietzsche and slave morality, or arguing that democracy
is a failure. Some conservative writers have elevated the concept of Caesar-

ism, that an autocrat should seize power and force the change that Americans want but can't achieve through democracy. A Republican Senate candidate in 2022 praised the Unabomber manifesto. The first time I saw a photo of a "drag queen story hour" was when a fascist troll sent it to me in 2017; in 2022 it became the obsession of the conservative movement, and in 2023, some five hundred bills targeting gay rights were considered in state legislatures across the country, according to the ACLU. Educated, upper-middle-class people have told me that "they" are cutting off eight-year-old boys' penises in gender confirmation surgery, and these people seem immune to my explaining that no medical guidelines recommend such surgery for young children. The Ron DeSantis presidential campaign shared a video showing the candidate as a Chad who was an enemy of trans people's rights; it included an incel meme.

In a congressional hearing about diversity in military academies in 2023, Republican congressman Matt Gaetz asked Lieutenant General Richard Clark, superintendent of the United States Air Force Academy, about the school's statement that "a diverse and inclusive force is a warfighting imperative." "Were the Mongols diverse?" Gaetz asked, raising his already pointy eyebrows. "Were the Vikings diverse?" Clark did not take the bait, and simply said he was building a fighting force from the nation's population, which was the most diverse in the world. Gaetz went on to grill him about a scholarship open to a variety of gender identities. The exchange came just six years after I had listened to a racist podcaster ridicule the idea that "diversity is our strength."

Alt-right trolls provoked "social justice warriors," while mainstream Republicans complain about "wokeness," but the script is nearly the same—that an irrational, emotional contingent of young people see bigotry when it's not there. The difference is Republicans generally argue America is good and mostly equal, while the alt-right claimed America was bad because it was not unequal enough.

Alt-right types occasionally try to infiltrate mainstream conservative events. At a Turning Point conference in West Palm Beach where Trump spoke to seven thousand cheering supporters, a young man asked to take a picture with me, and as he raised his phone to open his camera, I saw there were swastikas on his lock screen. Attendees had been invited to write their thoughts on the presidential candidates on Post-it Notes and stick them to cardboard cutouts of their heads. On the poster of Vivek Ramaswamy, nestled among notes saying "hero" and "brilliant" and "daddy" was one that said "1488" and another that had a Star of David crossed out with the word "Soon" underneath. Ramaswamy had frequently asserted that young people were obsessed with a secular religion of social justice and racial identity, and that it was a symptom of a cultural cancer. At a Ramaswamy happy hour afterward, another young man saw our crew's cameras, and, as many do, approached us with some questions. But instead of asking about the big bad liberal media, he asked what my ethnicity was. I stared at him for a second, and he said, "You look Celtic-Germanic." Then he turned to Sam and asked, "What are you?"

I do not like being ambushed by edgelords. But what is more disturbing is seeing their concepts penetrate the minds of normal people. I met a woman who lived outside L.A. and was a lifelong liberal until her kids' school being closed for Covid made her a supporter of Ron DeSantis. She'd been baffled when people on Twitter called her "alt-right" for advocating for open schools, and asked me what the alt-right was, and whether it really existed. She listened with genuine interest as I explained the last ten years of dark internet history. In the same conversation, she called herself blackpilled.

The question I asked myself as hundreds of tiki torches lit up in Charlottesville is still a question now: Are they going to win? I don't know. I don't believe that events are entirely dictated by sweeping economic trends beyond our control. It matters who decides to act. Employees of social media companies have to decide how much of their work they want to hand over to people who want to subvert democracy. Republicans who abhor racism have to decide whether they're willing to take personal responsibility to kick fascist infiltrators out of their party. Liberals have to decide whether they're willing to do anything to make the change they want to see in the world besides post about it online.

The people who stood up to the nazis in Charlottesville were students, activists, a trans woman—the very people disparaged by elite opinion as fragile, sensitive babies. Those were the brave people who faced down the torch march in Charlottesville. Not everyone has the strength to be the one to stand up for what's right. But if you don't have it in you, show some respect for the people who do.

On January 6, when I asked even the angriest people to tell me what had happened, "for history," their posture softened, and they told me everything. The reason it worked so well is that they understood immediately what I meant. They believed they were not just watching history but shaping it, taking their place in it. You can call it arrogance, or hubris, or cringe, but they pulled it off. They did shape history—for the worse.

Even in their blackpilled rage, the people I've reported on saw an opening in the fabric of history, and they dove into it to make the world they wanted. If you want to live in a very different world than they do, you have to throw yourself into history to stop them.

When I was fifteen, my family was driving on a nearly empty highway on a sunny winter day, and in front of us was a commercial truck with an open bed carrying grain or gravel, something with little pieces. Driving down a straight stretch of the road, the truck's load shifted, and it started fishtailing, its back half lurching left and right in wider and wider swings until the driver lost control. The truck spun 180 degrees and flipped, so it was now skidding backward down the highway, facing us and upside down. As it slid to a stop, my dad pulled our station wagon over and rolled down the window. "Hey, man, you okay?" The driver shouted back, "I can't turn it off!" A clear liquid was spilling out of the belly of the truck, past the driver's window, and onto the ground. My dad turned to me, sitting behind him on the back seat, and said, "That's gas. Elle, drive the car up a hundred yards in case it explodes." Then he opened the door and got out of the car.

I climbed into the front seat, put the car in drive, and as we rolled forward on the shoulder of the highway, burst into tears. Sobbing, I grabbed my dad's cell phone and called 911, and then my mom, brother, and I sat in silence while we waited. When my dad reappeared at driver's side door, he was happy. "I got the truck turned off!" he said. He'd pulled the guy out, and he was okay. Now we had to get going, he said, or we'd get stuck in the traffic.

Many of my sources, at the peak of their blackpilled fever, would have said my dad showed the masculine strength and courage that has been erased from society by feminism, liberalism, modernism, or whatever they want to blame for their problems. Of course I saw my dad as a hero. He was also a middle-aged man with a wife and two kids, a job and a mortgage. And when the moment called for him to act, he did.

ACKNOWLEDGMENTS

This book is the product of a decade of conversations with dozens of people. To everyone who took the time to speak with me, often for hours at a time: thank you. Thanks to the people who spoke despite fearing violent backlash, and those who could only speak anonymously. Thank you for being willing to take the risk of talking about such controversial subjects and disturbing events.

To my agent, Melissa Flashman: thank you for shaping this idea into something real, and for holding my hand through all the pain and suffering.

To my editor, Amar Deol: thank you for taking a giant pile of words and shaping it into something people could read.

To my colleagues from Vice—Josh Davis, Tracy Jarrett, Orlando de Guzman, Zach Caldwell, Joe LoCascio—thank you for going with me to Charlottesville. It was hard for us but important for the world.

To my colleagues from CNN, Sam Guff and Deb Brunswick, thank you for revealing the power of the all-girl crew.

To my friends: thank you for listening to me while I lay on the ground and stared at the ceiling.

To Mom: Thank you for teaching me the value of making a dossier in middle school and to not fear confrontation. And to my dad, who died when I was a teenager, thank you for teaching me to stand up for what's right.

To Jeremy: Thank you for reading, editing, advising, and making elixirs. Thanks for staying sane when it got crazy. Thank you for keeping me alive.

To Craig (my dog): Thank you for being so smart and cute.

A NOTE ON SOURCES

This book is based on countless hours of interviews from 2013 to 2023, as well as contemporaneous emails, text messages, social media posts, police reports, plane tickets, receipts, etc. Some of the internal communications between Unite the Right organizers were revealed as evidence in the federal civil lawsuit *Sines v. Kessler* in 2021. Facts reported by other news media are noted. Some names have been changed, including Anna and Lisa, in some cases to protect those who feared violence from the people they used to know.

———

I have reproduced the hateful comments of the people I interviewed only where necessary and to remove any doubt that terms such as white supremacist, misogynist, and fascist are accurate.

NOTES

AUTHOR'S NOTE

ix *It started when our neighbor built a fence:* My mom and I told part of this story on *This American Life* under pseudonyms at the suggestion of the show in 2006. My mom would have been happy to use her real name, birthday, photo ID, etc. *This American Life,* "With Great Power," October 6, 2006.

PROLOGUE: SURF THE KALI YUGA

2 *Pepe . . . on a hacked billboard in the UK:* BBC News: "Cardiff Billboard Offensive Images Display after Hack," August 2, 2017. https://www.bbc.com/news/uk -wales-south-east-wales-40802887

2 *in an official Russian embassy tweet:* Zack Beauchamp, "The Russian Government Just Tweeted an Image of a White Supremacist Frog," Vox, January 9, 2017. https://www.vox.com/world/2017/1/9/14212496/russia-embassy-pepe

2 *Anti-Defamation League's list of hate symbols:* "ADL Adds 'Pepe the Frog' Meme, Used by Anti-Semites and Racists, to Online Hate Symbols Database | ADL," September 27, 2016. https://www.adl.org/resources/press-release/adl-adds -pepe-frog-meme-used-anti-semites-and-racists-online-hate-symbols.

2 *He had been killed by his creator and reanimated:* Matthew Gault, "Rare Pepe NFT Is Not Rare Enough, $500K Lawsuit Alleges," Vice, March 25, 2022. https:// www.vice.com/en/article/dypj37/rare-pepe-nft-is-not-rare-enough-dollar500k -lawsuit-alleges

4 *Joe Rogan, one of the world's:* Joe Rogan, "We Are in Kali Yuga. The Age of Conflict. All of the Chaos We're Seeing Right Now Was Predicted in Hinduism Thousands of Years Ago. Civilizations Move in Predictable Cycles, and We Are in the Lower Left Hand Square of the Chart. Do Your Best to Elevate Yourself and the World around You from the Madness That Is in the Air, but Understand That This Insan-

ity Is All a Part of an Infinite Process," Instagram, November 27, 2021. https://
www.instagram.com/p/CWxaIYWFvfH/

CHAPTER 1: THE WIZARD

9 *"There are known knowns":* Errol Morris, "The Certainty of Donald Rumsfeld
    (Part 1)," *New York Times,* March 25, 2014. https://archive.nytimes.com/opinion
    ator.blogs.nytimes.com/2014/03/25/the-certainty-of-donald-rumsfeld-part-1/
9 *Then I send them a YouTube clip:* "Slavoj Žižek on Donald Rumsfeld (Unknown
    Knowns)," YouTube, 2016. https://www.youtube.com/watch?v=ql80Klk4pSU
20 *It was before Elliot Rodger posted:* Elliot Rodger, "My Twisted World: The Story of
    Elliot Rodger," 2014.

CHAPTER 2: NO COUNTRY FOR OLD RACISTS

35 *However, when the story was published:* Aram Roston and Joel Anderson, "This Man
    Used His Inherited Fortune To Fund The Racist Right," *BuzzFeed News,* July 23,
    2017, https://www.buzzfeednews.com/article/aramroston/hes-spent-almost
    -20-years-funding-the-racist-right-it
35 *Damigo had spent four years in prison:* Shane Bauer, "I Met the White Nationalist
    Who 'Falcon Punched' a 95-Pound Female Protester," *Mother Jones,* May 9, 2017,
    https://www.motherjones.com/politics/2017/05/nathan-damigo-punching
    -woman-berkeley-white-nationalism/; Hiuu Tran Phan, "White Supremacist
    Who Punched Woman in Berkeley Has Military, Criminal Ties to San Diego
    County," *San Diego Union-Tribune,* April 18, 2017, https://www.sandiegounion
    tribune.com/military/sd-me-nathan-damigo-20170417-story.html.
36 *She said under oath that Kline: Sines v. Kessler,* No. 3:17-cv-0072-NKM (United
    States District Court for the Western District of Virginia 2021).
37 *The distance between my pupils:* Julia E. Morris et al., "2012 Anthropometric Survey
    of U.S. Army Personnel: Methods and Summary Statistics," U.S. Army Natick
    Soldier RD&E Center, December 2014. https://dacowits.defense.gov/LinkClick
    .aspx?fileticket=EbsKcm6A10U%3D&portalid=48
42 *In the nineties, he met Buford Furrow:* Rene Sanchez, "L.A. Shooting Suspect Faces
    State, U.S. Charges," *Washington Post,* August 13, 1999. https://www.washington
    post.com/wp-srv/national/longterm/hatecrimes/stories/furrow081399.htm
42 *Schoep had been good friends with Jeff Hall:* Jesse McKinley, "Jeff Hall, a Neo-Nazi, Is
    Killed, and His Young Son Is Charged," *New York Times,* May 10, 2011. https://
    www.nytimes.com/2011/05/11/us/11nazi.html
43 *The next year, he talked to J. T. Ready:* "Arizona Militia Leader and Candidate for Sheriff

Killed Family During 911 Call," ABC News, May 3, 2012. https://abcnews.go.com/US/arizona-neo-nazi-sheriff-candidate-killed-family/story?id=16269803

43 *They'd waved swastika flags at a demonstration:* "Planned Neo-Nazi March Sparks Violence," CNN, October 15, 2005. https://www.cnn.com/2005/US/10/15/nazi.march/

CHAPTER 3: "ACCORDING TO FEDERAL COURT DOCUMENTS, I'M HIS BEST FRIEND"

47 *The products of obsessive and meticulous internet research:* Christie Welch et al., "Understanding the Use of the Term 'Weaponized Autism' in An Alt-Right Social Media Platform," *Journal of Autism and Developmental Disorders* 53, no. 10 (October 2023): 4035–46. https://doi.org/10.1007/s10803-022-05701-0

48 *Autism does not make someone more likely to commit violent crime:* Ragini Heeramun et al., "Autism and Convictions for Violent Crimes: Population-Based Cohort Study in Sweden," *Journal of the American Academy of Child and Adolescent Psychiatry* 56, no. 6 (June 2017): 491-497.e2. https://doi.org/10.1016/j.jaac.2017.03.011

48 *His defense team had hired Dr. Rachel Loftin:* Kevin Sack, "Court Files Raise Question: Was Dylann Roof Competent to Defend Himself?" *New York Times,* May 31, 2017. https://www.nytimes.com/2017/05/31/us/church-shooting-roof-charleston-hate-crime-.html

48 *Roof was isolated:* Rachel Loftin, "Psychological Evaluation of: Dylann Roof," December 29, 2016. https://www.nytimes.com/interactive/2017/05/31/us/document-Report-by-Loftin.html; United States v. Dylann Roof, 2016.

53 *What he found was the controversy:* Richard J. Herrnstein and Charles Murray, *The Bell Curve: Intelligence and Class Structure in American Life* (Free Press, 1996).

54 *The authors claim:* Evans, Gavin. "The Unwelcome Revival of 'Race Science.'" *The Guardian,* March 2, 2018. https://www.theguardian.com/news/2018/mar/02/the-unwelcome-revival-of-race-science.

54 *What is telling:* Yglesias, Matthew. "The Bell Curve Isn't about Science, It's about Policy. And It's Wrong." Vox, April 10, 2018. https://www.vox.com/2018/4/10/17182692/bell-curve-charles-murray-policy-wrong.

58 *At Towson University:* Joe Heim, "This White Nationalist Who Shoved a Trump Protester May Be the Next David Duke," *Washington Post,* April 12, 2016. https://www.washingtonpost.com/local/this-white-nationalist-who-shoved-a-trump-protester-may-be-the-next-david-duke/2016/04/12/7e71f750-f2cf-11e5-89c3-a647fcce95e0_story.html

58 *He led night patrols:* Carrie Wells, "Towson White Student Union to Patrol Campus

Looking for Crime," *Baltimore Sun,* March 25, 2013. https://www.baltimoresun
.com/maryland/baltimore-county/bs-xpm-2013-03-25-bs-md-towson-white
-student-union-20130325-story.html

59 *Who'd advocated for "exterminationism toward the Jews":* Buchanan, Susy. "Show-
down in Shelbyville: How Old School White Nationalists Failed to Deliver in
Tennessee." Southern Poverty Law Center, October 31, 2017. https://www
.splcenter.org/hatewatch/2017/10/31/showdown-shelbyville-how-old-school
-white-nationalists-failed-deliver-tennessee.

59 *He lives in Orlando, and reviews: BRUTALLY HONEST REVIEW OF GENIE PLUS
AT DISNEY WORLD,* YouTube, October 21, 2021. https://www.youtube.com
/watch?v=rURWbbPT9vg

CHAPTER 4: THE CONNIE SITUATION

61 *A friend wrote of her unbelievable frailty:* Ed Brayton, "A Sincere Plea for Help,"
February 8, 2007. https://www.patheos.com/blogs/dispatches/2007/02/08/a
-sincere-plea-for-help/

63 *In 2007, Connie got a website:* Connie Parrott, "Introduction: My Situation," February 28, 2007. https://web.archive.org/web/20070703185146/http://helpconnie
.blogspot.com/

63 *He went public as a white nationalist:* Matt Parrott, "Link Yourself to White Nationalism," Counter-Currents, August 13, 2013. https://counter-currents
.com/2013/08/link-yourself-to-white-nationalism

64 *Eventually, he wrote a manifesto:* Matt Parrott, "Hoosier Nation," 2009.

66 *One of those leading researchers:* Gareth Williams, "What Goes Around, Comes
Around," *The Lancet* 379, no. 9833 (June 16, 2012): 2235–36. https://doi
.org/10.1016/S0140-6736(12)60969-6

66 *Another brittle diabetes researcher:* Robert Tattersall, "Brittle Diabetes," Diabetes
on the Net, September 12, 2011, https://diabetesonthenet.com/diabetes-digest
/brittle-diabetes/; C. J. Garrett et al., "Recurrent Diabetic Ketoacidosis and a
Brief History of Brittle Diabetes Research: Contemporary and Past Evidence in
Diabetic Ketoacidosis Research Including Mortality, Mental Health and Preven-
tion," *Diabetic Medicine: A Journal of the British Diabetic Association* 36, no. 11
(November 2019): 1329–35, https://doi.org/10.1111/dme.14109; G. V. Gill,
"The Spectrum of Brittle Diabetes," *Journal of the Royal Society of Medicine* 85,
no. 5 (May 1992): 259–61.

66 *A factitious illness is:* Cheryl B. McCullumsmith and Charles V. Ford, "Simulated
Illness: The Factitious Disorders and Malingering," *Psychiatric Clinics* 34, no. 3

(September 1, 2011): 621–41, https://doi.org/10.1016/j.psc.2011.05.013; Gregory P. Yates and Marc D. Feldman. "Factitious Disorder: A Systematic Review of 455 Cases in the Professional Literature," *General Hospital Psychiatry* 41 (July 1, 2016): 20–28, https://doi.org/10.1016/j.genhosppsych.2016.05.002; Constanze Hausteiner-Wiehle and Sven Hungerer, "Factitious Disorders in Everyday Clinical Practice," *Deutsches Ärzteblatt International* 117, no. 26 (June 2020): 452–59, https://doi.org/10.3238/arztebl.2020.0452.

68 *Parrott wrote approvingly:* Matt Parrott, "Oratorical Terrorism: How Scott Terry Ruined CPAC," Counter-Currents, March 18, 2013. https://counter-currents .com/2013/03/oratorical-terrorism-how-scott-terry-ruined-cpac

69 *They floated more extreme action:* "American Renaissance Speakers Call for White Homeland," Southern Poverty Law Center, April 7, 2013. https://www.splcenter .org/hatewatch/2013/04/07/american-renaissance-speakers-call-white-homeland

71 *With a nod to his roots:* Matthew Heimbach, "Economic Suicide," Traditionalist Youth Network, June 11, 2013. https://web.archive.org/web/20130623073426 /http://www.tradyouth.org/2013/06/economic-suicide/

71 *"For decades our movement":* Matthew Heimbach, "The Death of White America: The Five Stages of Grief," Traditionalist Youth Network," June 14, 2013. https:// web.archive.org/web/20130614052710/http://www.tradyouth.org/2013/06 /the-death-of-rural-america-the-five-stages-of-grief/

71 *"I'm more welcome":* Matt Parrott "Never Leave a Fallen Comrade." Counter-Currents, April 22, 2013. https://counter-currents.com/2013/04/never-leave-a -fallen-comrade

72 *"In hindsight," he wrote:* Matt Parrott, "Terre Haute Victory Lap," Traditionalist Youth Network, October 12, 2013. https://web.archive.org/web/20131016162255/ http://www.tradyouth.org/2013/10/terre-haute-victory-lap/

73 *"The modern Western male":* Matt Parrott, "Lawrence of Suburbia: Coping with White Pathology," Counter-Currents, October 19, 2012. https://counter-currents .com/2012/10/lawrence-of-suburbiacoping-with-white-pathology

73 *In 2022, he posted a statement:* Evan McLaren, "A Statement from Evan McLaren," *Evan McLaren* Substack newsletter, April 28, 2022. https://evanramseymclaren .substack.com/p/a-statement-from-evan-mclaren

74 *By 2014, the CDC was warning:* "Opioid Painkiller Prescribing," CDC Vital Signs, July 2014. https://www.cdc.gov/vitalsigns/pdf/2014-07-vitalsigns.pdf

76 *Five years later, Brayton died:* Ed Brayton, "Saying Goodbye for the Last Time," *Dispatches from the Culture Wars*, August 10, 2020. https://www.patheos.com/blogs /dispatches/2020/08/10/saying-goodbye-for-the-last-time/

CHAPTER 5: SMART PEOPLE

79 *They found it to be very effective:* "Discord Leaks," *Unicorn Riot,* 2017.

CHAPTER 6: THE USEFUL IDIOT

84 *Any early video: Why Didn't You Just Leave (the Narcissist, Pychopath):* The Trauma Bond, YouTube, November 21, 2019. https://www.youtube.com/watch?v=PK10Sbtarlw.

84 *Nina Kouprianova was a child:* Nina Kouprianova, "If You're So Smart, Then Why Are You So Poor? Russia's 1990s Revisited," *Nina Byzantina,* November 19, 2015. https://ninabyzantina.com/2015/11/19/if-youre-so-smart-then-why-are-you-so -poor-russias-1990s-revisited/

84 *Kouprianova was twelve:* Diana Bruk, "Interview: Nina Kouprianova, Wife of Alt-Right Leader Richard Spencer | Observer," *Observer,* September 19, 2017. https://observer.com/2017/09/interview-nina-kouprianova-wife-of-alt-right -leader-richard-spencer/

86 *She was referring to a profile:* Lauren M. Fox, "The Hatemonger Next Door," *Salon,* September 29, 2013. https://web.archive.org/web/20131003002921/http:// www.salon.com/2013/09/29/the_hatemonger_next_door/singleton/?

88 *Afterward, Spencer and Scheunemann said:* James Kirchick, "A Racist's Crazy Ski Resort Smackdown," *Daily Beast,* October 18, 2014. https://www.thedailybeast .com/a-racists-crazy-ski-resort-smackdown

89 *In 1912, an American psychologist:* Henry Herbert Goddard, *The Kallikak Family: A Study in the Heredity of Feeble-Mindedness* (Macmillan, 1912).

89 *President Theodore Roosevelt had warned:* "Better Babies or More Babies?: Theodore Roosevelt, Margaret Sanger, and the Birth Control Movement," Theodore Roosevelt Center at Dickinson State University, July 16, 2015. https://www.theodore rooseveltcenter.org/Blog/Item/Sanger

89 *In 1927, the Supreme Court ruled: Buck v. Bell,* 1927.

92 *Despite their efforts:* Larry Keller, "Prominent Racists Attend Inaugural H.L. Mencken Club Gathering," Southern Poverty Law Center, November 26, 2008. https://www.splcenter.org/hatewatch/2008/11/26/prominent-racists-attend -inaugural-hl-mencken-club-gathering

92 *Four years later, Derbyshire:* Daniel Foster, "A Very Long Post About John Der-byshire," *National Review,* April 10, 2012. https://www.nationalreview.com/cor ner/very-long-post-about-john-derbyshire-daniel-foster/

94 *In 2011, the honoree was:* "Kistler Prize 2011 Recipient: Charles Murray," Founda-tion for the Future, 2011. https://www.futurefoundation.org/awards/kpr_2011 _murray.html

100 *The next day, the same Jobbik:* Margit Feher, "Hungary Bans Conference by U.S. Group It Calls 'Racist,' " *Wall Street Journal,* September 29, 2014. https://www.wsj.com /articles/hungary-bans-conference-by-u-s-group-it-calls-racist-1412021984

101 *A columnist for the* Daily Beast *wrote:* James Kirchick, "American Racist Richard Spencer Gets to Play the Martyr in Hungary," *Daily Beast,* October 7, 2014. https://www.thedailybeast.com/american-racist-richard-spencer-gets-to-play -the-martyr-in-hungary

101 *Greg Johnson, who ran:* Greg Johnson, "Budapest Conference Update," *Counter-Currents,* September 30, 2014. https://counter-currents.com/2014/09/budapest -conference-update

101 *In July 2018, he gave:* Richard Spencer and Nikolai Petroff, "Richard Spencer's Views on Russia—an Exclusive Interview with an Alt-Right Leader," *Russia Insider,* July 22, 2018. https://russia-insider.com/en/node/24250

102 *hacked emails show:* Anton Shekhovtsov, "Is Russia Insider Sponsored by a Russian Oligarch with Ties to the European Far Right?" *The Interpreter,* November 23, 2015. https://www.interpretermag.com/is-russia-insider-sponsored-by-a-russian -oligarch-with-ties-to-the-european-far-right/

102 *A few days later, Bausman:* Michael Edison Hayden, "Far-Right Propagandist Turns Up in Moscow After Jan. 6," Southern Poverty Law Center, September 1, 2021. https://www.splcenter.org/hatewatch/2021/09/01/far-right-propagandist-turns -moscow-after-jan-6

CHAPTER 7: THE FREE SPEECH PARTY

104 *A user said of one of the targeted:* David Futrelle, "Zoe Quinn's Screenshots of 4chan's Dirty Tricks Were Just the Appetizer. Here's the First Course of the Dinner, Directly from the IRC Log," We Hunted the Mammoth, September 8, 2014. https://web.archive.org/web/20141016102306/https://www.wehuntedthemam moth.com/2014/09/08/zoe-quinns-screenshots-of-4chans-dirty-tricks-were -just-the-appetizer-heres-the-first-course-of-the-dinner-directly-from-the-irc-log/

106 *(The phrase comes from a story):* Sam Biddle, "The Psychopaths of GamerGate Are All That's Left, and They're Terrifying," Gawker, February 2, 2015. https://web.ar chive.org/web/20150202202512/http://internet.gawker.com/the-psychopaths -of-gamergate-are-all-thats-left-and-th-1683271908

106 *When the* Daily Dot *asked:* Patrick Howell O'Neill, "8chan, the central hive of Gamergate, is also an active pedophile network," *Daily Dot,* November 17, 2014. https://web.archive.org/web/20180526154936/https://www.dailydot.com /layer8/8chan-pedophiles-child-porn-gamergate/

107 *In 2011, in an interview:* Amir Efrati, "Twitter CEO Costolo on Apple, Privacy, Free Speech and Google; Far from IPO," *Wall Street Journal,* October 18, 2011. https://www.wsj.com/articles/BL-DGB-23367

107 *For a sense of how:* Mat Honan, "Twitter Doesn't Give a Damn Who You Are," Gizmodo, September 9, 2011. https://gizmodo.com/twitter-doesnt-give-a-damn -who-you-are-5838414

108 *In 2009, Facebook defended:* Michael Arrington, "Facebook Remains Stubbornly Proud of Position on Holocaust Denial," *TechCrunch,* May 12, 2009. https://tech crunch.com/2009/05/12/facebook-remains-stubbornly-proud-of-position-on -holocaust-denial/

108 (*Facebook banned*)*:* Oliver Effron, "Facebook Will Ban Holocaust Denial Posts under Hate Speech Policy," CNN, October 12, 2020. https://www.cnn .com/2020/10/12/tech/facebook-holocaust-denial-hate-speech/index.html

108 *In 2012, amid a controversy:* Adrian Chen, "Reddit CEO Speaks Out on Violentacrez in Leaked Memo: 'We Stand for Free Speech,' " Gawker, October 16, 2012. https:// web.archive.org/web/20121218084850/https://www.gawker.com/5952349/red dit-ceo-speaks-out-on-violentacrez-in-leaked-memo-we-stand-for-free-speech

108 (*Reddit banned*)*:* Caitlin Dewey, "These Are the 5 Subreddits Reddit Banned under Its Game-Changing Anti-Harassment Policy—and Why It Banned Them," *Wash- ington Post,* June 10, 2015. https://www.washingtonpost.com/news/the-intersect /wp/2015/06/10/these-are-the-5-subreddits-reddit-banned-under-its-game -changing-anti-harassment-policy-and-why-it-banned-them/

108 *An NSM protest in Toledo:* FOX News Toledo, Ohio Riots 2005 (2020). https://www .youtube.com/watch?v=k24IlkFOVIY

109 *Christian yelled, "Free speech or die, Portland":* "Suspect in Fatal Portland Attack Yells about 'Free Speech' at Hearing," Reuters, May 30, 2017. https://www.reuters .com/article/us-usa-muslims-portland/suspect-in-fatal-portland-attack-yells -about-free-speech-at-hearing-idUSKBN18Q11F

109 *"On 8chan you are free":* Infinitechan, Twitter, 2014. https://archive.ph/Fg3i6

109 *The headline was:* Fredrick Brennan, "Hotwheels: Why I Support Eugenics," *Daily Stormer,* December 30, 2014. https://archive.ph/ftgkC

110 *In response to criticism:* Fredrick Brennan, "Infinitechan Comments on Hotwheels Gets Invited to Write an Article O . . . ," Reddit, 2014. https://archive.ph/oi2EJ

111 *Steve Bannon, who cofounded:* Joshua Green, *Devil's Bargain: Steve Bannon, Donald Trump, and the Nationalist Uprising* (Penguin, 2017).

111 *When Breitbart reported on leaked:* Milo Yiannopoulos, "Exposed: The Secret Mail- ing List of the Gaming Journalism Elite," Breitbart, September 17, 2014. https://

www.breitbart.com/europe/2014/09/17/exposed-the-secret-mailing-list-of-the
-gaming-journalism-elite/

113 *"I was, without a doubt"*: Joshua Goldberg, "First Public Statement from Joshua
Goldberg," *Medium*, March 18, 2020. https://medium.com/@MoonMetropolis
/first-public-statement-from-joshua-goldberg-8bb061aa56a0

113 *"I have been on the Internet"*: Joshua Goldberg, "How Social Justice Warriors Are
Creating an Entire Generation of Fascists," Thought Catalog, December 5, 2014.
https://thoughtcatalog.com/joshua-goldberg/2014/12/when-social-justice
-warriors-attack-one-tumblr-users-experience/

113 *If there was anything:v* Joshua Goldberg, "Why Censoring Speech Creates Extremists
and Causes Atrocities Instead of Stopping Them," Thought Catalog, November19,
2014. https://thoughtcatalog.com/joshua-goldberg/2014/11/why-censoring
-speech-creates-extremists-and-causes-atrocities-instead-of-stopping-them/

114 *On Fox & Friends*: Katherine Fung, "Fox News Panel Flips Out Over Father's Day
Hoax," *HuffPost*, June 16, 2014. https://www.huffpost.com/entry/fox-news
-endfathersday_n_5498861

114 *A few years later, Russia's troll farm*: Scott Shane, "How Unwitting Americans
Encountered Russian Operatives Online," *New York Times*, February 19, 2018.
https://www.nytimes.com/2018/02/18/us/politics/russian-operatives-face
book-twitter.html

114 *Though he said everything*: MoonMetropolis, Twitter. https://archive.ph/0EV5F

115 *One of Goldberg's personas*: United States v. Joshua Ryne Goldberg, 2018.

115 *As Australi Witness, Goldberg encouraged*: "2 Dead in Shooting at Muhammad Art
Exhibit in Garland," CBS Texas, May 3, 2015. https://www.cbsnews.com/texas
/news/breaking-shooting-in-garland/

116 *A CBS headline declared*: "Alleged Terror Plot Aimed at 9/11 Anniversary Foiled,"
CBS News, September 11, 2015. https://www.cbsnews.com/news/alleged-911
-terror-plot-florida-man-joshua-goldberg-posed-as-muslim-in-australia/

117 *In December 2017, Goldberg pled guilty*: "Florida Man Sentenced to 10 Years in Federal Prison on Bomb Charge," United States Department of Justice, June 25, 2018.
https://www.justice.gov/opa/pr/florida-man-sentenced-10-years-federal-prison
-bomb-charge

CHAPTER 8: THE GREAT MEME WAR

119 *It showed a handsome Donald*: Ben Garrison, "Dancing with the Star: The Trump Tango,"
GrrrGraphics, 2015. https://grrrgraphics.com/dancing-with-the-star-the-trump-tango/

124 *John Kerry ordered a sandwich*: Dana Milbank, "Steak Raises Stakes for Kerry in

Philly," *Washington Post,* August 13, 2003. https://www.washingtonpost.com /archive/politics/2003/08/13/steak-raises-stakes-for-kerry-in-philly/f59dd0f7 -20fc-4309-85fc-ac63cec7a123/

124 *"George Bush made a mistake":* Reena Flores, "Republican Debate: Donald Trump, Jeb Bush Spar over Bush Family Legacy," CBS News, February 13, 2016. https:// www.cbsnews.com/news/republican-debate-donald-trump-jeb-bush-spar-over -bush-family-legacy/

126 *In a presentation of his research:* Psnofsky, Aaron. "Citizen Scientific Racism: White Nationalist Appropriations of Genetic Research." UCLA Center for Behavior, Evolution, and Culture. January 4, 2021. https://bec.ucla.edu/event/aaron-pa nofsky-citizen-scientific-racism/.

129 *At the Republican National Convention:* Sarah Posner, "How Steve Bannon Created an Online Haven for White Nationalists," *Mother Jones,* August 22, 2016. https:// www.motherjones.com/politics/2016/08/stephen-bannon-donald-trump-alt -right-breitbart-news/

129 *Hillary Clinton addressed:* Tyler Prager, "Breitbart Mocks Clinton Speech," *Politico,* August 25, 2016. https://www.politico.com/story/2016/08/breitbart-mocks -clinton-speech-227420

130 *He told reporters the alt-right:* David Weigel, "Four Lessons from the Alt-Right's D.C. Coming-Out Party," *Washington Post,* September 10, 2016. https://www.washing tonpost.com/news/post-politics/wp/2016/09/10/four-lessons-from-the-alt -rights-d-c-coming-out-party/

132 *"I think the users of 8chan":* Craig Silverman and Jane Lytvynenko, "Meet the Online Porn Pioneer Who Created a News Site for Internet Trolls," *BuzzFeed News,* February 22, 2017. https://www.buzzfeednews.com/article/craigsilverman/meet -the-online-porn-pioneer-who-created-a-news-site-for-int

136 *Spencer gave a speech:* Daniel Lombroso and Yoni Appelbaum, " 'Hail Trump!': Video of White Nationalists Cheering the President-Elect," *Atlantic,* November 21, 2016. https://www.theatlantic.com/politics/archive/2016/11 /richard-spencer-speech-npi/508379/

CHAPTER 9: RIGHT-WING WOMEN

137 *"Day of the Rope":* Andrew MacDonald, *The Turner Diaries* (Barricade Books Inc., 1996).

139 *In 1987, Dworkin landed:* "The Spy 100," *Spy,* October 1987.

139 *In that book, Dworkin:* Andrea Dworkin, *Right-Wing Women: The Politics of Domesticated Females* (Women's Press, 1983).

141 *The* New York Times *headline read:* Liam Stack, "Attack on Alt-Right Leader Has Internet Asking: Is It O.K. to Punch a Nazi?," *New York Times,* January 21, 2017. https://www.nytimes.com/2017/01/21/us/politics/richard-spencer-punched-attack.html

142 *In February, a Milo Yiannopoulos:* Madison Park and Kyung Lah, "UC Berkeley Cancels Milo Yiannopoulos Talk after Violent Protests," CNN, February 2, 2017. https://www.cnn.com/2017/02/02/us/milo-yiannopoulos-berkeley-duplicate-2/index.html

142 *"March 4 Trump":* Rhea Mahbubani, Elyce Kirchner, and Pete Suratos, "Demonstrators Arrested at Berkeley 'March 4 Trump' Rally Await Charges," NBC Bay Area, March 7, 2017. https://www.nbcbayarea.com/news/local/american-hero-who-hit-anti-trump-protester-with-stick-at-berkeley-rally-to-be-arraigned/44755/

142 *It turned into a brawl:* Ryan Lenz, "The Battle for Berkeley: In the Name of Freedom of Speech, the Radical Right Is Circling the Ivory Tower to Ensure a Voice for the Alt-Right," Southern Poverty Law Center, May 1, 2017. https://www.splcenter.org/hatewatch/2017/05/01/battle-berkeley-name-freedom-speech-radical-right-circling-ivory-tower-ensure-voice-alt

142 *She was nineteen years old:* "Woman Punched During Berkeley Protest Describes Melee," CBS San Francisco, April 17, 2017. https://www.cbsnews.com/sanfrancisco/news/woman-punched-during-berkeley-protest-speaks-out/

143 *One RAM member texted another:* "Three Members of California-Based White Supremacist Group Sentenced on Riots Charges Related to August 2017 'Unite the Right' Rally in Charlottesville," United States Department of Justice, July 19, 2019. https://www.justice.gov/usao-wdva/pr/three-members-california-based-white-supremacist-group-sentenced-riots-charges-related

145 *Andrew Anglin described it:* Andrew Anglin, "What Is WHITE SHARIA and What Choices Do I Have in Accepting It or Not?," *Daily Stormer,* April 15, 2017. https://web.archive.org/web/20170418233712/https://www.dailystormer.com/what-is-white-sharia-and-what-choices-do-i-have-in-accepting-it-or-not/

151 *Schoep followed up in an email: Sines v. Kessler.*

CHAPTER 10: "WELL, HELLO, SWEETHEART!"

162 *In a January 2017 episode: Sines v. Kessler.*

165 *In a speech titled, "How":* Christopher Cantwell, "How the Libertarian Party Saved My Life," ChristopherCantwell.com, June 14, 2014. https://web.archive.org/web/20140617181139/https://christophercantwell.com/2014/06/14/libertarian-party-saved-life/

165 *According to the Free State Project:* "Christopher Cantwell," Southern Poverty Law

Center. https://www.splcenter.org/fighting-hate/extremist-files/individual
/christopher-cantwell

CHAPTER 11: CHARLOTTESVILLE

168 *"Anglin's gonna watch this": Sines v. Kessler.*

171 *But it was truly incriminating: United States v. Cantwell,* 2023.

CHAPTER 12: AFTERMATH

200 *He had not gone to the Iraq War:* Cott, Emma. "How Our Reporter Uncovered a Lie
   That Propelled an Alt-Right Extremist's Rise." *New York Times,* February 5, 2018.
   https://www.nytimes.com/2018/02/05/insider/confronting-a-white-national
   ist-eli-mosley.html.

203 *The feud intensified:* Hilary Sargent, "Christopher Cantwell Guilty of Extortion
   and Threats," *The Informant,* January 6, 2020. https://www.informant.news/p
   /christopher-cantwell-guilty-of-extortion.

204 *The affair ended, but in early: State of Indiana v. Matthew W. Heimbach,* 2018.

205 *He told the Southern Poverty Law Center:* Brett Barrouquere and Rachel Janik,
   "TWP Chief Matthew Heimbach Arrested for Battery after Affair with Top
   Spokesman's Wife," Southern Poverty Law Center, March 13, 2018. https://www
   .splcenter.org/hatewatch/2018/03/13/twp-chief-matthew-heimbach-arrested
   -battery-after-affair-top-spokesmans-wife

CHAPTER 13: "THE INITIAL PERIOD OF ABSOLUTE CHAOS"

209 *In his interrogation, Minassian: FULL Police Interrogation of Incel van Attack Driver,*
   YouTube, 2019. https://www.youtube.com/watch?v=VyHgtSy41VM

211 *Westphal testified:* Alyshah Hasham, "Forensic Psychiatrist Continues His Testimony
   for the Defence at Minassian van Attack Trial," *Toronto Star,* December 1, 2020.
   https://www.thestar.com/news/gta/forensic-psychiatrist-continues-his-testimony
   -for-the-defence-at-minassian-van-attack-trial/article_afae3c3b-8b1c-52d0-b5b5
   -24967a134ee0.html

215 *He told the* New York Times: Kevin Roose, " 'Shut the Site Down,' Says the Creator
   of 8chan, a Megaphone for Gunmen," *New York Times,* August 4, 2019. https://
   www.nytimes.com/2019/08/04/technology/8chan-shooting-manifesto.html

215 *He told the* QAnon Anonymous *podcast:* "Episode 63: Battle of 8chan feat Fredrick
   Brennan," *QAnon Anonymous* podcast, October 2019.

218 *He presented his evidence on the podcast:* "#166 Country of Liars," *Reply All* podcast,
   September 2020.

218 *the* New York Times *published a linguistic analysis:* David D. Kirkpatrick, "Who Is Behind QAnon? Linguistic Detectives Find Fingerprints," *New York Times,* February 19, 2022. https://www.nytimes.com/2022/02/19/technology/qanon -messages-authors.html

218 *Asked about QAnon by NBC:* Dylan Scott, "Trump Town Hall: President Says He Agrees with Part of the QAnon Conspiracy Theory," *Vox,* October 15, 2020. https://www.vox.com/2020/10/15/21518697/donald-trump-town-hall-what-is -qanon-conspiracy-theory

218 *When Trump campaign spokeswoman:* Max Cohen, "White House Press Secretary Says She's Never Heard Trump Talk about QAnon," *Politico,* August 20, 2020. https:// www.politico.com/news/2020/08/20/kayleigh-mcenany-trump-qanon-399273

CHAPTER 14: FANTASIZING ABOUT SELF-DEFENSE

224 *(Tarrio worked as a federal):* Aram Roston, "Exclusive: Proud Boys Leader Was 'Prolific' Informer for Law Enforcement," Reuters, January 27, 2021. https:// www.reuters.com/article/us-usa-proudboys-leader-exclusive/exclusive-proud- boys-leader-was-prolific-informer-for-law-enforcement-idUSKBN29W1PE

CHAPTER 15: FOR HISTORY

233 *He'd once written:* Matt Parrott, "The Color of Capitalism," Counter-Currents, February 13, 2012. https://counter-currents.com/2012/02/the-color-of-capitalism

237 *Sean Hannity repeated it:* "One on One with Sen Lindsey Graham," *Hannity,* Fox News, November 5, 2020.

237 *Minutes later, Hannity:* "One on One with Sen Ted Cruz," *Hannity,* Fox News, November 5, 2020.

EPILOGUE

241 *The most attention:* Laura Bassett, "Richard Spencer Listed Himself on Bumble as Politically 'Moderate,'" *Jezebel,* June 15, 2022. https://jezebel.com/richard -spencer-bumble-dating-profile-moderate-1849062955

242 *On a podcast, Cantwell:* "Brawl in Cell Block 88 (Interview w/ Chris Cantwell)," *Happenings w/ Jason Kessler* podcast, December 20, 2022.

243 *Milkshake, the large Proud Boy:* "Florida Man Pleads Guilty to Felony Charge for Actions During Jan. 6 Capitol Breach," United States Department of Justice, February 9, 2023. https://www.justice.gov/usao-dc/pr/florida-man-pleads-guilty -felony-charge-actions-during-jan-6-capitol-breach-0

243 *Barton Shively, who screamed:* "Pennsylvania Man Sentenced for Assaulting Officers

During Jan. 6 Capitol Breach," United States Department of Justice, June 2, 2023. https://www.justice.gov/usao-dc/pr/pennsylvania-man-sentenced-assaulting -officers-during-jan-6-capitol-breach-1

243 *The guy with the yarn beard:* "New York Man Found Guilty of Felony and Misde- meanor Charges Related to Capitol Breach," United States Department of Justice, August 31, 2023. https://www.justice.gov/usao-dc/pr/new-york-man-found -guilty-felony-and-misdemeanor-charges-related-capitol-breach-0

243 *Enrique Tarrio, who'd:* "Proud Boys Leader Sentenced to 22 Years in Prison on Seditious Conspiracy and Other Charges Related to U.S. Capitol Breach," United States Depart- ment of Justice, September 5, 2023. https://www.justice.gov/usao-dc/pr/proud -boys-leader-sentenced-22-years-prison-seditious-conspiracy-and-other-charges

243 *McCarthy said of the riot:* Stacey Shepard, "McCarthy Rebukes Violence at the Capitol," *Bakersfield Californian,* January 6, 2021. https://www.bakersfield.com /news/breaking/mccarthy-rebukes-violence-at-the-capitol/article_52cbd6ec -505e-11eb-8ccc-0ba728ef5ab0.html

243 *House Republicans withdrew support:* Dan Merica and David Wright, "GOP Con- gressional Committee Cancels Ad Reservations in Key House Race in Ohio," CNN, September 23, 2022. https://www.cnn.com/2022/09/23/politics/nrcc -ohio-9-jr-majewski/index.html

244 *Cassidy Hutchinson testified:* Jonathan Allen, " 'They're Not Here to Hurt Me': Former Aide Says Trump Knew Jan. 6 Crowd Was Armed," NBC News, June 29, 2022. https://www.nbcnews.com/politics/congress/jan-6-panel-looks-trump -white-house-cassidy-hutchinson-testimony-rcna35550

246 *Unabomber manifesto:* "Blake Masters—A New Kind of Politics," Alex Kaschuta podcast, March 2022.

246 *in 2023, some five hundred bills:* "Mapping Attacks on LGBTQ Rights in U.S. State Legislatures," American Civil Liberties Union, November 2023. https://www .aclu.org/legislative-attacks-on-lgbtq-rights

246 *The Ron DeSantis presidential campaign:* Nicholas Nehamas and Maggie Haberman, "DeSantis, Seeking Attention, Uses LGBTQ Issues to Attack Trump," *New York Times,* July 1, 2023. https://www.nytimes.com/2023/07/01/us/politics/desan tis-video-lgbtq-trump.html

246 *"Were the Mongols diverse?":* "BREAKING: U.S. Air Force Academy Superintendent Cannot Define Gender Ideology Terms Promoted on DoD Campuses," Office of Congressman Matt Gaetz, July 19, 2023. http://gaetz.house.gov/media/press -releases/breaking-us-air-force-academy-superintendent-cannot-define-gender -ideology

INDEX

ABOUT THE AUTHOR

ELLE REEVE is a CNN correspondent whose work has won numerous awards, including two Emmys and a Peabody for the documentary *Charlottesville: Race and Terror*, part of which was included in the movie *BlacKkKlansman* and the second impeachment of President Donald Trump (2021). Her writing has appeared in *Vice*, the *New Republic*, *New York* magazine, *Elle*, *The Atlantic*, and the *Daily Beast*. She lives in New York. You can follow her on Twitter @ElspethReeve.